The Practice of Godliness

VOLUME TWO

Composed from
Sacred Scripture

by

Johann Gerhard

translated by the Rev. Dr. Elmer Hohle, Em.

edited by Rachel Melvin

REPRISTINATION PRESS
MALONE, TEXAS

Copyright 2006 by Elmer Hohle. Published by permission of the translator. No part of this publication may be reproduced, stored in a retrieval system, or transmitted in any form or by any means, electronic, mechanical, photocopying or otherwise without the prior written permission of Repristination Press.

The artwork for the title page of this edition was inspired by that from the 1691 Leipzig edition of Valerius Herberger's Evangelische Herzpostille. *Originally this work would have been drafted with a quill using iron gall ink, then carved into woodblock or the like and used for printing.*

The original work for Schola Pietatis *was hand scribed and drawn on calfskin using quills, as would have been done historically. In our case, the original was drafted using vermillion in aged glair to replicate the color and texture of the original printing as well. The original was then digitally reproduced and homogenized to create the printed image you see in this edition of* Schola Pietatis.

Lucas Tucker, Scribe

Published in 2013.

Repristination Press
716 HCR 3424 E
Malone, Texas 76660

Email-HUNNIUS@MAC.COM

ISBN 1-891469-62-2

The Table of Contents

Dedication 9

Volume Two—Concerning the general style and manner as to the form in which a person can and should exercise himself in godliness. 19

Part One—Concerning certain salutary, auxiliary means that generally are of service for the exercise of godliness. 29

Chapter One—That the hearing or reading of God's Word motivates us towards godliness. 33

Chapter Two—In what manner a person should hear and read God's Word in order that it might convey and promote godliness. 40

Chapter Three—That the worthy reception of the holy Lord's Supper promotes us towards godliness. 48

Chapter Four—In what manner a person should use the holy Lord's Supper in order that it may serve to promote godliness. 51

Chapter Five—That holy, devotional contemplation promotes us towards godliness. 58

Chapter Six—In what manner holy devotional contemplation is to be employed in order that it may be conducive towards godliness. 62

Chapter Seven—Concerning that to which this contemplation should be directed so that it may promote godliness. 64

Chapter Eight—Concerning the control and directing of the thoughts that serve to promote a devotional contemplation. 104

Chapter Nine—That a zealous, diligent prayer and godly crying out prompting us towards godliness. 110

Chapter Ten—How prayer must be structured if it is to be of service in promoting godliness. 117

Chapter Eleven—Concerning the form of a daily prayer that is beneficial for the exercise and the increasing of godliness. 126

Chapter Twelve—That Controlling and Taming the Body is a Helpful Means Towards Godliness. 133

Chapter Thirteen—How these helpful means for godliness that have now been recounted are to be generally regarded. 140

Part Two—About the essential, necessary parts of godliness in general, as to how each individual Christian should exercise himself in them. 145

Chapter One—That true, proper repentance is an essential requirement for godliness. 147

Chapter Two—What should motivate a person to truly repent. 151

Chapter Three—In what manner a true Christian should exercise himself with true repentance. 169

Chapter Four—That true, proper repentance encompasses within itself contrition and sorrow over sin and a true, living faith in Christ. 174

Chapter Five—That true remorse and sorrow over sin is an essential part of repentance, and thus also of godliness. 181

Chapter Six—In what manner should a repentant heart exercise itself in the acknowledgment of, and remorse over, sin. 183

Chapter Seven—That a true, living faith in Christ is an essential part of repentance and also for godliness. 200

Chapter Eight—In what manner should a repentant heart exercise its faith in Christ. 204

Chapter Nine—That the new obedience is a necessary part of godliness. 220

Chapter Ten—In what way should a person exercise himself in the new obedience and good works. 225

Chapter Eleven—What it is that should motivate a true Christian to crucify and kill off his sinful flesh and be renewed by the Spirit. 229

Chapter Twelve—How a true Christian is to exercise himself in the crucifixion of the flesh and the renewing of the Spirit. 243

Chapter Thirteen—What should motivate a Christian to deny himself. 251

Chapter Fourteen—How a true Christian should exercise himself in the denial of self. 253

Chapter Fifteen—What should motivate a true Christian to follow after Christ His Lord. 261

Chapter Sixteen—How a true Christian should exercise himself in following Christ. 272

Schola Pietatis
The Practice of Godliness

i.e.,

Christian and salutary

Instruction

concerning the reasons why each individual Christian should be motivated to practice godliness and also as to the way he is to practice it.

VOLUME TWO

Composed from
Sacred Scripture

by

Johann Gerhard

Doctor and Professor at the highly esteemed University of Jena.

Even more so, it contains within it the sainted author's evangelical direction as to how to properly utilize these [instructions] to strengthen godly devotion, while at the same time increasing the beneficial use of the table of contents.

By the Approval of the King of Poland and the Noble Prince of Saxony.
****

Published by Wolfgang Moritz, Editor.
Printed by John Ernest Adelbulner. 1719 A. D.

Most worthy, enlightened, nobly born princes and ladies:

Lady Dorothy Sophia,

Duchess of Saxony, Landgravess in Thürin, to the Margravess at Meissen, the imperial free secular religious foundation of the Quetlinburg Abbey, etc.

As well as also the most highly enlightened, nobly born Princess and lady:

Lady Anna Maria,

Duchess of Saxony, Margravess at Meissen, etc.;

My gracious Princesses and Ladies,
    Most worthy abbesses and highly enlightened, nobly born princesses, my humble service to you most gracious princesses and ladies stands second only to my heartfelt obligation to wish for you long life, good health, and—above all else and foremost—eternal blessing from God. Gracious princesses and ladies: The holy Apostle Paul above all else required two things from all true Christians; namely, a genuine, true faith, and then clean, good consciences—which becomes obvious from all the very same passages in which a pure faith and good conscience are set side by side. In 1 Tim. 1:5, the main objective of this law or instruction here is love from a pure heart and from a good conscience, and from an unvarnished faith. In v. 18-19, **My son Timothy, I commit this instruction to you in keeping with the prior prophecies about you that you practice and exercise them with a good warfare. Also that you may have faith and a good conscience which can not be taken from you, so that your faith not suffer shipwreck. In ch. 3:8-9: The ministers of the Church should hold on to the mystery of faith with a pure**

conscience. Ch. 4:1: **In the last days some will step away from the faith.** V. 2: ... **and have the mark of the branding iron upon their conscience.** Tit. 1:15: **The conscience of an unbeliever is unclean.** Heb. 10:21: **Let us then step up with true hearts with total faith sprinkled into our hearts and be freed from an evil conscience.** These two parts [faith and a good conscience] are not only beneficial, but also necessary, for a true Christian. For in case one were to lack in either or to have one escape him, from then on he would no longer have this place where he is able to draw near to plead as a true Christian. For what pertains to the genuine, true faith is obviously that it simultaneously is *anima Christianismi* [*the soul of Christianity*]. It is the soul of true Christianity, **for without faith it is impossible to please God** (Heb. 11:6). And **what does not emanate from faith is sin** (Rom. 14:23). Through faith we obtain: **the forgiveness of sins** (Acts 10:43); **the righteousness that avails before God** (Rom. 3:22); **peace with God the Lord** (Rom. 5:1); **joy of heart and full access with confidence** (Eph. 3:12); **our being children of the heavenly Father** (Gal. 3:26); **the indwelling of Christ's kingdom of grace** (Eph. 3:17), **and the indwelling of the Holy Spirit** (Gal. 4:6); **the cleansing of the heart** (Acts 15:9); **life and eternal salvation** (Mark 16:16; John 3:16; 1 John 5:11). Wherever there is honest, upright faith, there will be these heavenly treasures and blessings at the same time. Where there is no faith, there also exists none of these treasures and blessings. Wherever true faith is lost, there also shall be lost the heavenly treasures and blessings. This genuine, true faith is encompassed with three parts: First, *notitiam* [*conception*], the conceptual knowledge and wisdom that out of God's Holy Word a person actually and truly recognizes God the Lord according to His essence and will, and His Son Christ Jesus according to His Person and Office. Next, *assensum* [*approbation*], the accompanying obligation for a person to commit himself to what is held before us about God and divine matters in the revealed Word with the same total faith, and to let obedience to Christ take his reason captive (2 Cor. 10:5). And finally, *fiduciam* [*trust*], the trust and believing, confident assurance so that one with true faith seizes the evangelical promise about the grace of God and the forgiveness of sins, and that one is certain God shall and will especially also make us partakers of these promises by grace. Such believing trust and accompanying confidence has no status without an accompanying, dutiful exercise [of it]. On the other hand, such an accompanying, dutiful committal has no status without knowledge and wisdom. As a result, it is obviously incumbent upon a Christian that he then confess God the Lord according to His essence and will, and His Son, Christ Jesus, according to His Person and Office as God the Lord has revealed Himself in His Holy Word. It is incumbent that he not add to, nor take away from, such revelation. Also, that he not draw up any false, erring teaching that goes against such revelation in the Word of God, and that would try to allow the drawing up—knowingly or unknowingly—of any [false] obligations. For through such misleading heresy the purity of faith, as well as the above-mentioned consequential heavenly blessings, would be stolen and taken away. It is for this very reason that God the Lord faithfully and zealously warns about false teaching not only in the Old Testament (Deu. 13:3; Jer. 23:16), but also through Christ and His beloved Apostles in the New Testament. In order that we do not believe or follow such [false teachings], He added a serious warning that everyone's salvation hangs in the balance if one does not take precautions and wards off false doctrine. Mat. 7:15: **Be-**

ware of false prophets who come to you in sheep's clothing but inwardly are ravaging wolves. John 10:7: I am the Door for the sheep. V. 8: All who came before Me were thieves and murderers. However the sheep did not listen to them. V. 27: My sheep listen to My voice. V. 5: But they do not follow a stranger, for they do not recognize the voice of the stranger. In Acts 20:28-29, St. Paul speaks to the presbyters at Ephesus: Watch over yourselves and over the entire flock. For this I know, after my departure gruesome wolves will come among you who will not spare the flock. Rom. 16:17-18: I admonish you, dear brothers, that you watch out for those who create divisions and offenses amidst the doctrine which you have learned, and steer clear of them. For such people are not serving the Lord Jesus Christ. Instead, they are serving their belly, and with sweet-sounding words and magnificent rhetoric they are misleading innocent hearts. 2 Cor. 11:2 - I have betrothed you to a Man in order to present you as a pure virgin to Christ. V. 3 - I, however, am afraid that just as the serpent seduced Eve with its shenanigans, so also your minds will go berserk away form the simplicity in Christ. Gal. 3:1 - O you mindless Galatians! Who has bewitched you that you don't listen to the truth? Christ Jesus was painted and portrayed before your very eyes; now He is being crucified by you. Eph. 4:14 - Let us not waver or be wafted about by every kind of wind of doctrine from man's trickery and doubts by which they try to cleverly mislead us. Phi. 3:2 - Watch out for the dogs, the evil doers, the circumcised. 1 The. 5:20 - Examine everything and keep what's good. 1 Tim. 6:3-5 - If anyone teaches differently and does not abide by the salutary words of our Lord Jesus Christ and with the doctrine of godliness, such a person is in the dark and doesn't know a thing. Separate yourself from someone like that. Shun a heretical person once he has been repeatedly admonished; v. 11 – and know that he is wrong and sins as someone who has judged himself. 2 Pet. 2:1-2 – There shall be false teachers among you who in your midst will introduce corrupt sectarianism and shall deny the Lord who has bought them. Also they shall lead themselves to their own destruction. And many will follow after their depraved corruption. 1 John 4:1 – You beloved ones, don't believe any individual spirit, but examine the spirits whether they are from God. For many false prophets have gone out into the world. 2 John 9-11 – Anyone who breaks ranks and does not abide by the teaching of Christ has not God. If anyone comes to you and does not bring this teaching, do not receive him into your home and do not greet him. For anyone who greets him makes himself a partaker of his evil deeds. Heb. 12:9 – do not allow yourself to be driven about with various, strange teachings. Jude 3-4 – fight for the faith which once was handed over to the saints, for there are certain people who have slithered into your midst who deny God and our only Lord Jesus Christ and only Ruler. Rev. 2:15 – You have those among you who hold to the teachings of the Nicolatians. I hate that, repent!, etc. These and similar passages of Holy Scriptures clearly testify that no one can approve of false teaching without outward danger to his salvation. And consequently good precaution and scrutiny is necessary so that one might see to it that he is properly following the right way in matters of faith. From this it also becomes obvious that it is a totally useless, mad delusion what many people think; namely that it is sufficient for one to busy himself with godliness and good works, even though he does not concern himself much about purity of doctrine and lets others do battle and fight over that. For true God-pleasing godliness and proper God-pleasing good works can have no status without faith. One can well observe this in sensible-minded heathen. They have also actually busied themselves with uprightness and—according to their thinking—also godliness. But since they lack a true knowledge of God and of His Son Christ Jesus, such uprightness and godliness (which of itself is not to be tossed aside) is unable to be of any use for their salvation.

So then, just as true godliness and proper good works apart from the foundation of faith and without purity of doctrine have no status, so also it is useless if a person wants to boast about pure doctrine and proper faith but does not show this by works and instead with his pure faith wants to knowingly lead an unholy, unclean, sinful life. This can likewise be concluded from the flowing passages. Mat. 7:21 - **Not all who shall say to Me, Lord, Lord, shall come into the kingdom of heaven; rather, those who do the will of My Father in heaven.** Luke 6:46 - **Why do you call me Lord, Lord and do not do what I tell you to do?** John 13:17 - **If you know this, blessed are you if you do it.** V. 35 - **By this shall every man know that you are My disciples, if you have love among one another.** Ch. 14:15 - **If you love Me, then keep My commandments.** Ch. 15:14 - **You are My friends [disciples] if you do what I command you to do.** Rom. 8:12-15 - **We are debtors not according to the flesh so that we should live according to the flesh. For if you live according to the flesh, you will have to die, but if you by the Spirit kill off the activity of the flesh, you shall live. For those who are motivated by the Spirit of God are God's children.** 2 Cor. 5:17 - **If** anyone is in Christ, he is a new creature. Gal. 5:6 – Neither circumcision nor foreskin is of any avail before Christ Jesus. Instead faith only—which is active in love. V. 24 – those who belong to Christ crucify their flesh, along with its lust and desires. 2 Tim. 6:8 – If anyone does not provide for his own, especially his own household, he has denied the faith and is more offensive than a heathen. 2 Tim. 3:5 – They have a façade of godliness, but they deny its power. 1 John 1:5 – God is a Light and in Him there is no darkness. V. 6 – If we say we have fellowship with Him and walk in darkness, we are lying and do not do the truth. But if we walk in the Light, as He is in the Light, then we have fellowship among one another. Ch. 2:3 – This is how we note that we know Him: if we keep His commandments. V. 4 – Anyone who says: I know Him and does not keep His commandments, he is a liar; and, in such a person there is no truth. V. 6 – Anyone who says that he abides in Him should also live as He lived. Ch. 3:6 – He who abides in Him does not sin. He who sins has not seen Him nor known Him. V. 9 – Whoever is born of God, His seed abides in him and he cannot sin, for he is born of God. V. 10 – Hereby is made known who are the children of God and who are the children of the Devil. Whoever doesn't do the right thing or love his brother is not of God. Jam. 2:14 – What does it help, beloved brethren, if someone says he has faith and yet does not have the works? Can faith also save him? V. 17 – **Faith is of itself dead if it does not have works.** V. 18 – **Show me your faith by your works.** You see, from these and similar passages it is crystal clear that it is not enough for a person to have and to believe pure doctrine. Rather, alongside the purity of doctrine, there must also exist a pure heart, a clean conscience, a pure life, so that it not be a false boast when one boasts with the mouth about one's faith and yet does not show this faith with love and good works. For true faith cleanses the heart and makes it possible for Christ and the Holy Spirit to reside in such a heart—as has been indicated above. There is no way that such a purity of heart and rich-in-grace indwelling of Christ and the Holy Spirit can continue to exist with godless teaching and deliberate sinning against conscience.

As a result then both parts—namely, purity of doctrine as well as a life of proper faith and eager zeal for godliness with true confession of God and a good conscience—belong to a genuine Christianity. From this it can readily be concluded that those whom God the Lord has placed into the teaching ministry of His Church should allow both faith and a good conscience to receive the highest priority in the congregation that has been committed to their care. To that end, Tit. 1:9 intends that it is required of a Bishop that he should hold to the Word, which is most certain. And, he should be able to teach it in order to be able to admonish powerfully with wholesome doctrine and correct those who contradict. If he does not want to take into consideration purity of doctrine but instead allow heretical doctrine and error to start to spread among his hearers, he would be allowing his office to be put into an awkward position. If He also would allow cocky self-assurance and godlessness to take root, he would once more not be beneficial for the office of his ministry. He has to guard and protect against both sides if the hearers are to be brought to salvation through faith. For this very same faith is a confession of the truth for godliness in the hope of eternal life (Tit. 1:1). The devil fights and battles against the Christian Church from both of these sides through false teaching and through godless living. That's why a teacher must guard the Church from both of these sides. Also it indeed takes great effort to uproot from the hearts of men the weeds of cocky self-assurance and godlessness, as well as heretical teaching and error. Experience well testifies to this.

Regarding this, I, relying on divine help, have undertaken to prepare some little treatises about godliness. Also, I want to share them with the Church of God through the public press so that the purity of doctrine in our Evangelical Church might by God's grace echo forth with other writings according to the measure of the few gifts that God the Lord has granted me. I am His most insignificant servant. Up to now I have held back and have up to now allowed myself to remains quiet against the opponents of divine truth.

Consequently, I have extensively recounted in Volume One the manifold reasons which can and should motivate each Christian towards godliness. Now there herewith follows a proper ordinance of instruction as to what manner a person should exercise godliness, since both knowledge and teaching are highly necessary. Actually, at the outset it was my intention to somehow bring together both of the reasons that admonish us toward godliness, along with the art and manner of how one should exercise oneself in godliness in one book. This despite the fact that I in the introduction of the first volume promised to only present the former. However, I soon discovered that this doctrine would not allow itself to be summarily written up and encompassed and grasped. Instead, it would have to be divided into various volumes. Hopefully nobody will be offended by this, since nobody holds it against a debtor if he pays back more than what he has announced and promised to do.

This my actual insignificant (but hopefully not needless or of no benefit) labor I submissively wish to dedicate and ascribe to you not only because I regard myself indebted towards Your Electoral Grace and my own beloved fatherland. Nor also my submissive indebted affection for the Imperial, free, secular sponsorship, and the state of Quedlinburg's authority, and for the many blessings shown to me and my relatives, nor just my thankful mindset for being able to show you something. No, I also did it above all else because I well know that Your Electoral Grace especially loves godliness and, along with other princely duties, daily exercise yourself in godliness. Your Electoral Grace's sainted father, the former highly enlightened, highly-born Prince and Duke, Duke Frederic Wilhelm, Duke of Saxony, etc., the Electoral Administrator and Guardian of Saxony, is remembered as a highly blessed Christian who obtained special praise from the whole world for his godliness. This can be seen to this very day in the Prince's Library at Alteburg. His Electoral Grace with particular diligence has read and commented on many exemplary Bibles and other beneficial theological books. Also he himself has composed godly mediations and prayers. Your Electoral Grace has with great fame followed in these praiseworthy footsteps. Also your attitude shows such godliness with your works. Consequently I have scooped up the hope that this my dedication, as well as your reading of this little volume, may not be rejected by Your Electoral Grace. Instead, by grace may it be pleasing to you. I herewith with submissive diligence pray and quite faithfully commend my inadequacies to your Electoral Grace under the protection of the Most High for every blessing. Dated at Jena on 17 October, 1622; on the 40th birthday of Your Electoral Grace.

Your Electoral Grace's submissive servant,
Dr. Johann Gerhard

Volume Two

Concerning the general style and manner as to the form in which a person can and should exercise himself in godliness.

In the first volume of this treatise I have related in an orderly way the main, important, and motivational reasons which should generally encourage and awaken every person towards godliness. Now, additionally, follows that we provide a sure form and good directions from the Word of God as to how and in what manner a person should and can practice godliness. It is necessary for us to know both, for God has prescribed both for us in His Word. For just as the holy Apostle Paul says in Rom. 8:26: **We know not for what we should appropriately pray. Instead, the Holy Spirit Himself intercedes for us most excellently with inexpressible groaning sighs.** So now we also, especially here, can generally say about godliness and all its essential parts: We do not know how we are to serve God the Lord and how we are to exercise godliness. But **the Holy Spirit is our teacher who teaches us everything** (John 14:26) **and guides us into all truth** (John 16:13). The heathen were able to recognize from the light of nature that there is a God and that one should serve Him. However, how and in what manner to serve Him so that it might be pleasing to God the Lord, that they cannot discover or obtain from the light of nature. God has provided counsel for this inborn blindness and ignorance of ours through the Light of His revealed Word.

Also, in the Word He has prescribed what He requires of us and in what manner we are to serve Him. Mic. 6:8 – **You, O man, have been told what is good and what the Lord requires of you; namely, keep God's Word, practice love, and be humble for your God.** For the Lord Christ prescribed a certain form and manner as to how to pray—as the disciples asked of Him while trying to find out the way: **Lord, teach us to pray like John has taught his disciples** (Luke 11:2). So also the Holy Spirit has prescribed for us in the revealed Word how and in what manner we are to practice godliness in every aspect. For He is the **Anointing who teaches us all things.** 1 John 2:27 – **The anointing which you have received from Him abides with you, and it is not necessary that anyone teach you. Rather, as the anointing teaches you all sort of things, they are true and are not lies.** As a result, it can be boasted about all true believers that they **have been taught by God** (Isa. 54:23; John 6:45). With such instruction, God the Holy Spirit wants to prevent us from attempting to serve God the Lord **according to our own discretion** and pleasure. Instead, we are **to let the divine Word be a lamp for our feet and a light upon our path** (Psa. 119:105).

For such self-prescribed spirituality, where one wants to serve God as he deems fit, strives against 1. *Dei praecipientis Majestas,* **God's commanding majesty and glory.** This glory belongs to God our Creator and Lord alone so that He might teach and prescribe for us how we are to serve Him. Isa. 33:22 – **The Lord is our Judge; the Lord is our Master; the Lord is our King.** Jam. 4:12 – **There is one Lawgiver who can save us and condemn us. This glory He shall give to no other**

(Isa. 42:8). That is why as He gives His holy Law as the norm and plumb line for all good works by His people, He preceded it with this serious and majestic Word: **I am the Lord your God** (Exo. 20:5). Understand this to mean: It is incumbent on Him alone to prescribe the form and the manner as to how one should serve Him with good works. In Eze. 20:19, He lets Himself be announced with great majesty: **I am the Lord your God. You are to live according to My commandments, and you are to keep My judgments and act according to them.** Consequently, the holy Apostle so faithfully warns us that we should not **become servants of men** (1 Cor. 7:23). That is to say, we should allow ourselves to be obligated to the commands which God the Lord has prescribed for us in His Word, and not allow ourselves to be regulated according to the commandments of men.

 2. *Prohibitionis divinae claritas*, the clarity of God's prohibitions, passages in which God the Lord expressly forbids that one should not serve Him according to **one's own preconceived notions**. He also clearly testifies that works that are motivated by one's own discretion do not please Him at all. Num. 15:39–41: **You shall behold and remember all the commandments of the Lord and do them. You are not to do as you see fit, not to do that which seems appropriate in your own eyes. Therefore, you should remember and do all My commandments and be holy before your God. I am the Lord your God.** (If one wants to serve God the Lord according to one's own good pleasure, that is a secret, forbidden idolatry which in Holy Scriptures is called spiritual harlotry and adultery. That's why God the Lord says: **You shall not whore around according to your eyes.** The whoring, adulterous women cast their eyes everywhere. So also those who want to serve God as they see fit are constantly looking about for new ways to serve God, and have nothing certain upon which to base it.) Deu. 4:2 – **You shall add nothing to that which I command you, nor shall you take anything away from same, in order that you may keep the commandments of the Lord your God which I command you** (man-made doctrines and self-elected spirituality are a hindrance to God's commandments. They lead away from the Truth, Tit. 1:14). Deu. 12:8 – **You shall never do that which each person thinks right for himself.** Isa. 1:12 – **Who is it that requires such of your hands?** Ch. 29:13 – **These folks draw near to Me with their mouths and with their lips. However, their hearts are far from Me, and they fear Me according to the commandments of man, which they teach.** (Christ references this verse in Mat. 15:9 and with it lays to rest **the recitations of the Pharisees.**) Jer. 7:24 – **They lived according to their own counsel and according to their own evil heart's discretion.** V. 31 – **They build the Altar of Topheth, which I had never commanded or had in mind.** Amos 5:25 – **Did you not offer up to Me sacrifices and food offering from the house of Israel as you wandered in the wilderness for forty years?** Yes indeed! V. 26 – **You carried Siccuth, your king, and Thiun, your image [idol], the star of your idols which you made for yourselves** (since they had no command for such worship, it could not please God and was not true worship). Mic. 6:7–8: **Should I give my first-born son for my transgression, or the fruit of my life for the sins of my soul?** (It was regarded as the greatest and highest form of worship by the idolatrous Israelites if they, in keeping with the intention of the **example of Abraham**, sacrificed their own children. But God the Lord rejected them on this through the Prophets). **It has been told to you, O man, what is good and what the Lord requires of you.** (It is as if He wants to say: You are not to think up any new worship. There actually has been more commanded to you than you are able to do, Sirach 3:25.) Zec. 7:5-6: **As you fasted and bore sorrows on the fifth and seventh month for these seventy years, did you actually fast for Me? Or, as you ate and drank, did you not actually eat and drink for yourselves?** (In the fifth month the Jews observed a universal fast in order to remind themselves that the Temple had been burned down in that same month. In the seventh month, they likewise observed a fast in order thereby to remind themselves that **Godolias** [Gedaliah] the captain, was murdered in that same month. Nebuchadnezzar had left him behind in the land of Judah, 2 Kin. 25. They regarded these fasts as a special, great **service of worship**. But the Prophet testifies that they did not fast for God the Lord, but rather for **themselves**. For they had actually instigated this worship without a command from God as they saw fit. If they had observed this fast for the sake of external discipline and as a **memorial**, and had not upheld it as a special **service of worship**, then God would have indeed tolerated it. But since they wanted to make this into a required service of worship and as a meritorious work, that's why God the Lord rejected it and directed them to His commandments in which were prescribed for their benefit what they were to do. Zec. 7:9 – **Thus says the Lord of Sabaoth: Judge justly and each person show goodness and mercy to his brother.** (This will please God for better then your self-chosen fasts out which you attempt to carve for yourselves a special service of worship and meritorious work.) Col. 2:20-23: **Since you then have died with Christ to the statutes of the world, why then do you allow yourselves to be taken captive to statutes as if you still were living with this world? Those who say to that you should not take hold, you should not taste, you should not touch, these are all underhandedly distorted and are commandments and doctrines of men. They have the appearance of wisdom through self-imposed spirituality and humility, and thereby they do not spare the body. And it does not give honor to the flesh with its self-indulgence.** All these passages clearly testify that God the Lord has no pleasure in the works that are performed at one's own discretion and in keeping with the commandments of men.

3. *Bonorum operum qualitas*, the distinctive characteristic of good works. The proper, God-pleasing works in the Holy Scriptures are described this way: that it is essential that they have the characteristic **that they have been commanded by God** and are prescribed for us [by Him]. If they lack this characteristic, they cannot be regarded as being truly proper good works. When in Mat. 19:16, Mark 10:17, and Luke 18:18 a ruler asks the Lord Christ: **Master, what must I do so that I may possess eternal life?** The Lord gave him this answer: **You indeed well know the Law? If you want to enter into life, then keep the Law.** By this is shown that no good work may occur unless it coincides with the commandments of God and is commanded by them. Once more, as a scribe asked Jesus in Luke 10:25: **What must I do that I may**

inherit eternal life? He gave him this answer: **What is written in the Law? How do you read it?** [He does this] to show that a person must concern himself with the Law of God and take note of what is written in it, if one wants to do something good. When St. Paul wanted to present the **doctrine of good works** to the Romans, he first stated the following admonition in Rom. 12:2: **Change yourselves by the renewal of your minds so that you may put to the test that which is the good, well-pleasing and perfect will of God.** And in the following chapter (13:9–10), he directs them to the divine commandments to indicate that the good, well-pleasing, and perfect will of God is prescribed in His Word. In Eph. 2:10, he writes that God has prepared us in advance for good works that we should walk in them, since He from eternity has elected us in Christ that we should be holy (Eph. 1:4). For He also in His Word has **outwardly** prescribed for us a certain rule for good works, and **inwardly** He motivates and moves us to every good work (Rom. 8:15).

4. *Legis divinae proprietas*, the distinctive feature of divine Law. Among other reasons, God the Lord has given us His Law in His holy Word for the purpose that He in it wanted to prescribe for a person a **perfect** rule and guideline for **good works.** Psa. 19:8 – **The Law of the Lord is perfect.** Gal. 6:16 – **All who follow after this rule** (as it is prescribed in God's Word)**, peace and mercy is upon them.** 2 Tim. 3:16 – **All Scripture is inspired by God. It is beneficial for doctrine, for exposing wrong, for improvement, for training in righteousness** (such a feature is beneficial for these kinds of parts of Christianity). V. 17 – **So that the man of God may have his skills honed perfectly skilled for every good work.** And God the Lord has actually also sternly commanded a person **not add to nor take away from** this rule and norm for good works (Deu. 4:2; 12:32; Pro. 30:6; Rev. 22:18-19). Since God's Law is a perfect rule and norm for good works, let a person also be satisfied with it and not perchance want to discover a **new work** and a **new worship**. Since God the Lord has given us His Word in order that it **should light up the way for us in this life** (Psa. 19:9; Psa. 119:105; Pro. 6:23; 2 Pet. 1:19), we should follow this **Light** both by **faith** and with **good works**.

5. *Rationis humanae coecitas*, **the blindness of human reason**. Ever since the Fall into sin, man's understanding has been **darkened** to such an extent that he is unable to grasp spiritual matter by his natural powers. 1 Cor. 1:14 – **The natural man receives nothing from the Spirit of God. It is a foolishness to him and he cannot understand it, for it has to be judged spiritually.** 2 Cor. 3:5 – **We are not capable to think anything** (good) **on our own. Rather, the fact that we are capable is from God.** V. 18 – **The lucid brightness of the Lord reflects itself in all of us with our veiled faces** (by means of the revealed **Gospel** through which we see the salutary face of God in and through Christ). **And with the same image, we are transfigured by the Spirit of the Lord from one brightness to another** (however not by the natural light of our understanding. Eph. 5:8 – **You were formerly in darkness** (prior to the conversion and enlightening by the Holy Spirit). **Now, however, you are a light in the Lord.** Since human reason is in sheer **darkness** about spiritual heavenly matters apart from and without the light of the divine Word, neither will our own natural powers be able to see or find out how a person may serve God the Lord so

that it pleases Him. That is why no new service of God or any new special way to practice godliness should be concocted.

6. *Peccati per electitios cultus commissi gravitas*, the gross sin that is initiated by self-chosen service to God. Not only has God **forbidden** us to serve Him according to how one sees fit, and has clearly testified that such self-selected service does not please Him; rather, He has also **shown by deed** that He regards this as a serious transgression in that He has always severely punished something like this. Psa. 106:39 – **they have defiled themselves with their deeds, and have committed prostitution with their actions.** *Fornicati sunt in adinventionibus suis*, they committed spiritual fornication in that they want to dictate and decide how they should serve God the Lord. V. 40 – **Thus the wrath of the Lord was inflamed against His people.** When the Israelites at their own **discretion** wanted to serve **God** with the **image of the golden calf** (Exo. 32), it caused them to fall into serious sin, and it resulted in a horrible punishment. When the hero Gideon made an **apron** and established it as a special service to God in the city of Ophrah, all of Israel **prostituted itself as a result of this. And Gideon and his family fell into a great offense** (Jud. 8:27). From the history of the Old Testament it is made known and revealed how displeased God the Lord was that the Israelites tried to serve Him with **Baal and Molech, with the golden calf in Dan and Bethel.** From all this it becomes clearly apparent that nobody should allow himself to become fond of serving God according to his own discretion nor let it be dictated by his own self-selected holiness. Instead, he should simply learn from **God's Word** alone as to what manner he should serve God the Lord and should practice godliness. For a dutiful adherence to same we only want to consider the form and manner of how a person should exercise godliness out of **God's Word** alone. And in no way do we want to mislead anyone onto the path of human commandments or self-selected holiness. God the Lord Himself wants to guide and lead us in this manner through His good Spirit in order that we be guided and led properly. Also, that we might be able to lead and guide others upon the pathway of godliness through Christ our Savior, AMEN.

Part One

Concerning certain salutary, auxiliary means that generally are of service for the exercise of godliness.

When the holy Apostle admonishes his disciple Timothy—and along with him, also all of us—that we (1 Tim. 4:8) **should exercise ourselves in godliness**, he requires two things from us. First, *adminiculorum usurpatrionem*, that we should take hold of the salutary *adminicula* or **auxiliary means** that generally can be of service to us in the exercise of godliness. Second, *pietatis juxta singulas partes exercitationem*, that we should exercise ourselves in a godly manner according to all the very same essential, necessary **parts**. For both parts are germane to this if we wish to properly exercise godliness. **The reason for each one** is because such salutary auxiliary means serve the purpose of godliness being implanted into our hearts by the Holy Spirit, as well as also sustaining in increasing godliness within us. For just as the Holy Spirit does not desire to work in us our **conversion, rebirth, and renewal without means, but rather through means**—in that He Himself has so ordained—so also He does not want to implant, sustain, and increase **godliness** within us without means. Instead, He wants to do it through specific means that He Himself has prescribed for us. Whoever neglects these **means**, or is found to be negligent in using them, in such a case it is no surprise that the zeal and diligence for godliness has grown cold or even has been totally extinguished and frozen to death. **This however** (namely, that we exercise ourselves in godliness according to all these essential parts) is required for this reason. On account of the fact that godliness is composed of **distinctive parts**, such as true, proper repentance, and then also proper **fruits of repentance**—namely, betterment of one's life, new obedience, and a holy life, as was in indicated in the foreword of this treatise.

Accordingly, as it is usually called, *ad constitutionem & integritatem totius sive essentialis sive integralis requiruntur omnes partes*, if a thing is assembled out of many parts, then it is necessary **that all those parts** be available and present if it is to otherwise be completed. Thus, it is likewise necessary that anyone who desires to exercise himself in godliness should also exercise himself in the essential, necessary parts. Concerning the **salutary means** that commonly are useful for the exercise of godliness, we first have to deal with the fact that they extend themselves over all the parts of godliness and are commonly required for the exercise of it.

Basically, there are five auxiliary means: **1.** *Verbi divini auditus, sive lectio*, **the hearing or the reading of God's Word. 2.** *Eucharistiae usurpatio*, **the reception of the Holy Supper. 3.** *Sancta meditatio*, **the sacred meditations. 4.** *Seria oratio*, **zealous, diligent prayer and calling upon God. 4.** *Corporis castigatio*, **the suppression and taming of the body**. Along with this, of course, is to be considered that all these auxiliary means are **not a character** and attribute, a dignity, and a power, as shall be further explained about each in its proper place. We want to summarily deal with each one in an orderly fashion, and see in what manner they will be useful for us to practice godliness.

Chapter One

That the hearing or reading of God's Word motivates us towards godliness.

Among other reasons, the ever-faithful, most loving God, who **desires that all men be helped and come to the knowledge of the truth** (1 Tim. 1:4), has, out of sheer, overwhelming goodness, revealed Himself to the human race in His Word. Also, He has entrusted it to His Church so that through the hearing and reading of it godliness would be ignited and awakened, implanted, sustained, and increased in the hearts of men. This becomes apparent from the following reasons.

    1. *Ex divino mandato*, from the command of God the Lord. God the Lord has commanded that every person should hear, read, and meditate His holy **Word**—even for the ultimate purpose and for the sake of this reason: that by all means he thereby be brought to fear God and brought to true godliness. For this end result and this benefit has been added on to such a command with definitive words. Deu. 17:18-19: **When the king shall sit upon the throne of his kingdom he should take this other Law from the priests of Levi and let it be written upon a book. It should remain at his side and he should read from it for the rest of his life.** And why is that? **So that he learns to fear the Lord his God in order that he may keep all the words of this Law and these judgments in order to do them.** Deu. 31:11-13: **When all of Israel comes to appear before the Lord your God at the place He**

shall choose, you are to let this Law be cried out to all of Israel for them to hear. In particular, [do this] **for the assembly of the people, both men and women, children and the stranger who is at your door.** And why is that? **So that they hear and learn in order that they thereby may fear their God and keep and do all the words of this Law. And that their children who do not know it may also hear and learn so that they may also fear the Lord your God for the rest of their lives.** Jos. 1:8 – **Do not allow this Book of the Law to depart from your mouth. Instead, meditate on it day and night.** Why is that? **So that you may keep and do everything according to how it stands written there.**

    2. *Ex Sanctorum Exemplo*, **from the example of the Holy Spirit.** The God-pleasing saints of God diligently listened to God's Word, read it, promoted it, and meditated one it—even to the end—so that they might thereby promote themselves and others towards godliness. In Gen. 18:19, God the Lord says of Abraham, the "father of all believers": **I know that he will command his children and his descendants after him that they keep the way of the Lord and do what is right and good.** That is, he will take My Word to heart and **make them more acutely aware** and speak to them about it (Deu. 6:6), so that they, too, may be brought up to fear God. In Psa. 78:1, David says: **I will open my mouth to speak and relate ancient history,** V. 3 – **Which we have heard and know about as told to us by our fathers,** V.4 – **so that we do not withhold from their children which shall come after us, and proclaim the glory of the Lord and His might and wonders which He has done. V. 5 – He established**

a testimony in Jacob, and gave a Law in Israel, which He commanded our fathers to teach to their children; V.6 – so that the descendants may teach it to their children, and the children yet unborn might—once they were grown—proclaim it to their children. For what purpose? V. 7 – **So that they might place their hope in God and not forget the deeds of God and keep His commandments.** What does the entire 119th Psalm deal with other than this: that David, by his example, diligently teaches us that the reading and contemplation of the divine Word is a salutary means which compels us towards godliness? V. 11 – **I keep Your Word in my heart so that I do not sin against You.** V. 16 – **I have a desire for Your judgments and do not forget Your commands.** V. 30 – **I have chosen the way of truthfulness, I have laid out Your judgments.** V. 38 – **May Your servant steadfastly keep Your commands at Your Word, so that I may fear You, etc.** It was the practice in the Israelite 'churches' that the writings of Moses and the Prophets were **read** in the synagogues on **every** Sabbath Day (Luke 4:16; Acts 15:21). This was so that people thereby would be brought to the true knowledge of God, to fear God, and be brought to everything godly. In Nehemiah 8:18, Ezra and Nehemiah read from the Word of the Law of the Lord to the people so that true worship of God might once more be reestablished.

    3. *Ex verbi nature & fructu*, from the nature and characteristic of the divine Word. The Word of God is not just a simple, plain, lifeless hull and book of impotent letters. Rather, **It is living and powerful and sharper than any two-edged sword. And it cuts through to separate soul and spirit, as well**

as marrow and bone (Heb. 4:12). **It is Spirit and life** (John 6:63), because it is God's Word that is Spirit and life. Consequently, whoever hears or reads God's Word, it does not leave him without benefit and fruit. **Instead, the Holy Spirit through it wants to be efficacious for godliness,** just so the person does not hinder himself over this and strive against the Holy Spirit. Isa. 55:10–11: **Just as the rain and snow falls from heaven and does not return but dampens the earth and make it fruitful and productive, so that it gives seed for sowing and bread for eating, so also shall be My Word which goes forth from My mouth. It shall not return to me empty, but shall do that which pleases Me and accomplish the thing for which I sent it.** In God's Word we find everything that we need for godliness. We are by nature lazy and reluctant to practice godliness, but God's Word gives us a **powerful admonition** and holds before us various reasons that are able to motivate and cheer us on towards godliness. We witness this in the examples of those who heard God's Word or read it. Acts 2:37 – As the **Jews at Jerusalem** heard the sermon of St. Peter about Christ, **it pierced their hearts, and they asked what should we do?** Ch. 24:25 – When Paul, standing before the Roman governor Felix, **spoke about righteousness and chastity and about the future judgement, Felix became terrified**, i.e., this sermon moved his heart and ignited in him a **fear and fright** which was a good beginning towards conversion and godliness. That's what would have happened had not Felix himself hindered and become distraught over this work of the Holy Spirit. We are **by nature in darkness as far as our knowledge is concerned,** so that we do not know how we are to serve God the Lord and how we are to exercise godliness. However, **God's Word is a lantern for our feet and a light for our path** (Psa. 119:105). In Pro. 6:23, we are directed to the pathway upon which we are to walk. It is the **blessed light** about which Psa. 36 states: **In Your light we see the Light**. Also, St. Peter speaks of this in his 2nd Epistle, 1:19 – **We have a sure prophetic Word, and you would do well to take note of it as a light that shines in a dark place, until the day breaks forth and the Morning Star arises in your hearts**. By nature we doubt whether our actions and being are pleasing to God. However, here God's Word gives us a **sure norm and guiding principle** by which we are to judge our actions and life—if it is to please God. Psa. 119:9 – **How shall a young person live his life blamelessly? When he clings to Your words** (cf. Psa. 119:5). And as a **rule** (Gal. 6:16; Phi. 2:6). Also, God the Lord has earnestly commanded that a person is to go forth according to this guiding principle and rule, and is not to add nor take away from it (Deu. 4:2; 12:28; Isa. 8:20, etc.). Yes indeed, the holy Apostles have ascribed such hearty praise and witness to the Holy Scriptures. In 2 Tim. 3:16, **for since they have been inspired by God,** they are not just beneficial for **doctrine and reproof** with articles of faith, but also for **betterment and for disciplining in righteousness** for life and conduct. V. 17 – **So that the man of God become perfectly equipped for every good work.**

Now then, God's Word is enclosed within the divine Sacred Scriptures in such a way as to be beneficial for our **betterment** that we by means of their instruction may be **equipped for every good work**. So obviously also, the reading of the Holy Scriptures and the hearing of the divine Word will indeed be a helpful means to promote godliness in our hearts. By **nature** we are **weak** and readily allow ourselves to be misled by tribulation and persecution for the path of true godliness. But then comes God's Word to our rescue. It **comforts** us amidst all trials and tribulations so that we do not allow ourselves to be deterred from godliness. Psa. 23:4 – **Your rod and staff** (Your holy divine Word) comforts me. Psa. 94:19 – **I had many cares in my heart, but Your comfort soothed my soul.** Psa. 119:50 – **This is my comfort amidst my afflictions, for Your word renews me.** V. 92 – **Had not Your Law been my comfort, I would have perished in my misery.** Jer. 15:16 – **When we find Your Word, may we be sustained by it. And this very same Word of Yours is the joy and comfort of our hearts. For we are named by Your Name, Lord God of Sabaoth.** Rom. 15:4 – **What has been previously written has been written for our learning, so that we, through patience and comfort of the Scriptures, may have hope.** We have powerful, mighty enemies who would gladly like to lead us astray from the way of godliness, namely the **devil** with his temptations, **the world** with its temptations, and **our sinful flesh** with its tempting provocations. However, we can arm and defend ourselves against these with the Word of God. For the Word of God is **the Sword of the Spirit.** With it we are able to resist the devil, and are able to chop off all evil lusts of the flesh (Eph. 6:17). When the devil tried to tempt Christ and attempted to misdirect Him from trusting God towards presumptuous idolatry, Christ took in hand this **Sword** and laid low all the cunning and might of this villainous rogue (Mat. 4:4,7 and 10). In similar fashion, God's Word is able to serve us against all might of the enemy, protecting us when he tries to mislead us from the pathway of godliness.

    4. *Ex opposito*, from the opposition. Experience shows that distorting true worship and all sorts of godlessness starts to spread carelessness and cocky self-confidence if one does not heed or pay attention to God's Word, but instead despises it and tosses it to the wind. When, at the **time of Eli, the Word of the Lord was rare** (1 Sam. 3:1), sin and godlessness gained the upper hand among the people of God. When, under the reign of Manasseh and Amon, the Book of the Law of the Lord had lain under the empty pew, massive idolatry and wickedness had started to spread among the people (2 Kin. 22:8; 2 Chr. 34:14*). In Pro. 29:18, Solomon says: **When prophecy has ceased, the people become wild and wasted**, i.e., where God's Word is no longer listened to and diligently promoted, there godlessness and sin spread like wild-fire. Why is it that so many actually **are earthly minded** (Phi. 3:19) and **strive only for what is earthly** (Col. 3:2)? Indeed, most of the time, it's because they do not diligently read the divine Word in the heavenly book [i.e., Bible]. Instead, they read and ponder only the books in which secular, worldly matters are dealt with. Why is it that many a person is attracted to **inordinate sexual lust** and carnal love? Truly, most often it emanates from the fact that he reads filthy, wicked books by which his heart is wounded with poisonous darts. Should not then the holy, divine Scripture—in which the Holy Spirit speaks of heavenly matters, of righteousness, chastity, and godliness—be able to serve the purpose of seeing to it

---

* Gerhard calls it '2 Parallel 24:14.'

that if we diligently read it and ourselves practice what we read, that therein, we thereby would be admonished and moved towards godliness, righteousness, and chastity?

Chapter Two

In what manner a person should hear and read God's Word in order that it might convey and promote godliness.

Pay attention to how you listen, Christ says in Luke 8:18. This teaches us that it is not enough that we just hear God's Word or read it. Rather, we have to also hear it properly and fittingly. In Mark 4:24, He says: **Watch out as to what you hear.** With this He teaches us that we should not to slander the neighbor with **shameful words and foolish gossip or jokes** (Eph. 4:4) and similar evil, shameful talk. Instead, we are to listen to **God's Word** and honorable, helpful talk. However, so that we do not think it is enough if we merely hear or read God's Word, He additionally states, **watch out as to what you listen to.** Namely, listen in a manner that is God-pleasing and serves to promote godliness and holiness in you. In similar manner, we especially can say here: **Watch out as to what you read.** However, if we want to hear or read God's Word properly so that it may convey godliness, then it has to take place—

    1. *Assidue & frequenter,* **often and daily.** For God the Lord commands this in Jos. 1:8 – **Let the Book of the Law not depart from your mouth, but instead meditate upon it day and night.** And St. Paul says in Col. 2:16 – **Let the Word of Christ live among you**

richly with all wisdom. David praises this in a pious person in Psa. 1:2 – **Blessed is he who has a desire for the Law of the Lord and speaks about His Law day and night.** Our inborn **blindness and ignorance** requires this. For we cannot at first glance immediately grasp the Holy Scriptures with a hurried reading of it. Instead, we have to make it **well** known to us and become very familiar with it. The very **Majesty and Glory of the Holy Scriptures** requires this. For in them are hidden such heavenly and godly mysteries about which we in this our entire lifetime shall never be able to completely finish learning. The tiniest letter and tittle in **God's Word** is full of heavenly wisdom and salutary doctrine. The Holy Scriptures are a rich **discovery of a mine** in which we continually must **search** (John 5:39) so that we may find in it the **golden nuggets** of salutary doctrine. The Holy Scriptures is a **living flowing spring** (Psa. 68:27; Isa. 12:3) which we shall never be able to scoop dry. The Holy Scriptures is a **deep ocean** whose bottom we shall never be able to fathom in this life, just as it is portrayed to us in Eze. 47:5: **from the water which flowed forth from the threshold of the Temple. When it was measured, it was so deep that one could not establish its depth. For it was so deep that one had to swim over it and could not touch bottom.** The Holy Scripture is a **Rock of Salvation and Life.** If this Rock is to spring forth the Water of comfort and life for us, then we must diligently read and ponder it often and knock on it.

    2. *Attene & dilgenter,* [with full] **attentiveness and diligence, so that a person does not perchance let his thoughts wander about.** Instead, one should with all diligence take note of what one is reading.

Christ calls for this in Mat. 24:16. **Whoever reads this**—from the Prophet Daniel—**let him take note of it** [not to forget it]. That which Christ says about the Prophet Daniel—that one should read him in such a way that one is aware of his meaning—one can say about the entire Holy Scripture. For all of Holy Scripture is **inspired by God and is beneficial for instruction in doctrine, in exposing wrong, in change for the better** (2 Tim. 3:16). The Prophet Isaiah calls for this in ch. 32:3, **the ears of the hearers shall take note.** Paul does the same in Heb. 2:1.* He writes, **Therefore, we should all the more discern† the Word** that we hear as **being true.** Thus we will keep it from sailing over our ears and hearts **like a ship** which gets off course and sails into oblivion. The sainted Apostle here uses a word‡ that can also indeed be translated as *ne perfluamus*, i.e., that we not drift away. That's why the sainted Apostle then compares mankind to an earthly vessel. If it has melted away so things run through it, then eventually nothing stays in it. Therefore he admonishes us that with diligence we should take note of the Word of God when we hear or read it. And, we should be like a vessel that is filled to the brim and not melted away. Instead, it retains that which flows into it. Such also evokes the **great danger** that confronts us if we do not hear and read God's Word with diligent attention. Christ

---

* Tr. note: Gerhard ascribes authorship of Hebrews to St. Paul; I personally go along with Luther and my favorite seminary professor, Dr. Martin Franzmann, that it more than likely was Apollos (possibly Paul dictated it to him).

† Tr. Note: προσεχω = pay attention to, hold a steady course—frequently used of steering a ship

‡ Tr. Note: παραρυωμεν, a word that conveys the picture of a ship that must stay the course so as not to miss its destination.

preaches about this very same danger in Mat. 13:19 – **If someone hears the Word about the kingdom and does not understand it, then the evil one comes and rips out the seed which has been sown into his heart. He is the one who has been sown on the road.** This really is frightening. The devil, like a hellish parasitic bird, is able to **rip out** the Word which has be sown **into the heart** when someone does not understand it or does not pay attention to it. How much more readily will he not be able to rip it **out of the person's ears** who has not yet had the Word enter into, and be sunken into, his heart? That's why the true hearers of the divine Word are described thusly. They **understand** God's Word, i.e., they listen to it with understanding and full attention (Mat. 13:23) **so that they may receive it with a good heart** (Luke 2:51; ch. 8:15), **so that may hear and keep it** (ch. 11:28). For just as they **are passionate in spirit** in other parts which pertain to godliness (Rom. 12:11), so also they hear God's Word with that kind of passionate desire and diligent attention.

3. *Devote & ardenter*, with prayer and devotion. For while we are unable to **understand** the mysteries of the divine Word by our own natural powers of our own reason, that's why the enlightenment of the Holy Spirit is required for this. However, we must obtain this by prayer. Luke 11:13 – **The Father in heaven shall give the Holy Spirit to those who ask Him.** In the same way, the Lord Christ opened the Scriptures to the disciples who were going up to Emmaus (Luke 24:32) and **opened up the understanding** of His Apostles so that they understood the Scriptures (v. 45). So also today He has to open one's understanding through the Holy Scriptures if we are to understand the Scriptures in a salutary way. For He is the One who has the **key of David** and opens (Rev. 3:7). He is the **Lamb who opens the Book that was inscribed on the outside and inside and sealed with seven seals** (ch. 5:1). That's why we first must pray to Him to ignite the light **of divine knowledge** and understanding in our hearts before we undertake to hear the divine Word or read it. And then too, when we have read God's Word we must once more pray that He would **seal** and empower the Word in our heart so that may bear fruit. The Holy Spirit is the **Gatekeeper** (John 10:3). He is the One who has to open and close. He has to **open** the door of our hearts. He has to open up the **mystery** that is hidden in God's Word. After that He has to once more **close** the door of our hearts, so that the treasure of the divine Word not be taken out our hearts. Without this Light of the Holy Spirit, we are incapable of a wholesome and edifying understanding a single tittle of **God's Word. For the natural man does not comprehend the things of the Spirit** (1 Cor. 2:14). Nor can they be obtained in any other way than by **prayer** (Jam. 1:5). That is the reason all the saints so longingly and inwardly sighed before God for the enlightenment of their understanding and for knowledge of His Word. This is how David prays in Psa. 119:10 - **I seek You with my whole heart, do not let me fail to keep Your commands. V. 12 – Lord teach me Your Law. V. 18 – Open my eyes so that I may see the wonders of Your commandments.** V. 19 – **I am a guest upon earth, do not hide Your Laws from me. V. 27 – Instruct me in the pathway of Your commands, thus I shall speak of Your wonders. V. 33 – Show me the ways of Your Laws so that I may keep them unto the end. V. 34 – Instruct me so that**

I may keep Your Law, and cling to it with my whole heart. V. 66 – Teach me salutary customs and knowledge, for I believe Your commandments. V. 68 – You are good and gracious, teach me Your Laws. V. 73 – Your hand has created and crafted me, guide me that I learn Your commandments. V. 108 – Let the willing sacrificial praise of my mouth please You, Lord, and teach me Your Laws. V. 124 – Deal with Your servant according to Your grace, and teach me Your Law. V. 125 – I am Your servant, instruct me so that I acknowledge Your testimonies. V. 130 – When Your Word is made know, it gladdens and makes wise the simple person. V. 135 – Let Your countenance shine on Your servant, and teach me Your Laws. V. 144 – The righteousness of Your testimony is eternal, instruct me so that I may live. V. 169 – Lord, let my lament come before You, instruct me according to Your Word. V. 171 – My lips shall give praise when You teach Your servant. The "master" of the Book of Wisdom* prays in ch. 9:10 as follows: **Lord, send down Your wisdom from holy heaven, and send it down from the Throne of Your glory, so that it may be with me and work within me so that I may know what is pleasing to You.** The holy Apostles step before the Lord Christ and ask in Mat. 13:36 – **Explain to us the parable.** The 24 Elders by whom the entire Church Militant upon earth and the entire Church Triumphant are signified **speak to the Lamb who sits upon the throne** (Rev. 5:9), **You are worthy to take the Book and open its seal.** This is the example of how we should at all times **longing sigh** before God the Lord and before Christ for the enlightenment of the Holy Spirit as we desire to read the Scriptures.

---

* *Wisdom of Solomon* in the Apocrypha.

4. *Submisse ac reverenter*, **with humility and reverence**, so that we ponder who it is that is speaking to us in and through this Word. Namely, it is **the Lord of lords and King of kings** (1 Tim. 6:15). The holy angels and Seraphim **cover their faces before Him** out of reverence (Isa. 6:2). St. Paul admonishes us, too, in 1 The. 2:13, as he lauds the Thessalonians for **receiving the Word of divine proclamation not as the word of men, but as it actually and truly is—the Word of God.** So also the prince Zerubbabel and the high priest Joshua, along with the rest of the people of Israel, are lauded that **they listened to the voice of the Lord their God and to the words of the Prophet Haggai with utmost respect** (Hag. 1:12). What else would you call reading the Scriptures and hearing God's Word other than wanting to **step before God the Lord** and enroll in His **school** in order hear and learn from Him? For this true **humility and reverence** are obviously a part. **Take note, you heavens, I will speak. And, let the earth hear the sayings of My mouth,** says Moses in Deu. 32:1. **Hear you heavens, and listen with your ears, earth**, Isaiah says in ch. 1:2. Should not man—whom God created as a rational creature—all the more so, with total humility and respectful reverence, hear and take note when God the **Lord speaks** in His Word? Amos say in ch. 3:8, **The lion roars, who should not be afraid? The Lord speaks, who should not prophesy?** As God the Lord was speaking to His people on **Mt. Sinai, the earth quaked** (Exo. 19:18; Psa. 68:9). **The mountains tremble and the hills fall apart** (Nah. 1:5). Should not mankind much more so fear before the Word of the Lord and hear it with total humility? In Jud. 3:20 is recorded about Eglon, the Moabite King, that when he heard from Ehud that he **possessed the Word of God**, he stood up from his throne. If a pagan king did something like that, how much more should not we get off of the high **throne of our arrogant heart** when we hear God's Word and listen to it with total respectful reverence.

  5. *Pie & obedienter*, **obediently**, so that we do not perchance foist our own **pre-conceived notions** upon the Scriptures and attempt to make Scripture comply with them. Instead, we are the earnest intention to learn **God's will from the Scripture** and follow it, so that we also **gladly take our reason captive to the obedience of faith** (2 Cor. 10:5; Rom. 1:5), and **willingly believe the Word of God**, even though we are unable to grasp it with our reason. And, yes indeed, that we also be **ready and willing to do** and to accomplish that which God bids us to do in His Word, so that we not **only become hearers of the Word, but also doers, so that we do not deceive ourselves. For if someone is a hearer of the Word and not a doer, he is like a man who looks at his physical face in a mirror. For after he has looked at himself, from that moment he goes on and forgets what he looked like**, says James in ch. 1:22-24. When the Israelites heard the voice of the Lord—who had spoken with them on **Mt. Sinai**—they said to Moses in Deu. 5:23, **Everything that the Lord our God says to you we want to hear and do**. That indeed was a good intention, if only they had abided by it. However, soon thereafter they fell away from God and His Word. We, however, should have the heart-felt, **steadfast intention** to do everything that God has commanded and prescribed for us in His Word.

Chapter Three

That the worthy reception of the holy Lord's Supper promotes us towards godliness.

In His wisdom and goodness, it not only pleased God to bestow His holy Word to mankind, but He additionally also provided **the holy Sacraments**. For in the New Testament there is **holy Baptism** and the **holy Lord's Supper**. Baptism is the *Sacramentum initiationis*, through which we are received into the Christian Church. That's why this Sacrament is applied only once in an entire lifetime. However, the **holy Lord's Supper** is *Sacramentum confirmationis*, through which we **become strengthened** in faith. We cannot and should not only use this Sacrament only once. Instead, we are to frequently use it for salutary purposes. The salutary use of the holy Lord's Supper is no less significant than is the hearing and reading of the divine Word. It is a good, **helpful means** towards godliness. This becomes apparent:

1. *Ex Eucharistiae natura*, **from the very nature and attribute** of the holy Lord's Supper. For the holy Lord's Supper is the second **Sacrament of the New Testament**. The holy Sacraments are *Verbum visibile*, a visible Word through which God the Lord especially wants to work and strengthen the very same thing in us which He works in us through the proclaimed and heard Word. Consequently, just as the hearing and reading of the divine Word promotes us towards godliness, so also the reception of the holy Lord's Supper can be useful in promoting us toward godliness.

2. Ex Eucharistiae materia, from the food of the holy Lord's Supper. In the holy Lord's Supper, **we do not just** receive **bread and wine.** Rather, by means of the blessed bread we simultaneously receive **the true body**, and by means of the blessed wine, **the true blood of Christ**—as is to be concluded from the words of the institution. But then Christ's body and blood is **personally united** with His **Godhead**. It is the **holy Temple in which the entire fullness of the Godhead dwells bodily** (Col. 2:9). And why should the reception and nurture of the body and blood of Christ not be promotional and helpful towards godliness? The assumed **human Nature of Christ has been anointed with the Holy Spirit without measure** (John 3:34). Since the Holy Spirit, who is a **Spirit of sanctification** (Rom. 1:4), resides with total fullness in the human nature of Christ, how should not then the reception of the true body and blood of Christ be of service for **sanctification by the Spirit**, and thus also for godliness? (2 The. 2:13; 1 Pet. 1:1) **The flesh of Christ is a life-giving flesh** (John 6:33). Accordingly, how then should the reception and partaking of it not be of service for us to **become partakers of the spiritual life which is from God**? (Eph. 4:18) However, if we then through the salutary and fruitful eating and drinking of the holy Lord Supper become partakers of the body that emanates from God, then it also obviously will transport us towards godliness.

3. Ex Eucharistiae fine, from the end result, on account of which the holy Lord's Supper was instituted. The holy Lord's Supper was not only instituted by Christ for the purpose that it **seal for us** the evangelical **promise of gracious forgiveness of sins and**

that it strengthen our faith, but that we also through it **should become embodied in the Lord and be fed for eternal life.** Even He Himself says in John. 6:56, **Whoever eats My flesh and drinks My blood, such a person remains in Me and I in Him.** Since the fruitful eating and drinking of His body and blood serves the purpose that **we remain in Him and He in us,** it then obviously will also served the purpose that we will be made **fruitful for every good work.** For He Himself also says in John 15:5: **Whoever remains in Me and I in him, such a person produces much fruit.** As Christ resides in our hearts through faith, we also by His Spirit become **strong in the inward man** (Eph. 3:16–17). If the holy Lord's Supper has been instituted for the purpose that we from this **fountain** of life **may scoop up the true spiritual life and be fed for eternal life** (John 6:33, 50, 51,etc.), then it will also serve the purpose that the **fruits of spiritual living** will be planted and promoted in us. For a **good tree** has been ordained for the purpose of producing good **fruit.** If the fellowship of the body and blood of Christ in the holy Lord's Supper has been ordained and instituted so that we may **obtain the fellowship of the spiritual body** of which Christ is the head (1 Cor. 12:13), then it also will obviously serve to **spiritually motivate and activate** us toward promoting godliness. For a living **body** lets its life shine forth through movement and activity. Just as **the body** receives life and activity from its **indwelling soul,** so also **our soul** receives its spiritual life and activity through the indwelling of Christ. If the holy Lord's Supper has been instituted for the purpose that through it we are transplanted and **established** into Christ—**the true Tree** of Life—then also the eating and drinking of the holy Lord's Supper serves the purpose of this Tree of Life **from henceforth greening up** within us, and then we produce all sorts of good **fruits of godliness** (Acts 22:2).

Chapter Four

In what manner a person should use the holy Lord's Supper in order that it may serve to promote godliness.

The sainted Apostle Paul testifies in 1 Cor. 11:27 that those who eat of the consecrated bread in the holy Lord Supper or drink from the chalice of the Lord **unworthily become guilty of the body and blood of the Lord**. Indeed, they eat and drink **judgment** unto themselves (v. 29). Therefore if the reception of the holy Lord's Supper is to promote godliness, it is not sufficient for a person to merely make use of the holy Lord's Supper, and along side others go to it out **sheer force of habit**. Instead, it is necessary that one partake of the holy Lord's Supper with an honest, **salutary preparation**; and, as the holy Apostle says, **examine oneself in advance**, and then to eat and drink from this chalice (v. 28). **Such an examination** consists of—

1. *Seriam contritionem,* **honest acknowledgement of sin.** Also, a heartfelt **contrition and sorrow** on account of the. For the holy Apostle teaches in the cited reference (v. 26) that this examination consist of **pondering and proclaiming** the death of Christ. **As often,** he says, **as you eat of this bread and drink from this chalice, you are to proclaim the death of**

the Lord until He comes. So as we then ponder **Christ's suffering and death**, we are thereby reminded of **our sin, for Christ died on account of our sin** (Rom. 4:23; ch. 6:10; 1 Cor. 15:3). Consequently, if we take to heart the underlying reason for Christ's death, we will acknowledge the magnitude and multitude of our sins from that, because they could never have been atoned for and paid for in any other way than through Christ's death. Also, from this we shall acknowledge the **burning wrath of God** against sin. For sin could not have been blotted away and expunged in any other way than through **Christ's blood.** From all this, inward **contrition and sorrow** over sin will grow within our hearts. To this Paul also teaches in this referenced place that to this essential examination pertains the fact that we are to **judge** ourselves (v. 32). That is, we are to present ourselves before **God's judgment** and admit our guilt before the **wrath** of His temporal and eternal punishment. At the same time, heartfelt, inward contrition will spring forth from this. In order for a person to be brought to such a genuine knowledge of his sins and **to a godly sorrow of contrition that none regrets which produces salvation** (2 Cor. 7:10) it is beneficial and also necessary for a person to do the following in using the Lord's Supper: He should from every earthly, temporal behavior force himself to examine **his inward life's conduct before the mirror of God's commandments.** He should diligently consider each one in particular order, one after the other, as to what God requires of us in each **individual commandment,** and how he has so frequently sinned against and behaved against each one in thought, word and deed. He also should recite within his heart the **penitential Psalms** of David, the

penitential prayer of the Prophet Isaiah (ch. 64) and Daniel (ch. 9)—or some other beneficial **little penitential prayer.**

2. *Fiducialem Christi apprehensionem,* **a true faith in Christ.** For the Apostle in a proper examination calls for a **man to discern the body of Christ** (v. 29). That is to say, one should not regard this as some ordinary, common meal. Instead, one should regard it as the kind of **heavenly meal** through which Christ Himself is present and by means of the consecrated bread and wine feeds us with His **true body and blood.** [All this] in order that we through this precious, priceless pledge of our redemption may be empowered in our hearts by the gracious promise of the forgiveness of sins and strengthened in our faith. This we must **believe with our whole heart.** And not only should we be certain and sure that the true body and true blood of Christ is distributed in the holy Lord's Supper, we also should be sure and certain that the **merits** that Christ won for us by offering up His body and shedding His blood are distributed, **imparted and sealed** to us. For here stand the clear words of the LORD Christ: **Take, eat; this is My body given for you. Take, drink; this is My blood shed for you.** Whoever **believes** these words is **worthy** and well prepared and possesses what they say and promise—namely, the forgiveness of sins. Whoever, however, does not believe, but doubts, is **unworthy** and unprepared. For the words **"for you"** call for pure believing hearts. To this also pertains the **proclaiming of the death of Christ** (v. 26). For as we ponder and proclaim Christ's death, we see shining forth from it His **love;** that He, out of heartfelt, incomprehensible love **gave Himself up into death for us** (Gal. 2:20). By this

we are strengthened in our faith inasmuch as for the sake of Christ, GOD the Lord **provides us with every good thing.** Also, we can be sure **that since we had been reconciled to GOD through the death of His Son while we still were enemies, much more so then we shall be saved through His life since we now are reconciled** (Rom. 5:10). In order that this faith be all the more strengthened, well-grounded, and increased in the heart of a person, it is essentially beneficial for a person to inwardly ponder, and hold and cling to within his heart the main **verses from God's Word** which speak about the **merits of Christ**, about gracious **forgiveness of sin**, about God's **compassionate mercy**, about the rich-in-grace **justification** of mankind before God the Lord, etc.

3. *Fraternam reconciliationem*, **brotherly reconciliation** with the neighbor. For if we examine ourselves, we find that we have sinned against God countless more times and more grossly than perhaps the neighbor may have behaved towards us. We are the ones who **owe ten thousand talents,** while our neighbor **barely owes us a hundred denarii** (Mat. 18:25 and 28). So then, if we desire that God should forgive us our debt so the reception of the holy Lord's Supper should serve to forgive us our sins and promote godliness, then we also have to forgive our neighbor his debt of sin (Mat. 6:14). Mark 11:25 - **Forgive your neighbor the wrong he has done you, and then pray so that your sin also be forgiven you.** Sir. 28:2-4 [Apocrypha]

---

* Tr. Note: Obviously Gerhard is here referencing Isa. 46:8b-9a; his quote is different from Luther's translation. I feel he was freely translating Isaiah from the original Hebrew from memory.

– A man holds a wrathful grudge against another person and wants to seek grace with the Lord. He is unmerciful towards someone like him and wants to pray for his own sin? He is merely flesh and blood and holds a grudge; who then would want to forgive him his sin? If we want to productively partake of the holy Lord's Supper, then we have to partake of it with **faith**, as has been indicated above. Now, however, true, genuine **faith is active through love** (Gal. 5:6). However, where there is **love**, there also is brotherly **reconciliation**. From this it indisputably follows that brotherly reconciliation belongs to the salutary, proper partaking of the holy Lord Supper. Christ directs us to that in Mat. 5:23-24: **When you offer your gift at the altar and there are reminded that your brother has something against you, then leave your gift there before the altar and first go out and reconcile yourself with your brother.** St. Paul reminds us of this when he demands in 1 Cor. 11:26 that we in the reception of the holy Lord's Supper should **proclaim the death** of Christ. However, if we ponder and proclaim Christ's death, we discover that He, our **great love,** gave Himself up for our debt of sin and gave up His life for us there. That's why it is proper that we also **pardon our neighbor.** Col. 3:13 – **Get along with each other and forgive one another. If someone has a complaint against another, you forgive just as Christ has forgiven you.**

4. *Reverentiae exhibitionem*, that we should not only in our **hearts** regard the holy Lord's Supper as highly precious and worthy and for the great heavenly meal in which Christ Himself feeds us with His body and blood, but that we also **show** this **with outward rever-**

ence and humble respect. For just as Christ says that that **which the heart is full of flows over from the mouth** (Mat. 12:34), so also we can say that the inward devotion and reverence shows itself and takes place in outward **respect. Indeed,** the upright examination and preparation does not actually and mainly consist of such outward reverence—which also the **hypocrites** are able to diligently pursue. Instead, it consist of the **inward motivation of the heart.** Yet it is still an excellent **outward discipline,** and shall not most certainly remain if the right inward examination and preparation is not within the heart. Therefore, then may she not be totally excluded from the very examination which the holy Apostle calls for,

5. *Vitae emendationem,* **that we have the earnest intention to henceforth step away from sins against conscience and to set in motion a life according to the will of God.** The holy Apostle likewise calls for the same thing; he says: **Let a man first examine himself** (v. 28). For if we properly examine ourselves, we shall find out that we are deeply in need of bettering our lives and abstaining from sin so that we do not load upon ourselves God's severe judgment. The holy Apostle likewise calls for this earnest intention for betterment when he says, **We should proclaim Christ's death** (v. 26). For that's why **Christ died:** in order that **sin might die in us and we henceforth no longer live for sin but for Him** who died for us (2 Cor. 5:15). Consequently, anyone who properly ponders Christ's death will also become an enemy of sin because it became so bitterly bloody for Christ to atone for and pay for our sin. However, anyone who still deliberately wants to proceed against conscience with deliberate sins,

thereby adequately indicates that he does not yet properly treasure **the death of Christ** (Heb. 10:28 [v. 26ff]). Additionally, to proclaim Christ's death then means to thank Him from the heart that **He loved us so much and give Himself up for into death** (Gal. 2:20). Such a thanksgiving must not merely take place with lips and with words. Instead, it also must take place **with deeds and with works**, that one **die to sin and henceforth live in righteousness** (1 Pet. 2:4). This thanksgiving has to be done with a sure, serious resolve. In short, we are to use the holy Lord's Supper *humiliter*, **with true contrition** and sorrow over our sin; *fiduciliter*, **with true faith in Christ**; *concorditer*, **with genuine love** and brotherly reconciliation; *reverenter*, **with dutiful reverence**; *obedienter*, **with earnest intention** to henceforth serve and be obedient to **God**.

These are the main parts that constitute the necessary examination and salutary preparation for a beneficial use of the holy Lord's Supper. They are also required for this if the reception of the holy Lord's Supper is to server to **promote godliness**. This was the practice in the Christian Church of the New Testament; namely, that those who wanted to partake of the holy Lord's Supper would first announce their intention to the preacher of the divine Word and **confess their sin** to him. As a result, he then could know whether they also had properly examined themselves in advance. Similarly, for some days prior to their partaking of the holy Lord's Supper they **refrained from all other activity** and directed their thoughts solely on this intention. Furthermore, on the day prior, they **fasted** or refrained from eating and drinking so that they might ponder their unworthiness and the worthiness of this heavenly meal; also, so that they might be better equipped for prayer. Finally, they also **let themselves be prayed for** in common Christian assembly so that God the Lord Himself through His good Spirit might make them diligently worthy and prepared so that they might receive this holy Lord's Supper not to their judgment but to their betterment and eternal salvation.

Chapter Five

That holy, devotional contemplation promotes us towards godliness.

By holy devotional contemplation we understand it to mean that a true lover of godliness daily sets aside a designated time during which he withdraws his heart's thoughts from all external, earthly, worldly affairs and enters his own heart and lifts it up to contemplate heavenly spiritual matters. That such holy, devotional contemplation is conducive towards promoting godliness can be concluded from the following reasons:

1. *Ex DEI mandato*, **because God the Lord requires such holy contemplation from us.** God the Lord said to Abraham in Gen. 15:5-6: **Look up to heaven and count the stars. Can you count them? So shall be your seed.** Here God the Lord places before Abraham the huge uncountable host of stars to contemplate so that they might be for him a prototypical portrayal and sign of the uncountable host of his spiritual seed. Job says in His book, ch. 12:7-8: **Just ask the cattle; they will teach you. And the birds under the heavens will tell you. Or speak with the ground; it will**

teach you, and the fish of the sea will tell you about it. Such teaching and questioning cannot occur in any other manner than through holy, diligent contemplation. Namely, that a person **contemplate** from these creations of God the Creator's **Wisdom, goodness and omnipotence.** Job 37:14 – **Take notice, see, and realize the wonders of God.** Psa. 4:5 – **Speak with your hearts upon your beds.** Ecc. 7:13 – **Take a look at the works of God, for who can make straight what He has bent?** Isa. 42:8* – **You transgressors, take it to your hearts; in due course remember previous things from ancient times.** In Mat. 6:26, Christ says, **Notice the birds under the heavens. Take a look at the lilies in the fields.** Luke 12:24 – **Consider the ravens.** Here Christ sets before us the little birds in the sky and the little flowers upon the earth in order that we should look at them and observe them. From this we will recognize God's marvelous, fatherly providence and rule.

2. *Ex Sactorum exemplo,* **because the saints of God have been described as having** such contemplation **ascribed to them.** In Gen. 24:63, it is written about **Isaac that he want out into his fields in the evening** *ad meditandum* [*to meditate*]—as it actually reads in the original Hebrew. He did so that **he might contemplate the wonders of God in** the work of creation and in the promises revealed in His Word. In Psa. 63:7, David says *in matutinis meditabor* [*in his early morning meditation*] **when I go to bed I think of You, when I awaken I talk**

* Tr. Note: Obviously Gerhard is here referencing Isa. 46:8b-9a; his quote is different from Luther's translation. I feel he was freely translating Isaiah from the original Hebrew from memory. Again, Gerhard appears to me to have been blessed with a brilliant mind and memory.

about You. In Psa. 63:7, Asaph says: **At night I think about playing my stringed instrument and speaking with my heart. My spirit must search. V. 12 – I remember the works of the Lord. Indeed, I think about Your previous miracles.** Psa. 119:15: **I behold Your ways. V. 52 – Lord, when I remember how You have ruled from the beginning of the world, I am comforted. V. 55 – Lord at night I think about Your Name and keep Your Law. V. 59 – I consider my ways and turn my feet to Your testimonies. V. 148 – I wake up early so that I may speak about Your Word. V. 172 – My tongue shall have its speech from Your Word, for all Your commandments are right.** However, the **cocky self-assured** and contemptible wicked are punished on account of the fact **that they do not look at the work of the Lord and do not behold the accomplishments of His hands** (Isa. 5:12).

3. *Ex meditationis fructu* [*on the basis of the fruit of meditation*], because such contemplation **is very beneficial, salutary and edifying,** for it brings us **to an understanding of God and of ourselves.** Such meditation immediately draws our heart away from the earthly towards the heavenly. It prepares and warms up our heart so that from henceforth we become all the more diligent in prayer. It guards against cocky self-assurance and wickedness, so that a person does not mindlessly, like some dumb livestock, pursue that and neglect God's Word. That's why David says in Psalm 1:3 – **Blessed is the man who has a desire for the Law of the Lord, and speaks about His Law day and night.** For, in the original Hebrew, David uses the sort of word which actually means *dilegenter meditari instar avium, quae mussitant, & perpetuo disserere* [*to diligently* *meditate like doves who while quietly cooing to each other endlessly discuss matters*]. So one is to **contemplate with diligence** God's Word in one's heart, and speak about it with one's mouth. Psa. 19:13; Psa. 37:30, etc. – **Whoever does this shall be rewarded** here in time and there in eternity. Rom. 1:20 – **God's invisible essence, that is to say, His eternal power and divinity is visible, so that a person can perceive and discern the truth from His works, namely, His creation of the world.** However, if a person truly wishes to perceive this, then this inward, heartfelt contemplation is needed.

    4. Ex typo.* In His Law, **God the Lord had ordained that all the animals that chewed the cud were to be regarded as being clean** (Lev. 11:3). He did so to indicate thereby that it is a true attribute of an upright Christian and of all God-pleasing people that they ruminate on God's Word and works and contemplate them with diligence and be motivated by them. The Word of God is a **holy Seed** (Luke 8:11). If the Seed is to bear fruit, that it must be received, implanted, enfolded, warmed, and moistened into rich soil. So also, if the spiritual Seed of the divine Word is to be fruitful for righteousness in us, it has to be implanted and preserved in the heart. The Word of God is the **true Bread of Life** by which God the Lord feeds our soul (Deu. 8:2). If physical bread serves to nourish the body it has to be chewed up and be digested. So also, if the **spiritual bread of the Word of God** is to feed and satisfy our souls, then it, too, must likewise, be chewed up and digested through contemplation so that it consequently becomes distributed throughout all the veins of the inward man.

---

* Tr. note: on the basis of type—Greek: τυπος.

Chapter Six

In what manner holy devotional contemplation is to be employed in order that it may be conducive towards godliness.

If this contemplation—the benefit and necessity of which becomes apparent from the previous chapter—is to beneficially promote godliness, then it has to be upright. It has to be both *ratione modi*, that it be carried out in **an upright manner;** and next *ratione objecti*, that it be directed towards **an appropriate purpose.**

Regarding the form and manner of this **contemplation**, it must diligently be *frequens & quotidiana*, it must take place **often and daily.** We are not to **undertake this** on a certain occasion on certain weeks or days. Rather, we are to at least daily—once we force ourselves to do this—see if there is not actually present a commandment about this in God's Word. Likewise also whether there is not a special commandment given as to how often one should pray and how often one should partake of the holy Lord's Supper. So then, there is enough to be concluded **from the benefit and necessity** of these contemplations that it is indeed appropriate that one rightly and ultimately take in hand—or even more so, take to heart—such contemplation in **the day,** as well as at night when we wake up. The most evil enemy actually knows all too well that such contemplation very much promotes godliness. That's why he constantly hurls hindrances in the way so that we do not achieve this. Isn't that why Christ expressly testifies in Mat. 13:22, Mark 4:19 and Luke 8:14 that the **cares of this world and this life choke out the seed of the divine Word** in the hearts of many people? There is no other reason for this other than that people allow the cares of this world and this life to actually engulf them to the extent that they consequently fail to achieve contemplating the divine Word and the works of God. Is not this even the same thing which our precious Savior has so clearly taught us in Luke 21:34, that **worries burden the nurturing of the heart** so that it is unable through the holy contemplation to lift itself up to God? That's why we should tear ourselves away from earthly affairs with which we become involved and to which we at the same time have become **enslaved.** We should completely sever ourselves for a while from the worries of this life and hasten to the closet of our hearts, lock shut its door, and with holy meditation **speak with God** (Mat. 6:6). The spiritual Bride of Christ speaks of this in Song of Solomon 1:4 - **The King leads me into his chamber.** Ch. 3:4 - **I found Him who loves my soul. I cling to Him and will not let go of Him until I can bring Him into my mother's home, into my mother's bed chamber.**

Secondly, this meditation must also be *ardens, & devota,* **diligent and devotional.** It is to be **begun and concluded** with a believing, longing sigh. Here we have to **begin** with David in Psa. 119:18 - **Open my eyes that I may behold the wonders of Your Law.** Also, we have to **conclude** with Isaiah (Ch. 8:16), **Seal the Law into my heart.** The High Priest **Eli** instructed the lad Samuel in this manner: When he was called, he was to say, **Speak Lord, Your servant hears** (Sam. 3:9). Of course, God does not speak with **us** through prophetic

revelations and visions. However, He does speak with us **in His Word**—not just only **externally,** but also **inwardly**—when through His Holy Spirit He reminds us in our hearts about what we heard externally from His Word or read from it. Here we should also like a true Samuel and hearers of divine **speech** say with true devotion: **Speak Lord,** for Your servant is listening. If it is to be a salutary meditation, then it must be carried out with true devotion. If an **image** is to be reflected in water, the water must not be disturbed, but rather remain still. So also must **our soul be still before God** (Psa. 62:2). Furthermore, through such contemplation the **glory of the Lord is to be reflected in us, with an uncovered face, and we are to be transfigured in the very same image from one glory to another, as from the Spirit of the Lord** (2 Cor. 3:18).

Chapter Seven

Concerning that to which this contemplation should be directed so that it may promote godliness.

Until now we have dealt with *de meditationis modo,* about the mode and manner, as to what kind of manner the meditation is to be carried out. From now on we must additionally deal with *de meditationis objecto* [*the object of the meditation*], that to which this contemplation should be directed so that it may be of service towards godliness.

The first kind of contemplation.

In the first volume of dealing with this, we proved that a person can be motivated towards godliness both through the **contemplation of the Creator**, and then also through [the contemplation of] **the creation** or the creatures. In God the Creator, a person especially should first of all contemplate His unending **goodness and mercy**. Secondly, in His immeasurable **righteousness**. Thirdly, in His **majesty and divine glory**. God's gifts and His goodness give testimony once and for all to His manifold, immeasurable **blessings** which He has shown to mankind on behalf of all other creatures. After this also come His sure, unfailing **promises** that He, in addition to these blessings, wants to bestow even more good things upon His beloved **children**. The divine blessings consist of **three** outstanding, special classifications. Certain ones belong to the Article of **Creation**, some to the Article of **Redemption**, some to the Article of **Sanctification**. The gracious work of sanctification encompasses within it the eternal **election by grace**, which took place before the foundations of the world were ever laid. Then there is also the **distribution and bestowing of the spiritual gifts** in this historical lifetime. As to the spiritual gifts and blessing that are bestowed upon us in the fullness of time, there once more are **three kinds of blessings** that belong this. First of all, there is the **divine call** into Christ's kingdom. Next, there is **justification and re-birth** which consists of the forgiving of sins and the imputation of Christ's righteousness. In the third place, there is the **renewal** and bestowing of the Holy Spirit. The **call** into Christ's kingdom takes place through **Word** and through the **holy Sacraments,** of which there are two in the New Testament. They are **holy Baptism** and the **holy Lord's Supper.** In addition to these blessings which are common for either **every human being,** or at least to **all believers and true Christians,** there still are certain **special** blessings that God the Lord particularly shows **in favor of someone else** from among us. The contemplation of these blessings should admonish towards godliness no less the than the prior blessings. The divine **righteousness** is to be understood only the inward, **essential** attribute that God the Lord is righteous in and of Himself. Also it is His unchangeable will that the rational creatures are to regulate themselves in accordance with the **norm and guiding principle** of righteousness that He has prescribed for them in the Law. Then there follows the **external actions** of divine righteousness which God the Lord directs His righteousness towards the rational creatures in that He rewards each individual according to his works: He rewards the good but punishes the wicked. The creatures of God's creation consist of two categories or kinds. Some kinds are **rational creatures,** others are **irrational creatures.** There are two groups of rational creatures, namely **angels** and **mankind. The angels** are either **good or evil** angels. Among mankind there are both we ourselves and there are other people who are generally grouped under the name of **the neighbor.** These other people are either **godly believers or godless unbelievers,** both in and outside of the visible church. Some have already **died** before us and have either gone **to the joys of heaven or to the pangs of hell.** However, some are **still living** around us and next to us here upon earth. The **irra-**

tional creatures are either **living** or they are **lifeless earthly** or **heavenly creations.** In what manner these creatures in **general or in special** contemplation are able to admonish and awaken us towards godliness, has already been extensively explained in the first volume. As a result, it will be of service to a true lover of godliness if he in accordance with such guidance of God the Creator, contemplates the creatures to thereby exercise himself towards godliness.

The second kind of contemplation.

The holy Apostle Paul divides true godliness into **three** parts when he says in Tit. 2:12: **We are to deny the ungodly essence and worldly lusts and live chaste, upright and godly lives in this world.** We are to conduct ourselves **blessedly** towards God the Lord who is over us, **justly** towards the neighbor who is next to us, and **chastely** within ourselves. According to this division, we can **raise three** *objecta* [*obstacles*] to which these holy **contemplations** may be directed, such as **God the Lord, we ourselves,** and **the neighbor.** **With God the Lord,** a person needs to contemplate the manifold **blessings** which he has received from Him. **With himself** he needs to contemplate once again the manifold **sins** which he has undertaken, as well as his manifold **needs** which he requires to sustain body and soul. Also, that he may receive and attain eternal life. With the **neighbor,** he needs to contemplate the very same manifold **needs** which he has brought before God in prayer [for himself]. To such an extent then especially are to be found **four** parts which each true Christian and lover of godliness should contemplate daily. First, of all his own **sin,** he should petition **the forgiveness of them** from God through Christ. The contemplation of sins consists of these **two** parts: the heavy burden of **inherited sin** and **actual** transgressions are to be acknowledged. The **actual** sins are initiated with thoughts, words, and deeds as one either undertakes to do that which is **evil,** or neglects to do the **good.** We sin against God, against the neighbor, and against ourselves. Here are to be found sins of our **youth** as well as daily transgressions. Our flesh and blood constantly tugs at us to sin. Many times we allow ourselves to be overcome by it. Frequently we allow ourselves to participate in **sin.** Also in many ways we ourselves fail. Indeed, all creation accuses us on account of our sins. And, in Christ's suffering and dying we especially see—like in a clear mirror the earnest—the burning wrath of God against sin, etc.

The **second** part consists of this: that we should constantly thank God for His **blessings.** For here a true lover of godliness should with constant contemplation of these divine blessings—like strolling through the beautiful pleasure gardens of **nature**—stroll through the garden of the Christian **churches** to gather from them various fragrant little 'plants' of divine gifts. He should gather them together in his memory, spiritually delight himself in them as over a physical fragrance, and bring to God the Lord the offering of his lips as a sweet smelling sacrifice for them.

Here every true Christian needs **to thank God** for creating, redeeming, and sanctifying him. Furthermore, that in this life He has poured out rich blessings on him. Also, that He has promised to bestow in the future an even greater blessing of eternal life, and that

He has enriched him in soul and body and outward blessings, that He has guarded and protected him in this life from all sorts of **dangers**. The misfortune from which God protects us by grace is a far greater blessing than all the other blessings He gives to us. *In Summa* [*To sum it all up*], a true Christian will discover with these contemplations that we neither with words nor by thought are able to achieve the numerous and honorable divine blessings for which we—along with all the elect—shall praise and glorify Him in all eternity.

Thirdly, a lover of godliness needs to daily contemplate his manifold **needs for which he needs to pray** in order to sustain and increase the gifts of the Spirit, as well as for a victorious overcoming of every anxiety. For the inward contemplation of our needs teaches us that we do not obtain even the most insignificant of any earthly or heavenly, bodily, or spiritual blessings on our own. Consequently, such meditation reminds us that we are to lay aside any and every **confidence** in our own worthiness and our own power, and solely seek refuge for gracious **help** in God's divine **mercy** which is promised to us in Christ. In addition, through this contemplation of our manifold needs, our heart is directed towards God and with longing sighs cries to Him to **kill off the old Adam** and to **renew** the **new** man within us. This is necessary for every regenerate person. Such **renewal** consist of nurturing and increasing faith, hope, love, humility, patience, meekness, chastity, and other virtues. All this has to be obtained with earnest prayer to God. Because of the fact that our **flesh** desires to move us to an inordinate love for the earthly; also, that the **world** with its hatred and **Satan** with his guile desire to conquer us—we have to despise and scorn earthly things. Also, we have to deny ourselves, victoriously overcome the world, find rest and renewal for our souls, be victorious over temptation. Furthermore, with zealous prayer, we have to daily grasp the gracious protection of the Lord of the armies as our war Lord and victory Lord against the devil's tricky ruses. Also, since we will have the greatest need for God's grace and help in the hour of **death** and on the Day of the Final **Judgment.** So we also must humbly seek and pray to God the Lord for a blessed **departure** from this life and for a blessed **entrance into** eternal life.

Fourthly and lastly, a true Christian should daily contemplate the need of his **neighbor.** For he should **pray for** all those things which the neighbor needs for this and the future life. For through such contemplation of the needs of the neighbor a Christian focuses in on the **common need** of the Church and the earthly authorities. Thereby, he also appropriately empathizes with the need of the neighbor as if this were his own need. The fruits of all this is a true, proper **love** which binds all of us members into one body, of which Christ is the Head. Also, it sees to it that we heartily accept the general **need** of the Church and all its members. Consequently, he prays daily for the upholding of the divine Word, for **teachers** and **hearers,** for **rulers and subjects,** and for **households.** God Himself has established these three institutions for the maintenance of this life and for the growth of the Christian churches. He prays for his relatives and benefactors which he otherwise is obligated to through the bond of natural law. He prays for his enemies and persecutors, whose conversion and salvation he seeks form the bottom of his heart. He prays for all sorts of people who are in need. Also, he cares for those whose misfortunes prick his heart and move him to Christian sympathy. Concerning this kind of divine, holy contemplation we have dealt with extensively in a special little pamphlet, the title of which is *The Daily Exercise of Godliness**. It is a prayer booklet that contains confessions of sins, thanksgivings, prayers, and petitions. It was first published by the Coburg Press, and later on in Jena.

The third kind of contemplation.

Saint David teaches us in the 19th Psalm that there are **two kinds of books** from which we may study God's knowledge. The **first** is *liber naturae,* the **book of nature.** He says of it: **the heavens declare the glory of God and the skies proclaim the work of His hands,** etc. Paul speaks about this same book in Rom. 1:20 this way: **God's invisible essence, i.e., His eternal might and divinity can be seen from observing His works, namely the creation of the world.** The **second** book is *liber Scripturae,* the **Book of Holy Scripture.** David speaks of this in the referenced place: **the Law of the Lord does not change and renews the soul. The testimony of the Lord is sure and makes the foolish wise.** Augustine in his *Enarr. Psal. 34: Duo sunt, quae in cognitione in DEI ducunt, Creatua & Scriptura.*† Just as we, to a certain degree, can study about the knowledge of God from both 'books,' so we are able to also use both books for the promotion of godliness. In the Book of Holy Scriptures

---

* Published in English with the title, *The Daily Exercise of Piety.*
† "There are two ways by which to acquire knowledge about God, creation & Scripture."

we find both **Law** and **Gospel**. If we contemplate God's Law, we find on the one hand: **1.** *Divina praecepta*, many frequently repeated **commandments** in which God the Lord admonishes us to godliness; **2.** *Divina promissa*, divine **promises** in which He promises temporal and eternal blessings to those who are obedient to Him; **3.** *Proemiorum exempla*, various **examples** of how God intends to keep His promises to richly reward the godly. On the other hand, we find: **1.** *Divinas prohibitiones* [*divine prohibitions*], namely, that we indeed are not to deviate from the pathway of godliness; **2.** *Divina comminationes*, divine **threats** in which God the Lord seriously threatens to temporally and eternally punish the godless and disobedient; **3.** *Poenarum irrogationes*, various **examples** of how God the Lord will punish the godless and disobedient for their stubborn rebelliousness. A true lover of godliness can daily present these points to his heart, and diligently mark the passages of divine Scripture which pertain to each part. This will be of service to him in promoting godliness within him.

To the **Gospel** belong the **prophecies** about Christ from the Old Testament, the **passages of comfort** that speak about Christ's blessings, the gracious **promises** about the forgiveness of sin and **God's** grace in Christ, etc. The contemplation of such passages cannot help but be of service in promoting godliness within a Christian—as has been extensively dealt with in volume one.

The contemplation of the **Book of the Holy Scriptures** is able to also instill the characteristic in a person to take note of how God the Lord in this Book is **speaking to a believing soul.** In other words, of how God the Lord is admonishing us and we obediently **re-**

spond. Of how God the Lord actually **is** promising grace and we are responding to Him by faith. Of how we cry out to God in prayer and God the Lord graciously answers us. Of how we lament to God with anxious hearts and God the Lord mightily comforts us—of all this we have extensively dealt with in a little handbook whose title is *Two Small Tracts on Comfort*. One of these covers the spiritual conversation between God the Lord and a believing soul; the other contains divine comfort. This one is especially directed towards twelve kinds of **needs.** They were first printed at Coburg and later at Jena.

Essentially, we can fruitfully study in the **Book of Nature** whenever we are contemplating **ourselves** or other **creatures** that were created by God. Within ourselves we find the **inner** book of **conscience** which constantly admonishes us that we are to diligently pursue godliness—if only we will give ear to this inward 'preacher.' He definitely would admonish us towards every good. In creation we find the external book that is there for us to constantly read, study and contemplate. As many creatures as are presented to us the heaven, in the sky, upon the earth, in the water, and below the earth, that's how many 'teachers' of godliness have been set before us—as has been indicated at the conclusion of the first volume of this series.

The fourth kind of contemplation.

God the Lord finished creating everything within **six** distinct days and rested on the seventh day—as **Moses** instructs us in the first and second chapter of his First book [Genesis]. So then, the contemplation of the creatures can justifiably be presented in keeping with such days of work, and the days can be divided this way each week. On the **first day,** God first created **heaven and earth,** i.e., a huge water-logged lump of dirt as the **material** from which He later formed heaven and earth. For Moses himself explains it this way in Gen. 1:2 – **And the earth was an empty wasteland, and there was darkness upon the depths of it.** With the work of this day please note the Creator's **Omnipotence** in that He could form such a beautifully built heaven and earth, and could **call forth into existence that which was not** (Rom. 4:17). Note that He could make that which one sees **out of nothing** (Heb. 11:3). Also contemplate the fact of the Creator's **wisdom,** in that He made everything in such an orderly way—and did not immediately finish everything like a flash in the twinkling of an eye. That's how He also handles our **conversion and renewal**—which, likewise, is the **second creation.** He crafts and renews us daily until we finally become perfectly finished in eternal life. Before such a mighty Lord who is able to create everything out of nothing and thereafter also once more turn it into nothing we indeed rightly ought to **fear** Him.

Before anything else, God created the **Light** on the first day (Gen. 1:3). It's a lifeless creature with which we would be unable to see any of the other creatures. With the work of this day please note that God the Lord is a most beautiful Light (1 John 1:5), **in whom there is no darkness, in whom there is no change or shifting between darkness and the Light** (Jam. 1:17). **For He resides in a Light that no man can approach** (1 Tim. 6:16). From His Substance and Essence, He from eternity beget **His Son** Who is the **Light** from Light (John

1:4). He is **the true Light that enlightens all men who come into this world** (v. 9), so that He, through the Light of His Word and through His Holy Spirit, might enlighten our darkened hearts and ignite within us the Light of divine knowledge. 2 Cor. 4:6 – **God, who called the Light to shine forth out of the darkness, has bestowed a bright shine into our hearts. Thus through this enlightenment about the knowledge of the glory of God in the face of Jesus Christ we were made into children of the Light.** Luke 16:8:1; 1 The. 5:5 – Hence, it is incumbent upon us that we should walk as **children of the Light** since we are a **light in the Lord.** Eph. 5:8–9 – Also, we are to **lay aside the works of darkness and put the weapons of the Light.** Rom. 13:12 – For He has also prepared for us **in eternal life** an indescribable, incomprehensible **Light** for which we long, and by faith we should strive for this with all godliness.

In the third place, the most outstanding ecclesiastical scholars maintain that God the Lord also created the **holy angels** on the first day [of creation]. The are heavenly lights and **morning stars** (Job 38:7). With this day's work the **goodness** of God gave consideration to providing such stately servants for mankind. We should acknowledge this with utmost thankfulness and with a grateful servitude towards God. But even more so, we especially should rightly follow the example of the steadfast **obedience of the holy angels.** A person can spend time with this particular contemplation on the first day of the week—or, as we say, on **Sunday.**

On the **second** day, **God** created the **firmament** of the heavens, the **skies** which He spreads out like a **carpet** (Psa. 104:2). He has stretched them out like a

thin skin and spread them out like a **tent** in which a person can live (Isa. 40:22; Ch. 42:5). On the same day, He **divided the water above the skies from the water under the sky.** With the work of this day, contemplate that God the Lord **made the heavens so orderly** (Psa. 136:5), that He has His sure course and never fails. That's why we should all the more rightly be **obedient** to God the Lord with sure, unfailing orderliness. Contemplate the fact that while **the visible, perishable heavens** are so beautiful and bright, **the invisible, eternal heaven** which He has prepared as a dwelling place for the believers and godly, will have to be far more beautiful and bright. Contemplate how the **heavens declare the glory of God and the skies proclaim the work of His hands** (Psa. 19:1), **how the water above the heavens praise God** (Psa. 148:4). That's why we, as rational creatures, should all the more **proclaim God's glory and praise.** A person can especially spend time with this sort of contemplation on the second day of the week—or, as we say it, on Monday.

On the **third** day, God created the **earth** and the **sea**, i.e., with His divine omnipotence He saw to it that the water under the firmament—which had wrapped and surrounded and intertwined itself around the earth—**gathered itself together in certain places so that one could see the dry part and He called the dry part "earth" and called the water "ocean."** With this day's great work, contemplate the great majesty and **omnipotence of God** the Creator, and let this move you toward an inward fear of God. God the Lord Himself points to this when He speaks about this day's work in His Word in Job 38:8-11 - **Who has unlocked** gates of the ocean so that it broke out as from a mother's womb? I have clothed it with clouds and wrapped it up with dark clouds like swaddling band. I set its course with My bounds and set its borders and doors. And I said, this far you shall come and no further. Here you shall lay down your proud waves. Psa. 33:7-8 – He holds together the water in the ocean as a heap, and lay its depths hidden away. Let all the world fear the Lord, and let everything that lives upon the ground be shy before Him. Psa. 104:5-9 – You who have set the kingdom of this earth upon its foundation so that it abides eternally from now on. You cover it with its depths as with a cloak, and waters stand above the mountains. But they flee from Your scolding, they run away from Your thunder. The mountains rise up and the broad valleys sink themselves down to the place which you have established for them. You have set Your boundaries over which they cannot cross, and they no longer can cover the earth. Jer. 5:22 – Are you not fearful of Me, says the Lord, and don't you tremble with fright before Me? I am the One who set the sand upon the shore for the ocean in which it must remain at all times. It dare not go over it. And though it tries to, it will be unsuccessful. Even though its waves rage, it still dares not pass beyond it.

Also on this same day God the Lord allowed the earth to grow **grass, leaves,** and fruitful **trees**. With this day's work, you are to also contemplate that you have **been planted** as a **fruitful tree** (Psa. 1:3) **planted in the house of the Lord** (Psa. 92:14) as **a tree of righteousness planted to the glory of the Lord** (Isa. 61:3). We are to bring forth **good fruits** that are well-pleasing to God the Lord and of service to the neighbor, and be fruitful with good works (Tit. 3:14). With this contemplation, one can especially increase one's spiritual joy the third day—or, as we refer to it, **on Tuesday.**

On the **fourth** day, God the Lord created both big **lights** in the vaults of the heavens—the **sun** and the **moon**—as well as the **stars.** With this day's work contemplate the fact that your Lord and Savior, Christ Jesus, is the **true Sun of Righteousness** (Mal. 4:2). He is **the Rising from on High** (Luke 1:78). **His countenance shines like the brightness of the sun** (Mat. 17:2; Rev. 1:16). He enlightens your heart so that you may receive from Him the **Light of Life**—just as the moon receives its light from the sun, so that you from henceforth also may **let your light shine before men so that they may see your good works** (Mat. 5:16). Also, so that **you may shine as a light of the world amidst a perverse and crooked generation** (Phi. 2:15). Contemplate that **Christ** is the beautiful **bright Morning Star** (Rev. 22:16) who sees to it **that also the divine knowledge of the Morning Star may arise in your heart** (2 Pet. 1:19). He also holds **you** in His **hand** like a beautiful **little star** (Rev. 1:15). That's why you must also let **the light of good works shine forth from you.** For what kind of star would it be which does not shine? Light is the nature and essence of a star. With this contemplation, one is able to especially be happy on the fourth day of the week—or, as we refer to it, on Wednesday.

On the **fifth** day, God the Lord created the **fish of the sea and the birds that fly around under heaven's vault.** Contemplate on the work of this day the **wisdom of God**, on the various kinds of fish and birds, as well as on His **goodness**—in that He created them **for the** benefit and good of mankind. Psa. 104:24-26 – **Lord, how great and many are Your works! You have provided them all so wisely, and the earth is full of Your goodness. The sea is so huge and wide that teems and crawls with both great and small animals without number. In it sail the ships. In it are the Leviathan that You have made so that they may playfully swim around in it.** With this contemplation, one may especially have great happiness on the fifth day of the week—or, as we refer to it, on **Thursday**.

On the **sixth** day, God created **cattle, creeping things and animals upon the earth—each one according to its kind.** Once again, contemplate the **wisdom of God** in regard to the various kinds of animals, and the **goodness of God** in that He **created them for the good of mankind** (Gen. 1:26). Some of the animals were created for the purpose of **feeding mankind**, certain others for **clothing,** others **to be of servitude and work,** others **for enjoyment.** However, all were created for his benefit and welfare. Also, contemplate the *simulacra virtutum*, the **virtue mirror** that God holds before us in these animals—as an example, the **diligence of ants.** Pro. 6:6-8: **You lazy one, go and observe the ant, take a look at its ways and learn. Although it does not have a ruler or commander or lord, it nevertheless prepares its bread in the summer and gathers food during the harvest.** We have another example, the **thankfulness** of the oxen and mules in Isa. 1:3 – **The ox knows its master and a mule the feed trough of its master, but Israel does not recognize anything, and my people notice nothing.** There's the example of the storks and cranes in Jer. 8:7 – **A stork in the sky knows his time; a turtle**

dove, crane, and dove note the time they are to return. However, My people want to know nothing about what the Lord wants. And the same applies to other animals. Also, on the very same day, God the Lord created man in His own **image.** He concluded His work of creation with man. With the work of this day, contemplate the fact that our **first Father** formed us out of **a clod of dirt!** This should **guide** you towards **humility.** *Adverte homo, quia limus es, & non sis superbus,*[*] Bernhard says in his *Sermon 3, in Nat. Dom. Col. 41.* **I have undertaken to talk with the Lord, even though I am dirt and ashes,** says Abraham in 18:27. Contemplate the miraculous **assemblage** of the veins, the bones, and all the members of the body, and from this learn that you are obligated to serve your Creator with every **member** of your body. Contemplate the great **goodness** of the Lord of giving you a **rational soul,** and from this learn that you are obligated to serve your Creator with all **the might of your soul.** With this contemplation, a person can happily take spiritual pleasure on the sixth day—or, as we refer to it, on **Friday.**

On the **seventh** day, God **rested** from all His work which He had done (Gen. 2:2). In this case, contemplate that God also **wants to rest in your souls.** Isa. 57:15- **Thus says the High and magnificent Noble One who lives forever, whose Name is holy. I live in the high and sacred place, and with those who are knocked down and are of a humble spirit in order to renew the spirit of the humble and the heart of the stricken.** Isa. 66:1-2: **Thus says the Lord: Heaven is My throne, and the earth is My footstool. What sort**

---

[*] "Take note, O man, because you are mud, and there is no reason for you to be arrogant."

of house is it you wish to build for Me, or where is the place where I should rest? My hand has created everything that exists, says the Lord. However, I look upon the one who is of a miserable and broken spirit and who is awestruck before My Word. It is as if He wants to say, I want to reside and rest in such a heart. Also contemplate the fact that you once more are **to rest in God,** and are to observe a spiritual **Sabbath** in that you rest from the works of the sinful flesh and allow God the Lord to work in You. Isa. 56:2 - **Blessed is the man who does this and the son of man who steadfastly keeps this: that he keeps the Sabbath and not defile it but watches his hand so that it does no evil.** Ch. 58:13-14: **As you turn your foot away from the Sabbath, you do not do that which pleases Me on My holy Day. It will be called a happy Sabbath of the Lord for sanctification and praise, if you do not go your own way or are caught in doing that which pleases you, etc. That's when you will you have your delight in the Lord.** Heb. 4:10 - **Whoever comes into His rest, rests from his labors—just as God did from His.** Contemplate the fact that God the Lord has prepared for you **the eternal rest** and peace in heaven as you continue to keep the **spiritual Sabbath** and let God rest in you. Isa. 66:23 - **They will come to worship before Me one Sabbath after the other, says the Lord.** Heb. 4:6 - **Accordingly it then is a given that certain ones shall enter this very same rest.** V. 9: **Therefore, there still is a rest that exists for the people of God.** V. 11: **So then let us diligently strive to enter into this rest so that nobody falls into the very same example of the unbelieving.** With this contemplation, one can especially delight one's spirit on the **seventh day**—or as we call it, on **Saturday**. And, one can, in an orderly manner, take a look at these kinds of works by God as if they were written upon a blackboard.

The fifth kind of contemplation.

One of the ancient church scholars often said that he daily read a book that had three pages: one was **red**, one was **white,** and one was **black**. From the **red** one, he read and contemplated **the bloody red suffering of Christ**. From the white one, he read and contemplated the **eternal joy of the elect.** For in Holy Scriptures the color white signifies **glory and joy.** Just as the **elect appear** before God's throne in **white robes** (Rev. 4:4; Ch.7:7, etc.), so also the holy angels allow themselves to be seen **dressed in white** (Mark 16:5; Acts 1:10, etc.). **In the Transfiguration of Christ**—which was a prototypical portrayal of the heavenly joy and glory—**His clothes became white** as a bright **light** (Mat. 17:2). **It was so white that no color upon earth could make itself so** white (Mark 9:3).

This ancient church scholar read and contemplated from the **black page the eternal torturous agony and pain** of the damned as they are being scorched in the hellish fires.

A lover of godliness is directed towards this kind of daily contemplation on these three points. He needs to contemplate: **1.** *Christi passionem,* **the bitter suffering of our Lord Jesus Christ;** 2. *Piorum glorificationem,* **the joy** and glory of the blessed and elect; and, **3.** *Impiorum damnationem,* the **pain of the damned** and their eternal **heartache.**

The contemplation of the **sufferings** of Christ can be presented **1.** *Historice*, the fact that we are to ardently contemplate the **history** of how things went with the Lord Christ in His sufferings. A person can be presented with such a historical description in various way.

First of all, it can be divided into **six** distinct *Actus* [acts], as one contemplates **1.** *Hortum*, how things went with Christ in the **Garden**, how there He sweated bloody sweat, was captured and bound, and was forsaken by all His disciples. **2.** *Pontifices*, how things went for Christ before the **ecclesiastical court** of Ananias and Caiaphas, how they brought witnesses against him, how He was shamelessly slapped in the face, mocked, spit upon, and condemned to death in an inexcusable manner. **3.** *Pilatium praesitem*, how things went for Christ before the **ruler Pilate**, how He was mainly falsely accused before him of being a rabble-rouser. **4.** *Herodem*, how things went for Him in the **house of Herod**, how he especially put a white robe on Him, how He was mocked and despised as an almost naked King. **5.** *Crucem*, how He, in **the judgment hall,** was scourged, crowned with thorns, spit upon, beaten, sentenced to death on the cross, how He was led out to place of the skull and there shamefully and painfully crucified. **6.** *Sepulchre*, what took place **after His death**, and how He was laid into the grave. The ancient little verse directs us to this kind of contemplation:

Hortus, Pontifices, Praeses, Crux atque Sepulchrum.
[Garden, Priests, Governor, Cross, and also Sepulcher.]

With this, one is able to divide up the contemplation of Christ's suffering according to a **time line.** The suffering of Christ began on the evening of **Maundy Thursday,** and it ended before the evening of **Good Friday**—and, in keeping with that, everything was completed in a single **Jewish day,** for the Jews count a day from one evening to the next. In this manner, the contemplation of **the history** of Christ's sufferings may be divided into two parts, so that a person can especially contemplate: **1.** What all took place with Christ from the evening of **Maundy Thursday** up to the morning of **Good Friday; 2.** What transpired from the morning of **Good Friday** until the evening of **that same day.**

With the **first part,** it is to be noted that the Jews divided the night into **four parts** or **night-watches,** as is also to be concluded from Mark 13:34. The **first part** began after sunset, and it lasts until nine o'clock—**calculated according to the hands of our clocks.** At that designated time, this was called **evening,** *ratione termini in quo* [*at which time it was calculated to end*]. **The second night watch** began at nine o'clock and lasted until midnight, or until twelve o'clock according to the calculation of the hands of our clocks. This same time period is referred to by Christ as **midnight** in regard to *ratione termini ad quem* [*the manner it was calculated to end*]. **The third night watch** began at midnight and extended itself out until three o'clock, our measurement of time. Christ called this period the **crow of the rooster,** since the rooster let himself be heard with his crowing at this time. The **fourth** night watch began at three o'clock and lasted until the rising of the sun, or until six o'clock. Christ called it **morning** because it extended itself until the morning.

During the **first night watch,** Christ ate the Passover lamb with His disciples at Jerusalem. Thereupon He instituted the Sacrament of the New Testament, washed the feet of His disciples, engaged His disciples in friendly conversation, and prayed His heartfelt prayer to His heavenly Father—which is recounted in John 17. He then went over the brook of Kidron up to the Mt. of Olives. He proclaimed to His disciples His forthcoming suffering, and as He came into the Garden with His disciples, He once more prayed His inward prayer to God and asked for the cup to taken from Him. Here His **inwardly severe** suffering began. It pressed upon Him so severely that He sweated bloody sweat and had to be comforted by an angel. When He had overcome this inward battle, He went out to meet His enemies. He knocked them to the ground with a single word. He was betrayed by Judas with a kiss, was forsaken by His disciples, and was taken captive and bound by His captives.

During the **second night watch**, He was led captive and bound through the Sheep Gate into the city of Jerusalem, first to the High Priest Ananias and later before Caiaphas. He was accused of false doctrine and of causing a rebellion. He was shamefully struck in the face and was denied by His own disciple, Peter. False witnesses were brought before Him, and He was condemned to die by the entire ecclesiastical counsel.

In the **third and fourth night watch**, namely from **midnight** until **morning**, He was mocked, spit in the face, struck with fists, and was blindfolded and struck by the servants of the High Priest who were guarding Him. Then, with taunting words, they required Him to prophecy or guess which of them had hit Him.

The Jews likewise divided the daytime into **four parts.** The **first part** began in the morning at six o'clock and extended itself until nine o'clock. **The second part** began at nine o'clock and extended itself until **noon,** or twelve o'clock. The **third part** began at noon and extended itself until three o'clock. The **fourth part** began at three o'clock and extended itself until the evening, or until it was six o'clock.

In the **first part** of the day, early in the morning, Christ was once more condemned by the High Priests and ecclesiastical council at Jerusalem, and thereupon He was led from the palace of the High Priest before the judgment hall. There He was accused of being a heretic and a rabble-rouser. And He was heard and examined by the governor, Pilate.

In the **second part** of the day, He was led before Herod, mocked by him, and with sarcastic derision and mockery He was cloaked with a white garment and sent back to Pilate. There He was presented alongside the evil murderer, Barabbas. Then He was scourged, crowned with thorns instead of a kingly crown, handed a reed instead of a royal scepter, and was cloaked with an old purple mantle instead of with a royal gown. They did this in order to deride and mock Him for the fact that He was called a king. Later, along with two murderers, He was condemned to death by Pilate and was led to the place of the skull. Then He Himself bore the heavy tree of the cross to which He was to be nailed. He was given to drink of vinegar into which bitter myrrh and gall had been mixed, and was stripped naked. He was crucified between two murderers with nails through His hands and feet. Then the soldiers also divided His clothing among themselves, they cast the die over His cloak, and He was slandered by the murderous thief, by the soldiers, by the High Priests, and by the common mob.

During the **third part** of the day, He hung upon the cross, prayed for those who had crucified Him, promised Paradise to the converted convict, commended His mother to the care of John, was forsaken by God, and complained that He was forsaken by God, and was thirsty. Also, as He gave witness that everything had now been finished and commended His spirit into the hands of His heavenly Father, at that time He died upon the tree of the cross as the Man who offered Himself there as the true atoning sacrifice.

During the **fourth part** of the day, He was taken down from the cross and laid into a grave.

Concerning the **third** one, with this kind of historical contemplation there actually enters into the picture the **seven hour contemplation** as it was observed by the ancients, as this was regarded in the ancient times in *Hymnis, Patris Sapientia, et Domine Jesu Christe.** Also later on transferred over and translated into the German Psalm: **Christ who has saved us, etc.** However, with this we need to take note that such [seven] hours are divided out according to **the Jewish clock:**† "Christ, who has saved us, initiated no evil. He was for us, **in the night,** led as a thief captive. Before godless men and falsely accused, He was laughed at, mocked and spit upon, just as the Scriptures say."

During the **first** hour of the day [6:00 A.M.], He was extravagantly presented to Pilate—a Gentile—as a murderer. Pilate found Him innocent, with no cause for the death penalty. As a result, He sent Him to King Herod.

* Tr. note: Two hymns, 'O Wisdom of the Father,' and, 'O Lord Jesus Christ.'
† Tr. note: Here upon Gerhard evidently is writing this hymn verse. Though written as a lengthy sentence paragraph, it seems to rhyme.

At the **third** hour [9:00 A.M.], God's Son was smitten with scourging and His head was pierced with a crown of thorns. He was dressed up for ridicule and mockery, was severely beaten, and had to carry the cross for His own death.

At the **sixth** hour [noon], He was nailed to the cross naked. He shed His blood on it. He prayed with painful lamenting. The onlookers mocked Him—as well as those who had been crucified with Him—until the sun also withdrew its light from such things.

Jesus cried out at the **ninth** hour [3:00 P.M.]. He complained that He was forsaken. Immediately there was gall in His mouth, laced with vinegar. Then He gave up His spirit and the earth quaked. The Temple curtain tore apart and many rocks split apart.

As they at **Vesper time** broke the legs of the criminals, Jesus' side was pierced with a **spear** so that blood and water flowed out of it, in order to fulfill the Scriptures—as John indicates solely for our sake.

As the day came to a close and **evening** had arrived, Jesus was taken down from the tree-trunk of the cross by Joseph. He was lovingly laid into a grave in keeping with Jewish custom. The grave was then watched over by guards as testified to by Matthew, etc. The very same German Psalm that begins with **O Jesus Christ, etc.** also especially applies here.

Fourthly, this historical contemplation of the sufferings of Christ can also be presented to such an extent of how all the **members** of Christ can contemplate, what He suffered in and on account of each of them, how His **head** was crowned with thorns, His face was splattered with spit, how He was beaten with a **rod**, how His eyes were blindfolded, and were darkened with death. Also, how His **cheeks** were slapped, how His **mouth** was given to drink of myrrh and gall, how His **hands** and **feet** were nailed to the cross, how His **side** was pierced with a spear, how His entire **body** was beaten and wounded with scourging.

To this historical contemplation of Christ's sufferings must be added on **2.** It be contemplated *mystice & practice* [*mystically and practically*], that a person contemplate and view Christ's suffering in a **spiritual** manner, as—

1. A **reflection of wrath,** for since sin is such an outrage to God the Lord that it could not be atoned for in any other way than through Christ's death, it must be concluded that God the Lord is a sincere enemy of sin. Peter says in Acts 4:28: **that with and through Christ's suffering, Herod and Pontius Pilate did what God's hand and God's council had previously considered that it should happen.** Therefore, we have to view everything Christ encountered with His suffering as if **God Himself** was opposing Him. And thus God bound Christ, scourged Him, crucified Him—not as if He personally was **such an enemy** towards Him, but because Christ took upon Himself the **sin** of the whole world in order to make payment for them. That's why God the Lord dealt with Him as if He were the greatest **sinner** of all. That's the reason Christ felt such anguish. He sweated bloody sweat because the burden of **our** sin and the divine wrath we deserved crushed Him like this. He lamented His **being forsaken by God, because God** the Lord wrathfully required Him to bear His divine judgment on account of our sins.

2. As a **reflection of love,** Rom. 5:8: **God revealed His love towards us in that Christ died for**

us while we still were sinners. John 3:16: **So much so God loved the world that He gave His only begotten Son** into the shameful death on the cross. As a result, Christ's suffering is a public testimony to the immeasurable **love of God in that God the Lord did not spare His only begotten Son. Instead, He gave Him up for us all** (Rom. 8:32). It is also a clear testimony to the invincible **love of Christ.** John 15:13: **No one has greater love than the person who gives up His life for a friend.** Gal. 2:20: **Christ loved me and gave Himself up for me.** How could there be any greater love than that Christ gave Himself over into that shameful death on the cross for our sakes? **He bowed His head on the cross** in order to kiss us out of love. He stretched out **His arms** in order to embrace us out of love. He opened His **mouth** in order to pray out of love for those who crucified Him. He allowed His **side** to be pierced open so that one might be able to see His loving heart. On the tree of the cross, He allowed Himself to be consumed by the **fire of love** as the true Lamb of God. Out of love, He **thirsted** for our salvation.

  3. As a **reflection of virtue,** St. Peter tells us in his first Epistle (2:1) that **Christ suffered for us, and left us a model for us to follow in His footsteps.** For in His suffering, Christ placed before us an example of **willing obedience** in that He **became obedient** to His Father **until death; indeed, to death on the cross** (Phi. 2:9). It is a **devout love** because out of love for us He suffered everything. It is a love of heartfelt **humility and patience** because he did not open His mouth as He was being punished and beaten. Instead, He conducted Himself as a patient **little Lamb that is being led to slaughter** (Isa. 53:7). It is a reflection of His **gentleness**

and kindness because **He didn't abuse as He was being abused, He didn't threaten as He was suffering** (1 Pet. 2:23, etc.). So you see, in this way a person can contemplate the suffering of Christ in a salutary manner. How to contemplate the **joy of the elect** and the **agony of the damned** has been sufficiently covered in the first volume in chapters 14 and 18.

The sixth kind of contemplation.

Another one of the ancient church fathers prescribes for us the following rule. We should daily contemplate **three things that are in the past, three things that are in the present,** and **three things that are in the future.** With the past things, we need to contemplate **1.** *Malum commissum,* **the evil which we have initiated,** i.e., our manifold **sins** which we have inwardly and outwardly so frequently committed against the first and the second Tables of the holy Ten Commandments of God, knowingly and unknowingly, secretly and publicly. **2.** *Bonum omissum,* **the good which we have left undone,** of how we could have accomplished many more good things with the might of our souls and bodies, but left them undone. **3.** *Tempus ammissum,* **the time that has passed us by,** especially about how already ten, twenty, thirty, forty, fifty, **sixty years** of our lives have passed us by. We are unable to retrieve or call back a **single hour** of that time.

Concerning the **present** things we need to contemplate **1.** *Vitae hujus brevitatem,* **the short time of our lives** here upon earth. Especially contemplate how quickly our time flies by. It is as if one year flies by after another like a month, or one day after the other slips by like an hour, and we ever draw nearer to the time when we will no longer notice it. **2.** *Salvandi difficultate* [*the difficulties of being saved*], how **burdensome it becomes when a person experiences doubts about his salvation** as he strives against the devil, the world, and the flesh. Then one has to contemplate how a person has to **wrestle** with them so that one is able **to enter through the narrow gate** (Luke 13:24). A person has to contemplate what one must **do with fear and trembling in order to be saved** (Phi. 2:12). **3.** *Salvatorum paucitatem,* [*the small number that are saved*], **how so few people shall be saved,** for the **gate is wide and the road is broad which leads to damnation, and those who journey upon it are many. And the gate is narrow and the road is small which leads to life, and those who find it are few in number** (Mat. 7:13-14).

In regard to the **future things**, we need to contemplate **1.** *Mortem, qua nihil horribilius,* **how we all must some day die,** and leave behind the shelter of this world. We need to contemplate how anxious and painful this experience will be. **2.** *Judicium, quo nihil teribilius,* how each of us will someday have to **be placed before the strict judgment throne of Christ** (Heb. 5:27). **3.** *Poenam inferni, qua nihil intolerabilius,* [*The infernal punishment, how it is nothing less than intolerable*], how many countless thousands of people **shall be shoved into hell,** and what an unblessed, indeed incomprehensible, torture that will be.

The seventh kind of contemplation.

This holy, devotional contemplation may then also be utilized for a person contemplating [these four points]. **1.** *Ea, qua suprano* [*that which is above us*], concerning **that which is above us** the ancient Hebrews said: "Three things are above us. They are **the Eye** that sees everything, **the Ear** that hears everything, and **the Book** into which everything is written." **2.** *Ea, quae intra nos* [*that which is within us*]. We find **good** and **evil** in that which is within us. We have received what is **good** from God. However, we do not always **thank Him for this from the bottom of our hearts**, nor do we always **use it** properly. The **evil** we have partly **inherited** from our parents and partly **initiated ourselves**. As a result, we find within ourselves the nagging of an accusing **conscience**. We still carry within ourselves the corrupt, sinful **flesh,** and in our **bosoms** we still carry **death** with us. **3.** *Ea, quae cira nos* [*that which surrounds us*]. In **what is around us**, we find the **holy angels** who gladly serve us when we are godly. We also find **the evil angels** who, in various ways, lure us into sin, **the world** which viciously accosts us from the right and the left, **the neighbor** whom we are obligated to serve in love, and **other creatures** who accuse us before God when we deliberately sin. **4.** *Ea, quae infra nos* [*that which is below us*]. In that **which is beneath us** we find **the grave** into which we will have to let ourselves be buried after our death, **hell** which spews out its rage and gnashes after us if we live in sin. So take note, no matter where you look, we will find avenues for saintly, good contemplation.

The eighth kind of contemplation.

Some have divided the **contemplation** by **the hours** and have proposed a spiritual time schedule for a lover of godliness. When the clock strikes **one**, we are to remind ourselves that there **is only One God** (Deu. 6:4). We are to honor and serve Him alone. **Everything emanates** from this One, and everything **hastens** to this One. [We are to contemplate] that there is **only One Mediator between God and man, namely the Man Christ Jesus** (1 Tim. 2:5), we are to cling to Him through faith and love. Also, that there is **One Spirit** Who binds together all spiritual members of the Body of Christ and motivates them to every good thing (Eph. 4:4). And **that there is One Lord, one faith, one Baptism, One God and Father of us all** (v. 6). Therefore, we **should be zealous to keep the unity of the Spirit through the bond of peace** (v. 3), that God the Lord has given to each one among us **just one soul** so that we take Him seriously. Contemplate that eternity hangs on **one moment. One** should remind us that we long with David in Psalm 86:11 and contemplate the word of Christ in Luke 10:41: **Martha, Martha, you have much worry and trouble, however only one thing is essential.**

When the clock strikes **two,** we need to remember that God the Lord has given us **two** great, wonderful **gifts of grace**—namely, His **Son** and His **Holy Spirit**—and thus we love Him because of that. We are to contemplate that there are **two** foremost **chief parts** of all divine teaching, namely the **Law** and the **Gospel.** They have been written down on **two stone tablets.** We are to write this down into our hearts through steadfast contemplation. We are to contemplate that **two commandments** are the chief and foremost of all the commandments, namely the **commandment about loving God** and the one about the **love of the neighbor** (Mat.

22:37-38). We are to busy ourselves with these two first. We are to contemplate that God the Lord has put man together of **two** essential **parts,** namely out of **body** and **soul** (Gen. 2:7) and we are to serve God the Lord with both. We are to contemplate that in the New Testament God the Lord has instituted **two Sacraments,** namely **Holy Baptism and the Holy Lord's Supper,** both of which lead and guide us towards godliness. We are to contemplate that our inner man has **two eyes** and that with the one eye he is to behold God's **mercy** and with the other God's **righteousness.** Contemplate that there are **two parts** to true repentance with which we are to busy ourselves every moment. One part is **the acknowledgment of sin** and the other is **faith** in Christ. Contemplate that there are two **breasts** which the spiritual Mother—the Christian Church—holds before us, so that we may suck from them the milk of divine Wisdom (Pro. 1:2), namely the Scriptures of the Old and New Testaments. Contemplate that there are **two things** that belong to true Christianity—a **good conscience** towards God and a **good reputation** with mankind. Contemplate that there are **two** homes that have been prepared for the after life: **Heaven** for the godly and **hell** for the godless.

When the clock strikes **three**, we need to remind ourselves that within the One Divine Essence there exist **Three** distinct **Persons—God the Father, Son, and Holy Spirit.** We are to serve Them in holiness and righteousness. We need to remember that in the first Table of the Law there are **three commandments.** The first addresses the fact that we should truly acknowledge, fear, love, and trust God. The second commandment addresses the fact that with our mouth we should not use the Name of God in an unnecessary way, the third that we should sanctify the Sabbath with all the might of our soul and every member of our body. We are to remind ourselves that in the book of nature there are **three** large **pages**. They are the **heavens**, the **earth**, and the **sea**. We are to read this book daily and study the knowledge of God the Creator. That we are to direct our daily contemplation in **three parts**, first of all as to what we **once were**, secondly as to what we **have now become**, thirdly as to what we **shall become**. In other words, what we were by **nature**, what we now have become by **grace**, and what we shall become in **glory**. That we from the heart deeply regret our past sin, despise the present things of this world, and with our whole heart long for the future eternal glory. We are to take note of **death's bitterness**. We are to remind ourselves of the final **Judgment's strictness** and of the inexpressible **heartache** of the **damned** in hell. We should remind ourselves to contemplate our **sin** in order to repent of it, to contemplate the divine **mercy** so that we do not despair, and to contemplate **death** so that we abstain in time from sin. We need to remember that we should give God the Lord **three things: glory** for being our Creator, **love** for being our Redeemer, and **fear** as our Judge. We should give our neighbor **three things: submissiveness** as our superior, **harmonious concord** as our fellow Christian, **kindness** as our fellow member. We should give ourselves **three things: purity** in our heart, **caution** in our mouth, **discipline** and moderation for each our bodily members. We need to evaluate each one of our deeds in **three ways**: first, if we are **allowed** to do it, then if it is **appropriate** for us to do it, and thirdly if it is **helpful** for us to do it.

The **three** foremost, chief efforts with which we are to diligently pursue for our entire life are **faith, love,** and **hope**. The **three chief enemies** against which we have to constantly strive are the **devil**, the **world**, and our sinful **flesh**.

When the clock strikes **four** o'clock, we need to remember that the day is divided into **four parts**, the night into **four night-watches**. Also, that in each night watch we are to await the **coming** of our Lord (Mark 13:34). We need to remember that **sin** gets started in our hearts in **four** different ways: through **irritability**, through **infatuation**, through **stubbornness**, and through **self-justification**. Remember that there are **four kind** of *gradus* or **steps** in sinning: First **evil thoughts** in the heart, secondly to **take a liking** to such evil thoughts, thirdly to **fulfill** these with outward **deeds**, fourthly to **defend** such deeds and not to desist from them with repentance. This is indicated to us with **Lazarus**, who lay in the grave for four days and had begun to **stink** (John 11:39). Remember that the seed of the divine Word falls upon **four kinds of ground**. For some of it falls along the **pathway** and is gobbled up by the birds. Some falls upon **rocky ground** and dries up. Some of it falls among the **thorns** and is smothered. Some of it falls upon **good ground** and produces fruit (Mat. 13:4 et. al.). As a result, we should indeed see to what kind of ground we are and as to how we hear. Remember that the **final end** particularly consists of **four** things: **death, Judgment Day, hell,** and **eternal life**. Remember that each individual at all times especially has **four things** to contemplate: **one's own death, Christ's death, the world's deceitfulness, and the eternal joy of the elect.**

Mors tua mors Christi, fraus terrae, gloria coeli,
Quatuaor haec semper sunt meditanda tibi.

That each individual be reminded by the **fourfold** striking of the clock of God the Lord, one's own **office, death,** and eternal **life.**

Numinis, officii, mortis vitae que futurae
Nos moneat praesens quae rapit hora diem.

When it strikes **five**, we need to remember the **holy five wounds** of Christ in His hands and feet and in His side, remember that in true faith we are to hide ourselves within them from the wrath of God. Remember that God the Lord has given us **five external senses—sight, hearing, taste, smell, and feeling**—that we are to use in keeping with God's will and commandments so that we will not with these external senses be punished in hell. We are to especially direct our contemplation in a **fivefold** manner, for we need to contemplate these five items: **ourselves, the world, Judgment Day, hell,** and **heaven.** Contemplate that there are **five enemies** that strive against us and the spiritual children of Abraham: **the devil, sin, the world, death, and hell** (Gen. 14:9). Also remember that Christ—as the **divine Joshua**—has overcome these five enemies and has stepped on and crushed their heads (Jos. 10:22). Contemplate that in the parable of the Lord there are presented to us **five wise and five foolish virgins** (Mat. 25:1), so that we diligently busy ourselves to be found among the wise ones.

When the clock strikes **six**, we need to remember that God the Lord created everything that is in heaven and on earth **in six days** (Gen. 2:1; Exo. 20:11). For this great goodness and blessing, we should offer Him thankful and grateful obedience. Contemplate that our life span is **divided into six parts**—namely into **childhood, youth, mature adulthood, the standstill of old age,** and to ultimate **incapacitation**—so that we then in all parts should direct our life towards serving God. Contemplate that spiritual circumcision should be performed on **six parts** of our body: on the **heart**, so that we may fight against evil lusts; on the **tongue**, so that we do not mock God nor speak derisively about the neighbor; on the **eye**, so that we do not look at vain or forbidden things; on the **ears**, so that we do not hear shameful words but have them be stopped up to the cry of the poor; on the **hands**, so that we do not use them to take what belongs to our neighbor or use them to preclude giving something to him; on the **feet**, so that we do not go to forbidden places. We are to contemplate that there are **six** kinds of weapons and armor required for the spiritual fight against the hellish enemy. As, for example, the **helmet of salvation**—which is Christ Jesus. Also the **breastplate or armor of righteousness, the girdle of truth,** this is a good conscience. Also the **boots or leg armor of the Gospel,** it equips us to pursue our calling. Also the **shield of faith,** with it we are able to extinguish all the fiery arrows of the villainous Rogue. And the **sword of the Spirit**, which is the Word of God, as well as **devout prayer** (Eph. 6:14ff.). We need to contemplate that especially in the Old Testament there were **six distinct sacrifices** by which are symbolized the spiritual sacrifices of the New Testament. Such as the **burnt offering,** by it is signified a **broken and crushed heart** (Psa. 51:19). **The Sacrifice of Atonement,** by it is signified the Atonement which took place through Christ on the tree of the cross (Eph. 5:2). We obtain possession of this Atonement by faith. Through the **daily sacrifice** is signified that we should daily present our bodies as a **sacrifice** that is alive and holy and pleasing to God. This is our reasonable worshipful service to God (Rom. 12:1). With the **spice sacrifice** is signified kind deeds to the poor (Heb. 13:16). With the **incense sacrifice** is symbolized a believing, devout prayer (Psa. 141:4; Rev. 8:3). And the **thank-offering** signifies the thanksgiving for God's blessings. We need to daily present these spiritual sacrifices to God the Lord if we actually want to be **spiritual priests** (Rev. 1:6).

When the clock strikes **seven**, we need to remember that God the Lord **rested on the seventh day and sanctified it** (Gen. 3:2). He reminds us with this that we should rest in Him. For just as God the Lord rested on the seventh day—after He had created everything in six days—so also after these up to now **six thousand years of this world** have been completed, the eternal Sabbath and Day of Rest shall begin. We should prepare ourselves for that Day with repentance and godliness. Contemplate that there are **seven commandments** in the **second Table** of the divine commandments. With this thought, we are to constantly endeavor that we should altogether direct the **seven days** which are in each week towards serving and glorifying God. Remind yourself that the Spirit of the Lord is present **with sevenfold gifts** (Acts 4:5). We should seek these from Him with believing prayer. Remember that there are **seven Petitions** in the Our Father [Lord's Prayer] in which is included everything necessary for us in this life and in the life to come. In true faith, we ought to speak these petitions hourly. Remind yourself that just as Christ fed his hearers with **seven loaves of bread** (Mat. 15:36), so He will also, in a spiritual manner, feed us with seven loaves in the future life. For example, as with the greatest **secure confidence**, safe **rest**, quiet **loveliness**, lovely **joy**, a joyful **eternity** eternal **salvation**, and a blessed **view** of the Holy Trinity. With longing, we should look forward to this.

When the clock strikes **eight**, we need to remind ourselves that Christ was **circumcised on the eighth day**, and received the most blessed Name of **Jesus** so that He might earn for us the spiritual circumcision of eternal salvation. For this we need to thank Him from the bottom of our heart. Remember that those whom Christ lauds as being blessed are **eight groups**. In Mat. 5:3-11, He bespeaks blessed those who are **spiritually poor**, for the kingdom of heaven is theirs. Blessed are those **who bear sorrows**, for they shall be comforted. Blessed are the **meek**, for they shall own the kingdom of this world. Blessed are those who **hunger and thirst for righteousness**, for they shall be satisfied. Blessed are the **merciful**, for they shall receive **mercy.** Blessed are the **pure of heart**, for they shall see God. Blessed are the **peacemakers**, for they shall be called God's children. Blessed are those who **for the sake of righteousness shall be persecuted**, for the kingdom of heave is theirs. **Blessed are you when men mock and persecute you on account of Me and say all sorts of evil things about you as the lie about it.** In every need and anguish, we can rejoice and comfort ourselves with these promised blessing from Christ. Remind yourself that **on the eighth** day, Christ was **transfigured** (Luke 9:28). Remember that on the 'Eighth Day'—after the completion of this temporal life which is divided into weeks—shall follow the blessed eternity and the eternal blessedness when we shall be transfigured in body and in soul.

When the clock strikes **nine**, we need to remember that Christ died in the **ninth hour** (Mat. 26:46), and therewith redeemed us from the death of sin and from eternal death so that we may from now on love Him and serve Him (2 Cor. 5:15). Remind yourself that in heaven there is more joy over one sinner who repents than **for the ninety-nine righteous** who do not need to repent (Luke 15:7). This should admonish and awaken us to repent. Contemplate that among the lepers whom Christ had healed, **nine were ungrateful** and only one was thankful (Luke 17:17). This should remind us to refrain from ingratitude.

When the clock strikes **ten**, we need to remind ourselves that God the Lord encompassed His holy Law in the **Ten Commandments** (Deu. 4:13). We need to learn and act upon them for the rest of our lives. Remember that God the Lord requires the **tenth** [tithe] for supporting divine services and the priesthood in order to remind us that from all that God has given us by grace we should give this back to Him and His servants [of the Word]. Contemplate that true godliness is so pleasing to God the Lord that He, **for the sake of ten righteous** persons, was willing to spare an entire city (Gen. 18:32).

When it strikes **eleven**, we need to remember that Christ gave to His **eleven disciples** the Keys of the Kingdom and the Holy Spirit (John 20:23). For these blessings we should thank Him, and use them for our comfort. If we however wish to fruitfully partake of this **key of redemption**, we have to truly repent, for without repentance the forgiveness of sins has no standing (Luke 24:47). If we wish to receive the gift of the Holy Spirit, we must **repent** (Acts 2:38) and live in true godliness—for the **Holy Spirit departs from the wicked** (ch. 1:5).

When the clock strikes **twelve**, we need to remind ourselves that Jesus, when He was **twelve** years old, let the beams of His divine Wisdom shine forth as He sat amidst the teachers in Jerusalem (Luke 2:41). He thereby sanctified the work of teachers [pastors] and hearers. Remember that He chose **twelve Apostles** who are indicated in the Old Testament by the **twelve sons of Jacob** (Gen. 35:22). This is so because in a spiritual manner they signify, via the **twelve fountains** which the Israelites found in the wilderness (Exo. 15:22), the New Testament Church. This is so because they, through the **twelve gemstones** that were on the official robe of the High Priest, guided the beautiful little fountains of Evangelical teaching into all the world (Exo. 28:21). Also, because they by their teaching and life shone through as **gemstones** with the **twelve stones** from which was built the **altar** (Exo. 24:4). Also, because the Church was founded in its teaching through the **twelve show breads** which lay daily before the Lord in the Ark of the Covenant (Lev. 24:5). Because with the heavenly bread of the Gospel, the hungry were fed by the **twelve oxen** upon which rested the honorary sea in Solomon's temple (1 Kin. 7:44). Because, with the **twelve stars** on the **crown of the Bride of Christ,** the sea of Holy Scripture is carried into the world (Rev.

12:1). Because its teaching is the Church's sure foundation (Eph. 1:20). We must abide by the teaching of the holy Apostles, follow it, and live by it. Consequently, we will someday eat **from the Tree of Life which bears twelve kinds of fruit and bears them every month** (Rev. 22:2). These fruits will be **health** without ailments, **youth** without aging, **overabundance** without spoilage, **freedom** without servitude, **beauty** without ugliness, **comfort** without pain, **surplus** without want, **peace** without strife, **security** without fear, **knowledge** without ignorance, **honor** without shame, **joy** without sadness. It is after such blessings that we should long for and strive after them with all godliness.

Chapter Eight

Concerning the control and directing of the thoughts that serve to promote a devotional contemplation.

Obviously this **holy and devout contemplation** has to be initiated by means of knowledge which have been imparted by the **Holy Spirit** and by means of good thoughts which emanate from the **Holy Spirit**. At the same time, it also is essential for a lover of godliness who wants to exercise himself in holy contemplation to discern **his thoughts** in order to control and direct them. In men, there exist **three kinds** of **thoughts**: Some are **holy, good thoughts**. These spring forth from **God the Lord** and the **Holy Spirit**, who alone create a holy mind-set, good counsel, and righteous works. The holy Apostle speaks of this in 2 Cor. 2:5 – **We are** incapable of thinking something of our own selves. Instead, the fact that we are able to do so comes from God. Phi. 2:13 – **It is God who works in you both the willingness and the doing of that which is pleasing to Him.** For every kind of insidious malice and striving of the heart of a man—insofar as it is contemplated outside of the realm of the re-birth and grace of the Holy Spirit—**is only and continually evil** (Gen. 6:6). Also, **the natural man**—who has not been born again by the Spirit of God—does not understand the things of the Spirit of God. It is a **foolishness to Him and he cannot grasp it** (1 Cor. 2:14). His thoughts become conceited and his ignorant heart has been darkened (Rom. 1:21). **He walks about with his conceited mind because his understanding has been darkened** (Eph. 4:18). However, if he is to think anything good, God the Lord has to take from him his **hard-as-rock, ignorant heart** and give to him a **soft, understanding heart of flesh** (Eze. 36:20). God has **to create in him a new heart** (Psa. 51:12). God has to **circumcise the foreskin of the heart** (Deu. 30:6), so that from henceforth good, holy thoughts come forth from the heart of man. However, one can determine the thoughts that actually are **good and holy** only if they are directed towards **the glory of God** and to the **benefit of the neighbor**. They must also agree with the **precepts of God's Word**. They must guide us towards **godliness**, holiness and righteousness. So then, the governor **Felix was frightened** when Paul spoke about righteousness, chastity, and future judgment (Acts 24:25). That was a good thought and the **initial foundation** for conversion that the Holy Spirit had laid. This conversion would actually have resulted if Felix had not hindered the work of the Holy

Spirit and quenched such a good thought. It was a **good thought** when the **hearers were pricked in their hearts** as they heard the sermon by **Peter** about the crucifixion and resurrection of Christ. They said, **What should we do?** (Acts 2:37). That was a **good thought** and a good beginning towards conversion, which also happened when they did not destroy the work of the Holy Spirit but instead repented and let themselves be baptized. Accordingly, if we feel a good thought in our heart that we should repent, abstain from evil, practice good works, etc., it is God the **LORD** who has brought such good thoughts to our minds **externally** by means of the Word and **inwardly** by means of His good Spirit. We most certainly should not subdue or toss to the wind such good thoughts. Rather, we should all the more cling to them and follow their guidance. The holy Apostle admonishes us to that end when he reminds us in 2 Tim. 1:6 - **that awaken the gift of God that is within us.** In the original Greek of this text, Paul uses the word **spark of fire** that lies in the ashes. Here he instructs that we are to again fan the fire instead of giving up so that the fire completely goes out and is extinguished. With this imagery, we are directed to the following prototypical portrayal: In the Old Testament times, it was, among other things, one of the duties of the office of the priesthood to **maintain** the **holy fire** that had fallen from heaven and with which the sacrifice had to be ignited. They had to continually place wood on the fire so that it would not go out. In the same way, true believers are also **spiritual priests** before God the Lord (1 Pet. 2:9; Rev. 1:6). Therefore, they should **never** allow **the spiritual fire of the Holy Spirit to be extinguished.** Nor should they ever allow it to be suppressed (1 The. 5:19). **Rather, they are to take note of the gift that has been given them** (1 Tim. 4:14). Consequently, when the **Holy Spirit warms up your heart** and places a good thought into it, you are not to pour upon it the ashes of the sinful, perishing flesh. Instead, one should all the more with devout contemplation **fan it into a blazing flame.** What else could such good, holy thoughts be other than a **work of the Holy Spirit** by which He wants to prepare us to become **His temple** and residence? **Whoever** subdues and hinders such thoughts within himself is destroying the work of the Holy Spirit and opposes the construction of that spiritual temple. What this means is written in 1 Cor. 2:17-18: **If anyone destroys this temple of God, God will destroy him, because the temple of God is holy. That's what you are. Let nobody deceive himself.**

In the second place, other thoughts are **misleading, evil thoughts.** These emanate from the evil devil. Thus, we read in Gen. 3:5 that the hellish snake **placed into the heart of Eve**, the first mother, **the thought** that she should eat of the fruit from the forbidden tree. Likewise, Satan placed into the heart of David that he should become haughtily proud and **allow the people of Israel to be counted** (1 Chr. 21:1). **He placed into Judas** [the idea] **that he should betray Christ,** his Lord and Master (John 13:2). He planted the idea in the heart of **Peter** that he should **restrain Christ** from His suffering. That's why Christ answered him so harshly in Mat. 16:23 – Get away from Me, Satan. You are an offense to Me. For your intention towards me is **not divine, but human.** Which of these thoughts are misleading and evil **can be identified by a person**—that is, if they strive against **God's glory** and the **neighbor's**

welfare—if they run counter to God's Word and command—if they lead us away from godliness, holiness and righteousness, etc. Consequently, if we notice such evil, misleading thoughts in our hearts, we should immediately **quench** them **by the power of the Spirit.** Also we should indeed not **bear** any affection for, or cling to, such thoughts. So then, when there **arose a thought** among the Apostles of the Lord Christ as to which of them **were the greatest,** Christ immediately took pains to squelch the thought and made the effort to root out this devilish weed that had been sown in their hearts (Luke 9:46). The ancient church fathers in a spiritual manner point to what is written in Psalm 137:9: **One should take the young children of the daughter of Babylon and smash them upon a rock.** That is to say, one should take tempting thoughts while they are still fresh and immediately smash and kill them before they start to grow and gain the upper hand. More appropriate would be to apply the saying of Christ in Mat. 18:8-9 here: **If your hand or your foot offends you, then chop it off and toss it away. It's better for you go on in life lame or as a cripple then that you have two hands or two feet and are hurled into the eternal fire. And if your eye offends you, rip it out and toss it away. It's better for you that you go through life with one eye than that you have two eyes and are hurled into the hellish fire.** That is to say, if an evil thought wants to sprout forth in your eye or another body member, then suppress it.

In the third place, there also exist the kind of thoughts that arise in one's heart which are *otiosae*—**idle, useless** thoughts that one **can easily push aside.** Others are *violentae*—**worldly thoughts** that are aimed at the things of this life; of how one might obtain **honor, riches, and blessings** in this **world**. A person should not cling to these with much intensity, lest things reach the point of which Christ speaks in Mat. 13:22 – **that the cares of this world and the burdens of riches choke out the seed of the divine Word so that it does not produce fruit.** Also, Luke 21:34 – **Guard yourselves that your hearts do not become overburdened with the cares for food.** Here the true warning of John in his first Epistle (2:15-17) should constantly flash before our eyes and hearts. **Do not love the world nor what is in this world. If a person loves the world, the love of the Father is not in him. For everything that is in the world, namely the lusts of the flesh and the lusts of the eyes and pride-filled life, is not from the Father but from the world. And the world will disappear along with its lusts. Whoever, however, does the will of God shall remain into all eternity.**

Some thoughts are *cogitationes immundae*—**impure, obscene thoughts** that tempt a man toward being unchaste, toward greed, and other sins about which Christ says in Mat. 15:18-20: **What comes out of the mouth of a man comes from his heart and the impurity of that person. For out of the heart comes evil thoughts, murder, adultery, fornication, theft, false witness, slander. These are the parts that make a man unclean.** Also St. Paul speaks about the same thing in 1 Tim. 6:9: **Those who want to become rich fall into temptation and strife, and many foolish and harmful lusts which sink a person into death and damnation.** If such thoughts want to crop up within us, we should immediately quench and kill them off by the power of the Spirit. We should do so in keeping with the admonition of the holy Apostle in Col. 3:5: **So then kill off your members that are upon this earth: fornication, uncleanness, harmful desires, evil lusts, and greed, etc.** Take note, whoever in this manner actually takes seriously his thoughts and directs them towards the right purpose will be able to proceed all the better in his devotional contemplation. For if he subdues his evil thoughts, **strikes down or defeats** his vain, futile thoughts, **curbs and restrains** his worldly thoughts, and **clings and hangs on** to beneficial, wholesome thoughts, then his holy contemplation will work spiritual knowledge in him. This knowledge will craft in him a **heartfelt contrition**. This contrition of the heart will craft in him **devotion**. This devotion will craft in him **faithful prayer and longing**. We now want to further consider this supportive means for godliness.

Chapter Nine

That a zealous, diligent prayer and godly crying out prompting us towards godliness.

Up to this point, we have dealt with **three kinds** of wholesome *Adminiculis*, or supportive means that can be of service in prompting us toward godliness. They are **the hearing or reading of God's Word, the worthy reception of the holy Lord's Supper, and holy, devout contemplation.** From this follows the **fourth** means of support. It is *seria oratio*, **a zealous, diligent prayer and godly crying out.** That a believing prayer needs to be included as a supportive means for godliness can readily be concluded from:

1. *Ex naturae nostrae corruptione,* **from the corruption of our nature.** Since the Fall into sin, by nature we have been corrupt. So then, we cannot by the power of our own reason or will rightly know God the Lord. Nor are we capable of rendering to Him service and pleasing works with godliness. Instead here the **Holy Spirit** has to bestow on us new, spiritual power by weans of rebirth, enlightenment and renewal. This can be proven with many sayings from Holy Scripture. Chap. 9:17-19*: **Who can experience Your wisdom unless You give wisdom and send Your Holy Spirit from on High. And thus the doings upon this earth shall become right and men shall learn what pleases You, and are saved through the Wisdom.** But if we wish to obtain such grace and the gift of the Holy Spirit, we must consequently seek Him **with devout, trusting prayer.** For **God gives the Holy Spirit to those who pray to Him for this very reason** (Luke 11:11). **Just as water** is escorted from a well through little pipes and canals, so also a devout, trusting prayer is a true, golden, tiny pipe through which the divine blessings that are necessary for the exercise of true godliness are escorted to us from the well of divine blessings. **Plants and trees** are unable to grow or bear fruit unless they draw sap from the roots, and are moistened with moisture from above. Also, similarly, we are unable to grow in godliness nor be fruitful with good works unless through prayer we receive the help of God and the gift of the Spirit.

2. *Ex renovationis imperfectione,* **from the imperfection of our renewal in this life.** Though the

---

* Tr. note: There is no Biblical book reference given, but Gerhard is quoting here from the Apocrypha, *The Wisdom of Solomon.*

Holy Spirit by His power renews our nature, yet, all the while **our inward man has to be renewed from day to day. This renewal is not immediately perfected** in this life (2 Cor. 4:16). We still daily have to busy ourselves with **putting off the old man and putting on the new** (Eph. 4:22, 24; Col. 3:9–10). Now once more, to this belongs a believing, daily prayer of our constant longing sigh before God **that He who began the good work in us** would **also complete it** (Phi. 1:6). He wants to strengthen His kingdom that He has established within us for it is His work (Psa. 68:29). **We shall be perfectly renewed** in eternity and be **empowered** with blessings. In this life, we still need to continually pray for the completion of the work that has been begun if we otherwise want to grow and increase in godliness.

3. *Ex hostium oppugnatione*, **from the enemies' manifold temptations.** As we travel on the pathway of godliness, we encounter many different enemies that want to drive us back, such as the devil, the world, and our sinful flesh. Against their cunning and power, we are unable to defend ourselves in any other way than through **God's Word** and with prayer. For a **believing prayer is the true shield of salvation with which we are able to extinguish the fiery arrows of the devil** (Eph. 6:16). It is as with the Israelites in the wilderness when they encountered the **fiery serpents** as they were sojourning to the Promised Land of Canaan. As they then cried out to the Lord they were protected and rescued (Num. 21:7). So also as we rush along upon the pathway of godliness to our heavenly inheritance, we encounter the **fiery, hellish snakes** that want to poison and kill us. But as we cry out to God in prayer, He will protect and rescue us. Similarly, **Amalek** fought

against the Israelites as they were leaving Egypt and wanted to hinder them on their way. However, **Moses overcame him through prayer** (Exo. 17:11). So also as we exit the Egypt of this world in a spiritual manner, the hellish enemy fights against us and wants to hinder us upon the pathway of godliness. However, through prayer we are able to subdue and overcome him.

    4. *Ex orationis conditione,* **from the nature and attribute of a believing prayer.** Through a believing prayer we can obtain that which is necessary for this and for eternal life. Mark 11:24: **Everything that you ask for in your prayer, only believe that you shall receive it and it will be yours.** 1 John 5:14: **this is the joy that we have before Him, if we ask for something according to His will, He hears us.** Therefore, through the power of prayer and the presence of the Holy Spirit, we shall be sustained in godliness and daily increase in it. Prayer draws our heart away from earthly things, guards us against sin, lifts our mindset towards heavenly things, and prepares us to receive the gifts of the Spirit. How, then, could not prayer serve to be a blessed means for promoting godliness? Through prayer, **Hezekiah**, that godly king, obtained **health and strength for his body** (Isa. 38:3). Should we not be able to **obtain health and strength for our soul** so that we **become strong in the inward man** (Eph. 3:16) and **grow in godliness?** David says in Psa. 138:3: **If I call upon You, hear me quickly and give my soul great strength.** In the original Hebrew, this actually reads this way: "When I called on You, You heard me and bestowed great strength upon my soul." Through prayer, we **draw near to God** and obtain from Him everything that we need. If we properly think this

through, we discover that all **Christian virtues** and everything that pertains to godliness are encompassed in prayer. Similarly, in the Old Testament **the incense offering** was prepared from expensive spices, balsam, gooseberries, ointments, and pure frankincense (Exo. 30:34). For a prayer contains within it **the knowledge of God**—for no one can properly call upon God unless he has properly come to know Him and tasted of His kindness. **Knowledge of Him**—because we have to acknowledge our need so that we, with longing sighs, may, from the bottom of our hearts, plea for help before God. **Faith**—for how shall they call upon Him in whom they do not believe (Rom. 10:14)? **Love**—because we do not just pray for ourselves, but also for the neighbor. **Hope**—because nobody truly prays unless he is hoping to receive something through his prayer. **Patience**—because we are not always immediately heard in every instance. **Obedience** to God the Lord—because without it God will not hear the prayer (Psa. 50:15). **True Humility**—because with prayer we have to humble ourselves before God (1 Pet. 4:7). **Righteousness**—because in prayer we present to God that which we are obligated to do for Him. **Spiritual Wisdom**—because we have to take into consideration *when* we pray, *why* we pray, *how* we pray, *what* we are praying for. **Thankfulness**—because we have to be thankful for the help we have received. Since a proper prayer encompasses all Christian doings and everything that pertains to godliness, how should it not be a means that is blessed, salutary and beneficial for godliness?

5. *Ex divina jussione*, **from the command of God the Lord**. God the Lord has **commanded us** to pray especially for the very purpose that we thereby might

be enabled to achieve the growth and increase of divine wisdom and spiritual power for godliness. Tobit says to his son in ch. 4:20: **At all times, give thanks to God and pray that He guide you, and that you in all your undertakings follow His Word.** Jam. 1:5: **If anyone among you lacks wisdom, let him ask of God who simply gives to every person and does not hold back from anyone. Thus it will be given to him.** The Lord Christ says in Mat. 7:7 and Luke 11:9-13: **Ask, thus it will be given to you. Seek, thus you will find. Knock, thus it will be opened to you. For whoever asks shall take. Also, whoever seeks shall find, and whoever knocks it will be opened to him. Where does a son ask his father for bread where he offers him a stone instead: And if he asks him for a fish, where does he offer him a snake in place of a fish? Or, if he were to ask him for an egg where he would offer him a scorpion instead? If then you who are evil can still give your children good gifts, how much more shall not your Father in heaven give good things and the Holy Spirit to those who ask Him?** The ancient church fathers explained this in this way: We should ask **for bread**, i.e., for the body of Christ which is the **Bread of Life** (John 6:48), and feeds and satisfies our soul. He will not give us a stone, i.e., a stone hard **heart.** We are to ask for a fish, i.e., for faith. For just as a fish is hidden under the water and cannot be seen, so also **faith is a certain assurance that a person hopes and does not doubt on Him whom one cannot see** (Heb. 11:1). He will not give us a **snake**, i.e. the poison of the old hellish snakes that unbelief gives. We are to ask for the **egg**, i.e., for **hope**. For just as in due time a living bird breaks forth from an egg, so also it will actually be fulfilled with what we hope for here. He will not give us a **scorpion**, i.e., **doubt**, so that we at the end of our life will have to carry doubt on account of our sin—like a scorpion has a poison in his tail.

6. *Ex probatorum exemplorum confirmatione*, **from the example of all the saints and God-pleasing people.** For these people, among other things, also prayed for godliness and the strength of the Spirit and for Christ-like efforts. David, in Psa. 51:12, prays, **Create in me God a pure heart, and give me a new, certain spirit. V. 17: Lord, open up my lips so that my mouth may proclaim Your glory.** In Psa. 86:12 – **Uphold my heart with Your own so that I may fear Your Name.** Psa. 143:10 – **Teach me to do according to Your good pleasure because You are my GOD. Your good Spirit guide me upon the even path.** Solomon prays in 1 Kin. 3:9, **Lord, You want to give Your servant an obedient heart so that he may understand what is good or evil.** Ch. 8:21 – **Since I realized that I could not be chaste any other way than that God gives it to me, I stepped before the Lord and petitioned Him, etc.** Sirach prays in ch. 23:4–6, **Lord God, Father and Lord of my life, protect me from an unchaste countenance. And turn from me all evil lusts. Do not let me fall into gluttony or unchastity, and guard me from a shameless heart.** The father of the demon-possessed boy in Mark 9:24 prayed, **I believe, dear Lord; help my unbelief.** The Apostles of Christ prayed in Luke 17:5, **Strengthen our faith.** Paul prays for the **Ephesians** in ch. 1:7, **that God the Lord would give them the Spirit of Wisdom and the revelation to know Him better. V. 18 – and enlighten their eyes of understanding.** Ch. 3:16–17, **That God**

the Lord would give them power according to the riches of His glory to become strong by His Spirit within the inward man. And for Christ to reside in their hearts through faith. Also, to become rooted and grounded through love. He prays for the Philippians, ch. 1:9-11, **that their love might become ever more rich in all kinds of knowledge and experience. That they may grasp what is the best thing, so that they might be pure and inoffensive until the day of Christ, that they may be filled with the fruits of righteousness which takes place through Christ Jesus to the glory and praise of God.** He prays for the Colossians, ch. 1:10-11, **that they might be filled with the knowledge of God's will, with all kinds of spiritual wisdom and understanding. That they walk worthy of the Lord, pleasing to all and be fruitful in every good work. And grow in the knowledge of God and be strengthened with all power,** etc. So you see, if a believing, sincere prayer were not a blessed, salutary means for growing and increasing in godliness, then these men of God would not have so longingly prayed to be strengthened in the inward man with these gifts of the Spirit.

Chapter Ten

How prayer must be structured if it is to be of service in promoting godliness.

It is not sufficient for a person to merely **outwardly speak the words of a prayer.** Rather, it must **flow from the depths of the heart** to be **right,** so that it does not called what is stated in Jam. 4:3: **You pray and receive nothing because you pray for evil reasons.** So then, if a prayer is to be pleasing to God and is to be of service in promoting us toward godliness, we must pray: 1. *Poenitenter,* **with true repentance.** For God the Lord does not listen to sinners, says the blind born man in John 9:31—take this to mean **unrepentant sinners.** God addresses such godless, unrepentant sinners in Psa. 50:16–17: **Why do you place My covenant into your mouth since obviously hate discipline and hurl My words behind.** Isa. 1:15: **Even though you spread out your hands out, I nevertheless hide My eyes from you; and, even though you pray a lot, I don't hear you. For your hands are full of blood.** How could God hear such a prayer with which a person actually calls upon and glorifies God with his mouth while slandering Him with his deeds be pleasing to God? It is written in Isa. 59:2: **The misdeeds separate God and mankind from one another, and sin hides God's countenance from mankind so that he is not heard.** How, then, can a person draw **near** to God through prayer if by his misdeeds and sins he **distances** himself from God? A **holy life** is a prayer that is truly God-pleasing—even though there are no words that show up in it. Godlessness and impenitence hinder a prayer—even though one were to pray through the entire Book of Psalms. An inward, repentant, **longing sigh** that arises from the bottom of the heart is far more acceptable to God than a lengthy prayer by an unrepentant person. We must **lift up holy hands** to the **holy God** (1 Tim. 2:8). For God says: **I am holy and you also shall be holy** (Lev. 11:44, 19:2; 1 Pet. 1:16). If a bride wants to weave her bridegroom an extravagantly beautiful little **gar-**

land wreath, she does not only gather together **lovely flowers** for this. Rather, she also washes and cleanses her **hands** with which she is going to weave together this little garland wreath. Likewise, if we want to weave together the **little garland wreath** of a devout prayer that will be a sweet-smelling savor for our heavenly Bridegroom, Jesus Christ, then we must not only use for this the prayers of saints—especially the beautiful Psalms of David. Rather, we must also **wash and cleanse ourselves** with true repentance (Isa. 1:16). All this **so that we lift up holy hands to Him** (1 Tim. 1:8).

2. *Fiducialiter*, with true faith and trust. Christ says in Mark 11:24: **I tell you, everything that you ask for in your prayer, simply believe that you will receive it; thus it will be so.** Jam. 1:5-7: **If anyone among you lacks wisdom, let him ask of God, but let him as in faith.** Faith is a spiritual fire that has to be burning in the heart if the **incense** of a God-pleasing prayer is to rise up. In the same way as no **incense** rises up and gives of a fragrance unless it is tossed upon **glowing coals,** so also a prayer before God has no **value as an incense offering** (Psa. 141:2) unless it has been ignited with the flaming fire of faith. Prayer without faith is like a dead corpse without a soul—like a **shadow** without a body—like a lifeless **image.** To pray in faith means a person has to pray in the **name of Christ** the only Mediator. Christ says in John 16:24: **Truly, truly I say to you, if you shall ask the Father for anything in My name, He will give it to you.** So also Daniel prayed in ch. 9:17, hear the prayer of Your servant as well as his plea **for the sake of the Lord.** The Israelites in the Old Testament had to turn **their faces towards the Temple and to the throne of grace.** So now also we with our

prayers have to turn with **true faith** to Christ the only Mediator and Throne of Grace (Rom. 3:25) in whom **the fullness of the Godhead** dwells **bodily** as in your own **temple** (Col. 2:9). In the Old Testament, the smoke from the incense had to be laid upon the altar of **incense offering** and be ignited if it was to please God. So also now our prayer has to be laid upon Christ—the sole Altar of the New Testament—in true faith if it is to be pleasing to God. *Nulla est grata DEO nisi Christus Filius ara**. About this it is recorded in Rev. 8:3-4: **I saw an Angel who stepped before the Altar and had a golden bowl of incense. And much incense offering was offered to Him, which He gave as a prayer for all the saints upon the golden Altar before the Throne. And the smoke from the incense offering of the prayers of the saints went up from the hand of the Angel before God.** Christ is the true golden Altar before the Throne of God in heaven. We have to lay the spiritual incense offerings of our prayers upon Him. He is also the **Angel** from whose hand the incense offerings of prayer from all the saints rises up before God, **for He intercedes for us** (Rom. 8:34), **and through His intercessions** He empowers our prayers so that they are acceptable before God. **God's grace** is the **foundation** upon which our prayer must ground itself. Psa. 119:149 - **Hear my voice in accordance with Your grace.** We can find and seize such **grace of God only in Christ** (John 1:16; Eph. 1:6). That's why our prayers must of necessity ground themselves upon Christ. **God's promise is the foundation of our prayer** (Psa. 27:8). However, now all the **promises of God are amen and yes through Christ** (2 Cor. 1:20). That's why our prayer must ground itself

---

* "Nothing pleases GOD except His Son, Christ, as the Altar."

upon Christ. That also means one must pray in faith, with the **sure confidence** of being heard. Jam. 1:6-7: **Let him pray in faith and not doubt that he will be graciously heard. For anyone who doubts is just like a wave in the ocean that is driven by the wind and is tossed about. Such a person dare not think that he is going to receive something from the Lord.** About the excellent, immovable foundation of prayer upon which we may with true faith build and about the hearing of which we can be sure, shall be dealt with in this portion later on.

3. *Reverenter*, **with complete reverence.** As we pray, we are doing nothing more than just **stepping before the throne of God** and **handing over** a supplication in which we lament our need and plead for **help** to this King above all kings and Lord above all lords. We must give thought to **what** kind **of great Lord** this is before whose eyes and throne we are stepping. **I saw the Lord**, says Michaiah in 1 Kin. 22:19, **sitting upon His Throne and all the huge heavenly army stood next to Him on both the left and right side.** Isaiah says in ch. 6:1-3: **I saw the Lord sitting upon a high and lofty throne, and His seam** [of His cloak] **filled the Temple. Seraphim stood over Him. Each one had six wings. With two they covered their faces. With two they covered their feet. With two they flew. And one of them cried out to the other and said: holy, holy, holy is the Lord of Sabaoth** [hosts of armies]. **All the lands are filled with His glory.** Daniel says in ch. 7:9-10, **This is what I saw until the Throne was established and the Ancient One sat down on it. His cloak was white as snow and the hair on His head was like pure wool. His throne was sheer fi-**

ery flames, and its wheels were burning with fire. And there went out from Him a long, fiery beam of light. **A thousand times thousand served Him, and ten hundred times a thousand stood before Him.** Who would not shy away before this great and glorious majesty, and step before the throne of God with total reverence? Job 26:11 – **The columns of the heavens tremble and are shocked by His scolding. During the time of prayer we step into the city of heaven.** In this city, the King of heaven sits upon the throne of His majesty, and standing around Him is the entire heavenly army of holy angels—the spirits who serve Him. With what **reverence**, with what **fearful awe**, with what **humility** ought not a person step before this One, since he cannot expect to be regarded before God as anything more than a **little frog** who crawls out of his puddle before the feet of a mighty King? How **attentively**, how **respectfully**, how **modestly** should not a poor sinner then speak when he appears with this great assembly of holy angels and souls of the saints before the Divine Majesty?

  4. *Frequenter*, **often and many times.** Pray without ceasing, says the holy Apostle in 1 The. 5:16. It is not enough for a person to pray maybe once or twice. Instead, he must pray **often.** Yes indeed, the entire life of the Christian is nothing other than a **daily prayer.** In the Old Testament, God had preordained that an incense offering was to be ignited in the tabernacle both in the **evening** and in the **morning.** So also all true Christians—who have **been made into spiritual priests before God** (Rev. 1:6)—are **to daily offer up the spiritual incense** of prayer before God the Lord. Prayer is nothing more than *familiare cum DEO collo-*

quium, **a friendly, lovely chat** with GOD the Lord. Psa. 19:17 – **May the words of my mouth and the conversation from my heart be well pleasing to You.** If we wish to show ourselves to be true lovers of God we must also speak with God the Lord through prayer often and gladly. How often did not Moses enter into the tabernacle to speak with the Lord as the mediator of the Old Testament? Also, the people of Israel spoke with the Lord through him (Exo. 19:8). **Christ, only Mediator** of the New Testament, has **opened up the way** for us so that we are able to step before the Throne of God with a believing prayer—**as often as we need help** (Heb. 4:14). **Since we then have a great High Priest— Jesus, the Son of God who ascended up to heaven,** v. 16, **let us step up to the Throne of Grace with joy so that we may receive mercy and grace in the time when we are in need of help.** Ch. 10:18–21, as we then now possess the **joy for entry into the holy place by means of the blood of Jesus, which He has prepared for us for a new and living way through the curtain, i.e., through His flesh. Also we have a High Priest over the House of God. So let us approach with true hearts in perfect faith.** If you remind yourself of how in every hour and moment you are hovering in great danger, you will pray often and diligently.

     5. *Ferventer*, **devoutly and passionately.** Prayer is not to work the lips of the mouth. Rather, it is a **lifting up of the heart** to God the Lord. *Ascensius mentis ad DEUM**, as *Damascenus*†, that ancient ecclesiastical teacher, calls it in *lib. 3. Orth. Sis. Cap. 24*‡. Or, as David

---

* "the ascending of the mind towards GOD"
† John of Damascus († A.D. 749)
‡ Tr. note: Vol. 3 of *On the Orthodox Faith*, Chap. 24.

describes it in Psa. 19:17, a **conversation that the heart has with God the Lord**. Consequently, if a prayer is to be proper and pleasing to God, then the **inward heartfelt devotion** has to accompany it. **When you pray**, says Christ in Mat. 6:7, **you should not keep on babbling or express lots of words**. Take this to mean praying without a devout heart, for with many words there commonly is very little devotion. **The Lord is near to all who call on Him**, David says in Psa. 145:18, but with this there is also the statement **of all those who** call on Him **sincerely**. **The prayer of a righteous person accomplishes much**, James says in ch. 5:16. However, alongside it is also written, **if it is sincere**. Likewise, the Lord says to Samuel in 1 Samuel 16:7, **A man sees what is before his eyes, but the Lord looks upon the heart**. Thus we may also say, a man **hears** what comes to his ears, but the Lord **hears the longing sighs of the heart**. Just as God the Lord speaks **to and in our hearts** with His Word, so we also with our prayers must speak with Him **from within and from the bottom** of our hearts. If you want to serve God, says Sirach in ch. 18:23, **then take the matter seriously so that you do not tempt GOD**. Or, as it actually reads in the original language, **before you pray**, prepare yourself and do not be like someone who tempts God. If you want for your prayer to be heard, it has to arise from the **inward man** (Eph. 3:16). True petitioners have to pray **in spirit and in truth** (John 4:23). Now, nobody can pray unless he prays with **devotion. Whoever prays without devotion does not pray in truth**. For the heart does not totally agree with the words. That, then, is **hypocrisy and falsity**.

6. *Humiliter*, with true **humility**. A prayer must

not found itself upon its own **worthiness** but solely and alone upon God's gracious, sure promises, and upon the **precious merits of Jesus Christ.** Dan. 9:18 – **We lay before You our prayer not based upon our righteousness, but upon Your great mercy.** Prayer can be called nothing other than confessing one's need, one's misery, one's weakness before God. How, then, could it be a true, God-pleasing prayer if one wants to rely upon one's **own merits** and worthiness? **Just look at how your Lord and Master, Christ, humbles Himself with prayer. Out of humility, He falls upon His face** before His heavenly Father (Mat. 26:39). How much more is it not incumbent upon us that we should in prayer inwardly humble ourselves before God? Look at how the **repentant publican** humbles himself in prayer. **He did not dare lift up his eyes towards heaven. Instead, he smote his breast and said, God, be gracious to me, a poor sinner** (Luke 18:12). Such a humble prayer pleases God the Lord. For thus says the Lord: **Heaven is My throne and the earth is My footstool** (Isa. 66:1). **My hand has made everything that exists, says the Lord. I, however, look after those in abject poverty and whose heart is broken, and to him who trembles before My Word** (v. 2).

8. *Instanter ac perseveranter*, **with urgency**, that we hang on with prayer. In Luke 18:1, Christ admonishes that one should at all times pray and not become lax. He gives the example of **the widow** who, with her urgent persistence, moved the **judge to become kind like the friend who got up in the middle of the night and granted the person his request** in Luke 11:5. **Ask, says the Lord** in Mat. 7:7; Luke 11:9, **and it will be given to you.** Does not God the Lord want to hear

immediately? **Seek and you will find.** If that doesn't help, then **knock** on the gates of heaven with the **hammer of prayer** and **it will be opened for you. Keep on praying**, says St. Paul in Rom. 12:12, Col. 4:2. For God at times tests us for noble reasons with His response. That's why we must **wait on Him** (Psa. 27:14; Hab. 2:4). If the desire of the heart of the petitioner is sincere, it will not immediately become lax if God does not immediately respond. Instead, it thereby will increase all the more.

Chapter Eleven

Concerning the form of a daily prayer that is beneficial for the exercise and the increasing of godliness.

Whether or not prayer actually and principally consists of reading or speaking **specific formulations**, nevertheless there is no way that such recitations and speaking of specific formulations are to be neglected or despised. For Christ Himself actually used a **specific** form for praying (Mat. 26:39 John 17:2), and prescribed for us the **Our Father** [Lord's Prayer] (Mat. 6:10; Luke 11:20). The saintly people used certain forms in their prayers, as the entire Holy Scriptures repeatedly testifies—but especially the **Psalms of David**. Thus, it can hardly fail for the heart to be ignited with devotion by the Holy Spirit. Thus it, in turn, will break forth with **words. For that which the heart is filled with, flows forth through the mouth** (Mat. 12:34). In addition, such forms serve the purpose of giving good guidance to the simple of how and for what they should ask of God, and because these forms are taken **from God's Word—which is Spirit and Life** (John 6:63). Thus, they also are a blessed **powerful means** by which the Holy Spirit wants to warm up and inflame our hearts so that we become all the more fervent in inward prayer and longing sighs. Therefore, let nobody get the notion about such high and great devotion that he consequently can set aside external verbal praying. Instead, he should also **carry them out with words.** For God did not only form **the heart** in us, but He also formed the **tongue**, so that we use both members for prayer and praise of God. Such a daily form for prayer is prescribed for us in the **holy Our Father.** It is the prayer in which Christ with His divine, wondrous **Wisdom** has briefly summarized what is necessary for us for this life and for eternal life. And even though at times we actually use other words in prayer, yet we are praying for nothing other than what is contained in this prayer of our Lord—even though we may properly pray differently. So also Augustine teaches in his *Epist. 121. Cap. 12.* Whenever **other forms of prayer** are presented—which are either found in Holy Scripture or taken from divine church doctrine—they are to be regarded as nothing more than **an explanation of the Our Father** [Lord's Prayer]. However, since not everyone immediately discovers the heavenly Wisdom which has been summarized in this brief **prayer of the Lord**—the Our Father—it is **not inappropriate** that at times also **other forms of prayers** be used in keeping with windows of opportunity and other circumstances. They then may be taken from the Psalter of David or other books of the Holy Scriptures, or from faithful, godly teachings of the

Church. To that end the little prayers, which have previously been mentioned, have been collected together from Holy Scripture in a book with the title: *The Daily Exercise of Godliness**. It could pleasingly serve a person to that end. Or each individual person may use a different **prayer book** by a Christian teacher to this end. Also, no one is prevented from **assembling** for his own benefit one or more of certain forms of prayer—just so long as they all diligently follow the divine guidelines of Holy Scriptures. Of course, it might complicate one's time schedule for a person to read through the entire previously mentioned little book **every day**. And yet at the same time—in order to hold up to one's heart each and every point of this booklet's content so one may present it to God in prayer—the **sum and content** of this entire booklet has been briefly summarized in the prayer that now follows.

O holy and righteous God, merciful Father, You are One, eternal, true GOD in three distinct Persons. God Father, Son, and Holy Spirit, I confess and lament from the bottom of my heart that I, a person **conceived and born** in sin from infancy on up to this present hour, have sinned against You daily and frequently. I have sinned knowingly and unknowingly, inwardly and outwardly, in **thought, word, and deed**. I have sinned against the **first** and the **second** table of Your holy Ten Commandments. I have never kept them properly and perfectly. Instead, I have sinned against all of them. I confess that I additionally have made myself a partaker of **various sins**. As a result, all creation accuses me before Your judgment. Also, my own heart and con-

---
* i.e., *The Daily Exercise of Piety*.

science cause me anxiety for so shamefully **abusing** Your manifold, great blessings with my sinning. Also, I have **stirred up against me** Your righteous wrath. From my heart, this grieves me. And I pray You, **O my Lord and God**, from the bottom of my heart, that You would pardon and forgive me all this for the sake of Your beloved Son, my true Savior, Jesus Christ, and for the sake of His precious merit and His perfectly availing payment.

Along with this, I thank You, O **gracious and faithful God!** I thank You for all Your blessing which You have so richly and abundantly shown me, that You have so wondrously formed me in my **mother's womb** and allowed me to be born into this world alive. I thank You that You have graciously **sustained** me and provided for every need of my body and life in a fatherly fashion. That You have redeemed me from sin, death, devil, and hell **through Christ**, that You sent Your only begotten Son into the flesh for my benefit and gave Him up into death—even death on the cross—for me. That You, **through Your holy Word, have called me** into the fellowship of Your kingdom of grace. I thank You that You waited with great patience for my conversion, that my heart's conversion through the Holy Spirit was so mighty. That by grace all my **sins are forgiven.** That You have **sustained** me with good resolution and have richly bestowed on me **all sorts of blessings** in body and soul. That You, in **holy Baptism, received** me as Your dear **child** into Your covenant of grace. Also, that You, in the holy **Lord's Supper**, have fed and given me to drink of the true body and blood of Jesus Christ. That You up to now have **protected** me from many kinds of dangers and misfortunes and that You, by grace, have given me the sure promise of **eternal** life in Christ Jesus, my Savior.

Furthermore, I ask of You, O almighty God and Father, that You would subdue and kill off the **old man** [old Adam] in me. Give to me and increase in me faith, love, hope, humility, patience, meekness, chastity, and all other **Christian virtues**. Grant that I, in my heart, spurn temporal things and truly long for eternal things. Through Your Holy Spirit's implantation of Your grace, confer on me that I may deny and overcome the world. May I at all times find comfort amidst tribulation, **true rest for my soul**. Grant that I overcome in every adversity. May I be guarded against the **devil's power** and cunning. Grant that I may finally **depart** from this life in peace and joy, and someday **arise** on Judgment Day to eternal life.

Last of all, I commend to You, **O faithful God**, Your **holy Christian Church**. May You graciously uphold it, increase it, and rule over it. Give us faithful **teachers and preachers** in schools and churches in order to open the hearts of **the hearers,** and direct them to follow Your **Word** with child-like **obedience**. Also, may You also grant that **rulers and subjects, house fathers and house mothers,** children and relatives, servants and maidens all faithfully fulfill their duties and Your will. I especially commend to You the authorities over me, my relatives and benefactors. May You please reward them for all the good they have shown to me. I also pray to You for all my **enemies and persecutors.** May You please overcome and convert them. I pray to You on behalf of **all those who are in need.** May You graciously grant counsel, comfort, and help to anxious and sorrowful hearts. Also, **in general, may You have**

mercy upon all mankind. O faithful God and Father, would You please give ear to this prayer for the sake of Jesus Christ, Your beloved Son and our Savior and Redeemer. Amen.

Should this form of daily prayer become too lengthy because of time restraints and other circumstances, then let a person take in hand the prayer which follows, in keeping with his opportunities.

I thank You, my **dear heavenly Father**, that You have created and nurtured me, and have continued to graciously protect me for many dangers. I thank You that You have gifted me with Your beloved Son and through Him have redeemed me from sin, death, devil, and hell. That You have made it possible for me to know this through Your Word, and have through Your Holy Spirit re-birthed me and renewed me. For this and all Your blessings which You have shown to me in body and soul, I thank You from my heart. And, I humbly ask of You that You would, by grace for the sake of the precious merits of Jesus Christ, Your beloved Son and my Savior, forgive me all my sins. May You from henceforth rule and guide me by Your Holy Spirit, so that You give to me and increase in me faith, love, hope, humility, patience, gentleness, chastity, and all Christian virtues. Finally, also, grant to me a blessed moment of death and a joyful resurrection to eternal life, and may You have mercy upon all mankind through Christ, Your Son and my Savior and Redeemer. Amen.

Another form for daily praying.

Merciful, eternal God, Comforter of the distressed, Healer of the sick: let our prayer come before You with whatever anxieties and needs we cry to You, so that all mankind may rejoice in Your help and thank You. May You also graciously forgive Your Christian people their sins, and rescue them from all error and evil. Keep them in true faith and obedience. Give them faithful teachers. May all authorities lead and rule to Your glory and for the common peace. Protect all heads of households along with their wives, children, and household members. Cleanse the air of all pollution, pestilence, disaster, sickness, fires, and war. Graciously avert all the aforementioned, well-deserved punishments from us—or otherwise sustain us through them with Your mercy. Give us fruits of the fields and protect us. Take care of the imprisoned. Help those who have been shipwrecked back to land. Comfort the distressed. Grant the expectant mother a happy view of a new fruit from her body. Grant health to the sick. Grant grace to sinners to better their lives. And show mercy to all believers in Christ. Impart Your Holy Spirit and eternal life through Jesus Christ our Lord. Amen.

Chapter Twelve

That Controlling and Taming the Body is a Helpful Means Towards Godliness.

Thus far, we have dealt with the matter of hearing and reading the Sacred Word, of the reception of the holy Lord's Supper, of the holy and devout contemplation of prayer, and of calling upon God. There now remains the fifth and final *Adminiculum* or **helpful means** that promotes the exercise of godliness. It consists of **controlling and taming the body.** St. Paul writes about this in 1 Cor. 9:24 as follows: **Don't you know that those who run within the bounds, they all are racing. Yet only one obtains the jewel. So then run so that you seize it. V. 26 - I, however, do not run as someone who is unsure. Nor do I fight as one who is striking out at the air. V. 27 - Instead, I control my body and tame it so that I do not preach to others and I myself end up cast aside.** In these words, the holy Apostle compares true believers and lovers of godliness to those who are running in bounds, and to those who **fought in the public arena**—as was the practice of the Romans and Greeks, but it is not a practice with us Germans today. For a person who **runs** [in a race] overtakes the rest in order to obtain the jewel. Also a person who **fights** receives the **crown** with great glory if he **overcomes** the rest. So also true **believers**—if they properly run in the race of praying to God and practice their faith, if they properly and bravely fight against the devil and all his allies—will obtain the jewel and the imperishable crown of eternal life. However, a runner who wants to race properly has to overtake others and wants to reach the goal set before him has to **choose the right way, not stand still nor turn back.** He must not pay attention to the unjust judgments of the spectators. He has to **get rid of** any load that is slowing him down. With patience, one has to **endure** difficulties and **sneering enemies.** Similarly, a spiritual 'runner' has to be a person who is a true Christian who exercises himself in godliness. He has **to place before himself the righteous path of God's commandments.** As David says in Psalm 119:30 **- I have chosen the path of Your truth, I have set before me Your judgments. V. 32 - If You comfort my heart, I will run the way of Your commands. V. 106 - I swear and will keep the oath that I will keep the judgment of Your righteousness.** Also, he must **never stand still** on the pathway of blessedness. Instead, he must constantly stride forward and gain ground. Even more so, he should never **turn back.** Isa. 1:4: **The corrupt children have turned back.** Luke 9:62: **Whoever lays his hand on the plow and looks back is not fit for the kingdom of heaven.** Phi. 3:13-14: **I forget what is behind and stretch out for what lies ahead and I chase after the set goal of the jewel which holds in store the heavenly calling of God in Christ Jesus.** He must not deviate from the true pathway. Deu. 17:11: **You shall not deviate from the Law, neither to the right nor the left.** 1 Sam. 12:20: **Do not turn away from the Lord, but serve the Lord with your whole heart.** Job 23:11-12: **I set my foot upon His track and keep His way and do not deviate from it. And I do not step** away from the commandment from His lips. **Psa. 125:5: Those who deviate upon their own crooked ways the Lord will drive away with the evil doers.** He must not pay attention to the wrong judgments of the children of this world. **Jer. 17:16: You know that I have not desired to have the days of men, i.e., I have not sought praise from men. 1 Cor. 4:3: It is an insignificant thing that I should be judged by you or be brought to court by men.** He has to lay aside the **burden of sin** with true repentance. **Heb. 12:1: Let us lay aside sin, which constantly sticks to us and becomes a burden, and let us run with patience the race that has been set before us. Heb. 12:3-4: Think about Him who endured such accusations against Him by sinners so that you do not become worn out in your mind and give up. For you have not yet resisted to the point of blood letting.** A warrior has to **precisely take note** of his opponent, not retreat from his position, nor engage in lots of failed battles (1 Cor. 9:26); instead, he must protect himself well and diligently strive to demolish his opponents on every side. In the same way also, a spiritual warrior has to **properly fight** (2 Tim. 2:5), in such a way that he seriously takes note of the **evil attacks by the devil. 2 Cor. 2:11: We know what Satan has in mind.** One must never **give up the fight**. A person must never engage in failing battles and faithless deeds of failure. One must protect himself well with the **armor of prayer** and valiantly strike down the enemy with the **sword of God's Word** (Eph. 6:11ff.). Here, however, the holy Apostle draws special attention to the fact of how a runner or a dueling fighter [fencer] practices restraint in all things (v. 25). In other words, he practices moderation in what he eats and drinks, gets the right amount of sleep, etc., so that he does not ruin the strength of his body. He **does not overindulge himself** with all sorts of sweet foods. Rather, he abstains from many of them so that his body does not become overweight, or his mind become dehydrated. Instead, he restrains his eating and drinking and all other external matters in order that his body remain finely honed and lean, and so that his mind remain nimble and alert. Thus he may parry, neutralize, and strike down his opponent's thrusts, while at the same time deftly thrusting back at him. So also a spiritual runner and fighter, says the Apostle, has to **subdue and tame** his body to the same degree he here in v. 27 presents to the lovers of godliness with his **own example**. With such subjugation and taming of the flesh, he obviously does not mean a **Baal-styled scourging and cutting of the body!** (1 Kin. 18:28). (God has forbidden this in Lev. 19:28 and Deu. 14:1.) Instead, he hereby first of all and foremost means the **taming of the old man** [old Adam]. Elsewhere he calls it **crucifying the flesh** along with its lusts and desires, Gal. 5:24, **the crucifying of the old Adam, the putting aside of the sinful body** (Rom. 6:6). He calls it **the killing off by the Spirit of the works of the flesh** (Ch. 8:14), **the killing off of the members which are upon earth** (Col. 3:5), **the laying aside of the old and the putting on of the new man** (Eph. 4:22 and 24; Col. 3:9–10). Christ calls for **chopping off the hand and the foot** if it offends us, **to rip out an eye** which offends us (Mat. 18:8). Also, it is nothing other than that one by the power of the Spirit fight against the evil lusts which still rule in our members, subdue them, and never agree to let them come to fruition.

Next, with such subjugation and taming of the body, the Apostle means **the essential, beneficial control of the natural body** by which a person keeps the body under control with moderation, work, watchfulness, and also at times with fasting, so that **the flesh does not strive against the Spirit.** Also, so that the body does not become lazy and negligent towards works of godliness. For here it usually happens like what Moses said about the people of Israel in Deu. 32:15 – **After he became fat and satiated, he became sexually aroused. He became fat and obese and strong, and he neglected the God who had made him. He regarded the Rock of his salvation as insignificant.** The Apostle speaks about such necessary, beneficial control of the body in Rom. 13:14: **Yet guard the body so that it does not become sexually aroused.** Or, as it actually reads in the original Greek, "Guard the flesh against lusts." In other words, guard the body in such a way so that you do not at the same time fulfill the lusts of the sinful flesh.

However, the fact that both forms of subjugation and taming of the body are essential for godliness is to be concluded from the following instruction. For first of all, one dare not have any doubts that the **crucifixion of the flesh** and the killing off of the old Adam is essential for godliness. For the **holy Apostle** instructs with clear words in Rom. 6:12-13, **Do not allow sin to reign in your mortal bodies, nor become obedient to the desires with their lusts. Also, do not with the sins of your members give in to the weapons of unrighteousness. Rather, give yourselves up to God as those who have been made alive from the dead. Also make your members from God weapons of**

righteousness. He [St. Paul] powerfully promotes this doctrine throughout the entire chapter. Ch. 8:12–14: **We are debtors not to the flesh to live according to the flesh, for if you life according to the flesh, you shall die. If you however by the Spirit kill off the affairs of the flesh, you shall live.** Gal. 5:16–17, 19–24: **I however say, conduct yourself in the Spirit. Thus, you will not fulfill the lust of the flesh, for the flesh lusts against the Spirit and the Spirit against the flesh. These two are in opposition to one another so that you do not do what you want to. ... However the works of the flesh are obvious, such as adultery, harlotry, uncleanness, fornication, idolatry, witchcraft, enmity, hatred, greed, wrath, argumentation, discord, envy, hatred, murder, drunkenness, revelries, and the like. I have spoken to you about this before and tell you once more, that those who do such things will not inherit the kingdom of God. However the fruit of the Spirit is love, joy, peace, patience, kindness, goodness, faith, meekness, and chastity. There is no law against such things. But those who belong to Christ crucify their flesh along with its lusts and desires.** Ch. 6:8 – **Whatever a man sows is what he will reap. Anyone who sows onto his flesh shall from the flesh inherit death. However, whoever sows to the Spirit shall inherit eternal life from the Spirit.** There are many other such apostolic admonitions to be found elsewhere, especially for example in Eph. 4:22; Col. 3:9, etc. From them, we can clearly see that the killing off of the sinful flesh is essential for godliness. One also finds the same thing when one considers the future harm that ensues if one does not fight against the evil, sinful lusts of the flesh. For anyone who follows the lead of his sinful flesh, he **sins against his conscience.** But anyone who sins against conscience **stands to lose his faith, God's grace, the indwelling of the Holy Spirit, and eternal life**—which, of course, is most harmful to his godliness.

However, that controlling the body is essential for godliness is to be concluded from the fact that all the while the soul of a person in this life mostly accomplishes its deeds through the service of the body is the reason that it is necessary that the body also be controlled in order that the deeds may be able to serve the souls at the Judgment. Thus it is to be tamed so that it not strive against the soul. *Ita nutrienda est caro, ut serviat, ita domand, ut non superbiat.*[*] Sirach says in ch. 33:24, **The mule is due his fodder, whip, and burden. So also the servant is due his bread, chastisement, and labor.** To a certain degree, this may also be applied to the body of a man. Thus, he is due his fodder, i.e., his nourishment. He is due his burden, i. e. his labor. He is due his **chastisement**—not so that one perhaps should beat and whip him. Rather, so that one might take the opportunity to **deter** him from lowly food and drink so that he be humbled. However, this point about how the evil lusts of the flesh are to be killed off and how to control the body with moderation shall be dealt with extensively and comprehensively in another place.

---

[*] "Not only is the flesh not to be nurtured, but also to be made subservient. Not only is it to be dominated, but also to be made subservient."

Chapter Thirteen

How these helpful means for godliness that have now been recounted are to be generally regarded.

This is how the helpful means that are of service in the promotion of godliness are to be generally regarded.
1. They are not *liberi arbitrii in naturalibus relicti opera*. *[works left to the natural powers of the free will]*. Unless he has been born anew by the Spirit of God, such **deeds** cannot be performed by natural man. **By his own natural powers,** he cannot perform them in the way God requires nor in a way pleasing to Him. Quite obviously he can outwardly avail himself of the Lord's Supper, outwardly say prayers, as well as outwardly guard himself from gross sins. However, it simply does not exist within the natural powers of one who has not yet been born again to do the following: to hear God's Word in such a manner that through it the heart of a man is changed, conversion is effected, and rebirth is accomplished. Also, to partake of the holy Lord's Supper so that its reception is received by the inward man from the heart and with the kind of devotion that pleases God, prayer, the subjugation of the evil lusts of the flesh, etc. The power to do all this does not exist in a person who has not yet been born again. Instead, the Holy Spirit has to work this in our hearts. However, at the same time, the Holy Spirit **will not do this without a means** for doing so. Rather, He actually works

through the means of the hearing, reading, and contemplation of the divine Word and through the use of the Holy Sacrament—just so long as a person does not willfully resist His gracious workings.

2. Much less is it an *opera meritoria,* **a meritorious work.** For we are already in so many ways **obligated to God** (Luke 17:10). For God the Lord works every good in us through His Holy Spirit (Isa. 26:12). Thus we are much more obligated to God the Lord because our works in this life are **imperfect.** And we do not keep the commandments of God with very much inward and outward obedience as it actually should be done. It is because our works are unclean and splotched with many sinful stains and blemishes (Isa. 64:6). How possibly could our works thus ever be regarded before God the Lord as meritorious?

3. Much less are these helpful means *aequalia,* **of the same kind of nature and attribute**, of the same worthiness, and of the same **power or impact.** For concerning **bodily exercise,** i.e., the controlling of the body, St. Paul says in 1 Tim. 4:8 – **that they are of little benefit,** that, contrariwise, **godliness has the promise of this and the future life.** We explained this passage of the Apostle very extensively in the introduction to this Tract. The diligent, inward **contemplation** of God's Word and a devout, inward prayer avails much more for the promotion of godliness than does some outward **control** of the body, although that, too, has it own benefit in its proper place. Heb. 11:9 – **It is a precious thing for the heart to become steadfast. That takes place by grace, not through eating from which there comes no benefit about which to brag,** i.e., those who make of this an outstanding **service to God.**

4. That the parts that have been related up to this point are not just *Adminicula*, salutary **means for help** that are essential for godliness. Rather, they are also in certain measure and manner *Requisita* for the kind of things that **are essentially required** for godliness. For whoever does not hear the Word of God, partake of the holy Sacrament, does not diligently pray, does not fight against the lusts of the flesh, shall not be able to obtain true godliness. For the whole time **he is despising these means** by which God the Lord wants to craft godliness in the heart of a person. Indeed, the means of help in certain measure and manner are also **essential parts** of the godliness that God the Lord has called for in His Word from all lovers of godliness. So then, nobody should be surprised that this thing is simultaneously a means that is of help in promoting godliness and is called the essential part of blessedness. Christ says the same thing. **God gives the Holy Spirit to those who ask the Spirit of Him** (Luke 11:13). Also, **no one may call Jesus 'Lord' except through the Holy Spirit** (1 Cor. 12:3). Nor can anyone in a proper fashion and in a way pleasing to Him call on God the Lord without the **pleas of the Spirit** (Zec. 12:10). (This can be compared to a believing prayer that is **motivated by the gracious workings** of the Holy Spirit ... and yet along with this there exists a blessed means by which the rich in grace gifts of the Spirit are **increased in a person**.) Thus, there is this helpful means that is partly essential and a necessary part of godliness while, at the same time, there are also salutary means by which a person can grow and increase in godliness. Still, everything happens out of the sheer **grace and goodness of God the Holy Spirit**.

5. If these means for help are regarded as *requisita studii pietatis*, as a part that **of necessity** belongs to godliness, than one can appropriately include and add on *recta intentio* [*righteous intentions*]. Thus, a person should not view his works as being for **his own glory or benefit.** Rather, they are to be viewed as being **to God's glory** and for the **benefit of the neighbor.** On this point, Christ admonishes in Mat. 6:22–23: **The eye is the body's light. If your eye is simple-minded, then your whole life will be light. But if your eye is a rascal, then your entire body will be in darkness. But if the light that is in you is darkness, how great then will be the darkness itself?** The eye of the soul is the intention for a person not to seek or intend to seek his own glory with his good works but, instead, the **glory of God the Lord.** If this proper intention is not present, then no proper good works can be performed. Instead it is all filled with the inward **darkness** of sin and nothing can result from it other than that one continually fail and give offenses just like a person who walks in darkness. Actually, true intention does not **make for good works.** In the same way, everything that a person does with good intention would be good and God pleasing. For also this must reach the point that the works **have to be commanded by God** and agree with the seal of the divine Word. Nevertheless, it will still of necessity promote good works, and where they do not exist there can be no true good and God-pleasing works taking place. With this we conclude the First Part of the Second Volume of the *Exercise of Godliness*.

Part Two

About the essential, necessary parts of godliness in general, as to how each individual Christian should exercise himself in them.

Thus far we have treated and discussed the matter of the salutary *Adminiculis* or **helpful means** that can be useful on the whole in the exercise of godliness. Now we must also address in an orderly and explanatory manner the matter of the **essential, necessary points** of true **godliness.** It is not sufficient for a builder to only assemble together the lumber, bricks, and other essential items for erecting the building. Instead it is quintessential that he **initiates the construction work** of **properly laying the foundation** and then **builds** upon it. In the same way also, it is not sufficient for **godliness** that a person have in hand these **helpful means**. Rather, one must also initiate taking in hand the task of building this godliness **upon** the sole **foundation and rock of Christ.** King David provided all the necessary items required for the building of the Temple. **See,** he says to his son, Solomon, in 1 Chronicles 22:14 – **I, in midst of my deprivation, have provided a hundred thousand talents of gold and a million talents of silver. In addition also, bronze and iron without number, for it is not too much. Also, I have provided wood and stone.** Nevertheless, at the same time, the building of the Temple was not initiated. Instead, Solomon **built** the Temple in keeping with the Lord's command (2 Sam. 7:13). So also with the building of godliness, it is not undertaken or completed when a person makes all sorts of good preparations and takes in hand the blessed means of help. Instead, the entire construction project has to be carried out according to the Word of the Lord. However, there are **two essential chief parts** in true godliness. This has been extensively demonstrated in the introduction to this study; namely, true, **proper repentance** and then also true, proper **fruits of repentance. True repentance** contains within itself **contrition and sorrow** over sin; and then also **true faith in Christ.** The fruits of repentance are composed of child-like obedience towards each and every commandment of God the Lord. Whoever diligently exercises himself with these essential parts of godliness is to be regarded as a true lover of godliness. **Knowledge** of this is not enough for this. Instead, there also belongs to this the **doing or practice** of it. In the same manner, it is not sufficient for a master to know how he is to carry out his work. Rather, he must strive with 'hands on' application to apply himself to the task. **If you know this,** Christ states in John 13:17 – **blessed are you if you do it.** Likewise, knowledge is of necessity required for this if the activity or deed is to be the result. Consequently, so that a lover of godliness may know how he should exercise himself in godliness, we want to consider the essential parts of godliness in an orderly manner.

Chapter One

That true, proper repentance is an essential requirement for godliness.

If our first parents, along with all of their descendants, had remained in the **state of innocence with holiness and righteousness** in which God had created them (Eph. 4:24) they would not have needed any **repentance**. Nor would repentance have been required of them as a necessary **part** of true godliness. For where there **is no sin,** there is no way that **acknowledgement of sin and true repentance** of it would have been necessary. Nor would **forgiveness of sins** through faith in Christ have been necessary. Instead, their godliness would only and solely consisted of holy, **perfect obedience** of God's command. That's why before the fall into sin the **Law of God** had not been given them for the purpose that they were to **acknowledge** their **sin** from it and **regret it**—as the Law today is preached to mankind for this end (Rom. 3:20; 4:15; 7:7). Instead, it would have been only and solely for the purpose that they were to learn from it in **which works** they were to exercise themselves. Also, that they were to demonstrate their service and obedience to God the Lord. However, because they had separated themselves from God their Creator through deliberate disobedience—and also all their descendants inherited sin—that's why true, proper repentance is of necessity required of them and all of us. The holy **angels** do not require **repentance,** for they are without sin. However, we humans need to repent if we otherwise desire to properly exercise oneself in godliness. This becomes apparent:

1. *Ex peccatis originalis propogatione,* **from the propagation of inherited sin by which through one person,** namely through the first **man sin came into the world because we all have sinned** (Rom. 5:12). **There no longer is any difference; we are altogether sinners, and we lack the glory that we are to have before God** (Rom. 3:23). **We have been conceived and born in sin** (Psa. 51:7), **and thus by nature children of wrath** (Eph. 2:3). With true repentance and humility, we must acknowledge such shameful misery, and with pleading sigh before God the Lord for the forgiveness of this inherited sin.

2. *Ex peccatorum actualium perpetratione,* **from the performing of actual sin.** Things don't just stop with **inherited sin.** Instead there also gets added on many and all sorts of **actual sins. For before God the Lord there is nobody who is innocent** (Exo. 34:7) **There is not a single person who does not sin** (Exo. 34:7). **There is nobody who does not sin** (1 Kin. 8:46). **How could a man be righteous before God?** (Job 4:17). **Look, among His servants there is none who is without blame, and His commandments are foolishness to him** (v. 18). **How much more shall not those who live in glued together houses that are founded upon dirt** (in reference to sin) **be gobbled up by worms?** (v. 19). **A human being cannot stand justified before God** (Job 9:2). **If he wishes to try to quarrel with Him, he is incapable of giving a response to a thousand things** (v. 3). **Who is able to find a clean thing where there is nothing clean?** (Job 14:4). **What is man that he should be clean and be righteous since he has**

been born of a woman? (Job 15:14). **Look, among His saints there is not one who is without fault, and those who are in heaven are pure only because of Him** (v. 15). **How much more so will a person who is an abomination and is despicable** (v. 16). **He drinks unrighteousness like it were water** (v. 17). **Who can keep a record of how often he fails?** (Psa. 32:6). **All the saints have to plead for forgiveness of sins** (Psa. 32:6), and have to cry out with David: **God be gracious to me according to Your goodness, and expunge my sin according to Your huge mercy** (Psa. 51:2). **If You, Lord, were to keep an account of sin, who would be able to stand?** (Psa. 130:3). **Do not enter into judgment with Your servant, because before You no living person is righteous** (Psa. 143:3). **Who can say, I am clean in my heart and purified of my sin?** (Pro. 20:9). That is the reason why Christ has taught us altogether to pray thus: **Forgive us our debt as we forgive our debtors** (Mat. 6:11; Luke 11:4). **For all of us fail in manifold ways** (Jam. 3:2). **If we say we have no sin, we deceive ourselves, and the truth is not with us** (1 John 1:8). **Since then in particular sin sticks to us constantly** (Heb. 12:1). That's why it is necessary that we acknowledge such weakness and failures, and with true repentance, daily petition God the Lord for forgiveness of them. That is, if we wish to be found in true godliness.

    3. *Ex Christi & Apostolorum praedicatione*, from **the preaching of Christ and His Apostles.** There can be no doubt about it: the sermons of Christ, John the Baptist and all the Apostles were all directed to the goal that their hearers might be brought to true godliness. **We proclaim to and admonish all people and teach**

all people with all wisdom so that we may present each individual person perfect to Christ Jesus, Paul says about himself and other Apostles in Col. 1:28. Now, however, Christ, John the Baptist, and the holy Apostles all faithfully admonished their hearers to repent. **Jesus began to preach and He said, Repent! The Kingdom of heaven has come into your midst** (Mat. 4:17; Mark 1:15). John the Baptist came and preached in the wilderness of the land of the Jews. He said, **Repent, the kingdom of heaven has come into your midst** (Mat. 3:2; Luke 3:3). **So it has been written and so must Christ suffer and arise from the dead on the third day. And there has to be preached in His name** (through the holy Apostles) **repentance and the forgiveness of sins among all nations and beginning at Jerusalem,** Christ says in Luke 24:46–47. **The Apostles went out and preached that people should repent** (Mark 6:12). **Repent and each of you let yourselves be baptized in the name of Jesus Christ for the forgiveness of sin,** Peter says in Acts 2:38. **Repent and turn yourselves around so that your sin be polished off,** Peter says once more in Acts 3:19. Indeed, he expressly testifies that God the Lord specifically **raised Christ from the dead and sent Him to the Israelites in order to bless them,** so that each individual might **turn away from his evil ways** (v. 26). **With His right hand God exalted Jesus to be a Prince and Savior in order to give Israel repentance and the forgiveness of sins,** he likewise states in Acts 5:31. **God command all people in every place to repent,** Paul says in Acts 20:21. **I proclaimed to Jews and Gentiles that they repent and turn back to God and do works appropriate for repentance,** he says in Acts 26:20. From this it is to be concluded that for true godliness it requires repentance as an essential, necessary part thereof. Still more grounds from which to conclude that for a true godliness repentance is called for may be drawn from the chapter that follows.

Chapter Two

What should motivate a person to truly repent.

One can find any number of vital and important **reasons** why **we** should altogether truly repent and turn ourselves back to God the Lord. Among such motivating reasons the following are the most important.

1. *Dei praecipientis majestas*, **God the Lord's order and command.** In Acts 17:30, the Apostle says, **God bids all mankind for all of them to repent.** This order of God is frequently repeated in the preaching of the holy Prophet John the Baptist, the Lord Christ, and the holy Apostles. Through the prophet (Jer. 3:7), God the Lord states: **Turn yourself back to Me. V. 12 – Turn back again, You unfaithful Israel. V. 14 – Turn yourselves back, you defecting children.** Ch. 4:1 – **If you wish to turn yourself around, Israel, then turn yourself back to Me, says the Lord.** Ch. 25:5 – **Each one of you turn yourself back around from your evil ways and away from your evil existence.** Ch. 35:15 – **I have continually sent to you all My servants, the prophets, and had them tell you: Each one of you turn yourself back from his evil existence and improve your life.** Eze. 18:30–32, **You turn away from all your transgressions so that you may not fall on account of your iniquity. Throw away from yourselves**

all transgression with which you have transgressed, and make for yourself a new heart and a new spirit. Do turn yourselves back from your evil existence. Hos. 12:5 – **The Lord is the God of Sabaoth. The LORD is His name. So turn yourself back to your God.** Ch. 14:2, **Turn yourself back, Israel, to the Lord your God. For you have fallen because of your iniquity.** V. 3 – **Take these words with you and turn yourselves back to the Lord and say to Him, Forgive us our sin.** Joel 2:12-13, **Thus then says the Lord: Turn yourselves back to Me with your whole heart, with fasting, with crying, with lamentation. Rip apart your hearts and not your garments, and turn yourself back to the Lord your God.** Jon. 3:8 – **Each individual turn himself back from his evil ways and from the deceit of his hands.** Mal. 3:7 – **Turn yourselves back to Me. Thus I will turn Myself back to you, says the Lord.** Sirach 5:8 – **Do not pass up the opportunity to turn back to the Lord, and do not put it off day after day.** Ch. 17:20 – **Turn yourself back to the Lord and forsake your sinful life.** V. 21 – **Petition the Lord and refrain from evil.** John the Baptist proclaims in Mat. 3:2 – **Repent.** In ch. 4:17, Christ proclaims, **Repent.** In Acts 2:38, Peter proclaims, **Repent.** In ch. 3:19, he once more says, **Repent and turn yourselves back.** In Rev. 2:5, the Son of God says, **Repent and do the original works.** V. 16 – **Repent.** Ch. 3:19 – **Be diligent and repent.** Note that these are not commanding words from an **earthly king,** but from God the Lord, **the King of all kings** and **Lord of all lords** (1 Tim. 6:15). Indeed, we are obligated to be obedient to Him and follow Him so that He will not have reason to lament about us from the prophet, Mal. 1:6, **A son should honor his father** and a servant his lord. Now I am your Fathers, where then is My glory? If I am the Lord, where is there anyone who fears Me? says the Lord of Sabaoth.** It is God's unchangeable, **sincere** desire that we should repent. That is why He has so very often repeated in His Word this command that we should repent. If we do not fulfill this gracious desire of God through **contrition** and **repentance**, then He fulfills His will over and against us with **punishment**. *Si non impletur DEI voluntas 'a nobis salutari conversione, DEUS eam implet de nobis nostri eversione, quia voluntate Dei jubentis currimus ad volunatem DEI punientis.** If the servant does not do what the Lord requires of him, then the lord fulfills that with which he had threatened the disobedient servant.

2. *Mandati divini universalitas* [*The universality of divine commands*], since this **command extends itself upon all mankind.** Acts 17:30–31, **God bids all men in all the ends** [of the earth] **to repent. Because He has set one day in which He shall righteously judge the whole world.** This is a beautiful closing argument; the Final Judgment applies to every human being. **For we all will have to stand before Christ's Judgement throne** (Rom. 14:10; 2 Cor. 5:10). That's why the preaching of repentance goes out to all humanity in every nook and cranny of the world. The reason is this: **because all of them are sinners**—as was indicated in the previous chapter. If all of them are sinners, then all of them are in need of repentance. In Luke 24:47, Christ required that **repentance and forgiveness of sins had**

---

* "If we don't fulfill the will of God with salutary conversion, God, i.e., His will, fulfills it with respect to us with our turning away, because by the will of God who commands, we run to the will of God as He punishes us."

to be preached among all peoples, also beginning at Jerusalem. The preaching of repentance in the New Testament indeed began at Jerusalem. However, from then on it was spread out to the **entire world** among all nations. The fact, however, that it is written in Luke 15:7 - **the righteous do not need repentance,** is to be taken to refer to the incorrect intended judgments of the Pharisees, with whom Christ Himself is here speaking. For they regarded themselves **to be pious and righteous on their own** (Luke 18:9). To them, Christ sets this parable against them in which He teaches that God and all the holy angels bear a greater approval upon a repentant sinner than upon such who think they are holy and righteous. Consequently, since the proclamation about repentance applies even more so since the Fall of all mankind into sin, we should not deceive ourselves as if we did not need repentance. Rather, we must most certainly view ourselves as all being in need of repentance.

   3. *Dei beneplacitum & bona voluntas,* **God's gracious pleasure.** Those things that God the Lord has bidden and required of us, He also has a gracious pleasure in. Now, however, God the Lord has commanded that we should repent and turn ourselves back to Him—as has been shown up to this point with many verses of divine Scripture. From this it follows that He also has a gracious pleasure over our repentance. He Himself says of this in Eze. 18:23 - **Do you think that I have pleasure in the death of the godless and wouldn't rather that they turn themselves from their evil ways and live?** Ch. 33:11 - **As surely as I live, says the Lord of lords, I have no pleasure in the death of the godless, rather that the godless turn back from**

his ways and live. **So you then turn away from your evil ways.** Likewise, God the Lord sincerely **hates sin** and it is His heartfelt enemy. So also, He has a heartfelt **pleasure** in mankind's **repentance** and conversion as that through which a person turns away from sin and draws near to God. A man heartily loves a person and regards him as his best friend when that person hates, persecutes, and kills off his denounced enemies. In the same way, God the Lord loves that person and regards him as His friend who through **true repentance** hates, subjugates, and kills off within himself **sin as God denounced enemy.** Sin is the **biggest evil**, the biggest shame. It's the most repulsive thing over which God and the holy angels bear utter disgust and disapproval. Contrariwise, God the Lord is the highest Good, the most Beauteous, the most Blessed. He is the ultimate Kindness. It can sufficiently be concluded from this how dear and acceptable repentance of men must be to God the Lord. For through repentance a person turns away from the greatest evil—namely, from sin to the highest Good—to God the Lord. Since God the Lord has such a heartfelt pleasure in the repentance and conversion of a man, it should indeed also be incumbent upon us to once more have a heartfelt love to do that which is acceptable and pleasing to God. We should rightly examine that **which is good, pleasing and a fulfillment of God's will** (Rom 12:2). We should pray with David in Psa. 143:11 – **Teach me to do according to Your pleasure, for You are my God. Your good Spirit leads me upon the even road.**

    4. *Dei promittentis benignitas,* **God's promises.** The good and multitudinously faithful God does not only want to encourage us to repent through His command, but He also wants to tug and lure us to do so through His promises. Eze. 33:11 – **Do turn yourselves back to Me. Thus you will live, says the Lord.** Mal. 3:7 – **Turn yourselves back to Me. Thus I will turn Myself back to you, says the Lord of Sabaoth.** Christ says in Mat. 11:28: **Come here to Me all of you who are weary and overburdened. I will renew you.** John 6:37 – **Whoever comes to Me I will not push him aside.** The Prophet Joel directs us to such gracious promises of God in ch. 2:13, and then takes an admonition to repentance from it in that he says: **Turn yourselves back to the Lord your God who is gracious, merciful, long-suffering, and of great goodness, and immediately He regrets the punishment.** Also the Apostle, St. Paul, points us to such a promise in Rom. 2:4 – **Are you despising the reign of His goodness, patience, and long-suffering? Don't you know that God's goodness guides you to repentance?** Obviously, it is a great goodness, patience, and long-suffering that God the Lord sees and knows how mankind provides lodging in his heart for God's renounced enemy, **sin.** Mankind treasures it, serves it, follows it, and clings to it—even though his heart is supposed to be **God's house.** And, at the same time, GOD the Lord sustains such a sinful person with His might. God does not immediately allow him to be destroyed with His zealous fire, but instead He waits for him to turn back. A person should once more acknowledge such great goodness, patience, and long-suffering and hasten to repent, so that this renounced enemy of God might be driven out of one's heart and a residence for God the Lord may prepared within it. The heavenly Bridegroom, **Christ Jesus, knocks at the door of our hearts** through the preaching of repentance (Rev. 3:26), and He **calls** us to Himself as His beloved bride. From the Song of Solomon (5:2), **Open up for Me, beloved lover, My sister, My dove, My pious one.** Open for Me the door of your heart through **repentance**; thus I will enter into you with grace. Such knocking and calling takes place through the **preaching of the divine Word.** St. Paul addresses this point in 2 Cor. 5:20 – **We are messengers in Christ's place, for God is pleading through us. So then we beg of you in Christ's stead: Let yourselves be reconciled with God.** Is not this a great goodness and grace that GOD the Lord not only **promises** us reconciliation and offers it to us, but that He still instead **begs us** that we should let ourselves be reconciled with Him? Indeed, there is still more. The fact is that Christ not only calls out to us with **words** and begs us to repent, but that also His **holy blood** cries out to us that we should yet repent so that His power and meritorious benefit not be lost on us. For the power and meritorious benefit of the precious blood of Christ can have no effect on an unrepentant heart in the same way that **precious balsam** can be of no benefit to a hard **stone**. Since Christ not only shed **tears** for our good, but that He also shed His precious **blood** in order to thereby call us to repentance, should we ourselves not then much more shed tears of true repentance?

5. *Poenitentiae necessitas,* **the necessity of repentance.** Repentance is not perchance a mediocre thing left to our free discretion, something that we may take in hand or set aside. Instead, with the utmost, unchangeable necessity it calls for us to repent if we otherwise wish to obtain God's grace, forgiveness of sin, and eternal life. In Luke 13:3, Christ says, **If you**

do not improve yourself through true repentance, **you shall all perish.** *Aut poenitendum, aut ardendum.** Either we must in **this life repent**, or else be separated from the **future life** and be shoved off into **hell.** Why? Because **without repentance** we cannot **draw near** to God. Instead we remain **separated** from Him. If we are separated from God, then we also are **separated** from **the life** that is in and from God (Eph. 4:18). If we are separated from the life that is in and from God, we must be eternally lost and damned. There is no third alternative or middle ground to be found. Consequently, since this unchanging necessity requires that we repent, we then should not postpone it or put it behind us.

  6. *Poenitentiae utilitas,* **the great benefit** that we receive from true repentance. For true repentance brings with it the following fruits and benefits. (1) *Deo nos reconciliat,* it **reconciles us with God the Lord and through the same brings us once again into grace.** Psa. 51:19 – **The sacrifices that please God are a distressed spirit. A distressed and crushed heart You, God, will not despise.** In the same way that our **sin and wrongdoing separate us from our God and from each other** (Isa. 59:2), so contrariwise through **repentance we draw near** once again **to GOD**, and find grace with Him. For He wants to **reside** (by grace) **with those who are of a crushed and humble spirit so that He may renew the spirit of the humble and the hearts of the crushed** (Isa. 59:15). **He desires to look** (with favor) **upon one whose heart is miserable and crushed** (Isa. 66:2). Indeed, there will be **joy in heaven** (before God the Lord) **over one sinner who repents—more so than over ninety-nine righteous persons who do**

---
* "Either repentance or fiery torment."

not need repentance (Luke 15:7). Christ Himself quite masterfully and comfortingly explains this through the portrayal of the very loving **father** who ran out to meet the lost son. He hugged and kissed his neck as he was coming towards him, v. 20.

(2) *Angelos exhilarat,* **Repentance makes the holy angels rejoice.** Christ Jesus teaches us this with clear words in Luke 15:10, **I tell you, there will be joy before the angels of God over one sinner who repents.** *Lachimae poenitentium sunt vinum Angelorum*. Just as **wine gladdens the heart of mankind** (Psa. 104:15), so also the tears of repentance make glad the holy angels in heaven. What causes this *first of all* is because through repentance we **fulfill God's will** (Eze. 33:11). However, that which pleases God also thoroughly pleases the holy angels on account of the perfect similarity between the will of God and the will of the holy angels.

In the *second place*, because we through repentance **become partakers of the protection of the holy angels.** The unrepentant are outside the realm of the protection of the holy angels. That's why the holy angels rejoice when a person repents so that they from then on may serve him. For they are **serving spirits** (Heb. 1:14).

In the *third place*, through repentance we **become partakers of eternal life.** The unrepentant have no hope of eternal life. Instead, they are locked out from the fellowship of the holy angels and all the elect. That's why the angels rejoice when a person through repentance obtains the hope of eternal salvation, and thus his contribution consists in praising and glorifying God.

---

* "tears of the repentant are wine for the angels."

In the *fourth place*, because we through repentance **escape temporal and eternal punishment.** The holy angels are overflowing with love. They have a heartfelt sympathy with us humans. They see and understand our misery and tribulation far better than we humans do. It also pierces their hearts all the more on account of the **perfect love** that shines within them. They know that the unrepentant are bodily possessions of the devil, and that they cannot escape the hellish agony and pain except through true, proper repentance (Mat. 3:7). That's why they rejoice when a person through repentance **escapes the temporal and eternal punishment**.

In the *fifth place*, because we through repentance **become the recipients of the fruit of Christ's suffering.** Christ's merits come to no good for the unrepentant person. That's why the holy angels rejoice when the precious medication of Christ's suffering—which the angels highly regard as being of great worth—comes to the person with its power and is received. It's just like a faithful mother rejoices when she sees that her unappreciative child now continually accepts and uses the medicine that he has previously rejected.

In the *sixth place*, because through repentance **the kingdom of the devil is destroyed within us.** The unrepentant are servants of sin and bodily possessions of the devil. That's why the holy angels—as denouncing enemies of the devil—rejoice when they see that through repentance the devil's kingdom is destroyed in people.

(3) *Diabolum contrista*, **repentance distresses the evil devil.** The devil has his desire for sin. There can be no doubt that he becomes distressed by our repentance. The devil's incipient mind-set is totally opposed to the will of God and the holy angels (as the denounced enemy that he is). Accordingly, since God and the holy angels have great pleasure in the repentance of a person, it can easily be concluded that the repentance of a person really distresses the devil. Through impenitence there is prepared in a person's heart a soft pillow for the devil. That is why he is so highly opposed when he has to leave this previous lodging.

(4) *Omnis generis bonis so cumulat*, **repentance brings us everything good.** For through repentance we first of all obtain **forgiveness of sin.** Psa. 32:5 – **I said, I will confess my transgressions to the Lord, then You forgave me the iniquity of my sin.** Jer. 36:3 – **Write this saying in a book so that perhaps the House of Judah might turn back—each person from his evil ways—so that I can forgive them their iniquity and sin.** Ch. 12:19 – **With this you will give your children to understand that they should be of good hope in that you desire to undertake to repent of sin.** In Mark 1:4, John preaches **about the Baptism of repentance for the forgiveness of sin.** Luke 24:47 – **Christ thus had to suffer and in His Name have preached repentance and forgiveness of sin.** Acts 3:19 – **Repent and turn yourselves back so that your sin may be forgiven.** Ch. 5:31 – **God exalted Jesus in order to give to Israel repentance and forgiveness of sin.** 1 John 1:9 – **If we confess our sin, He is faithful and righteous and cleanses us from all vices.** In these and similar passages, **repentance** and **forgiveness of sins** are placed side by side, because upon true, proper repentance there follows forgiveness of sins. A beautiful prototypical portrayal of this is presented to us in Lev. 16:21,29, where upon a particular day the

Israelites in true repentance chastised their bodies, and the **atoning-ram bore** their sin into the wilderness.

In the second place, the miserable tax-collector in Luke 18:14, with heartfelt repentance, longed for **the righteousness that avails before God. "God be gracious to me a poor sinner!"** Thereupon immediately follows, **This one returned home justified** before that arrogantly proud Pharisee.

In the third place, the **gift** of **the Holy Spirit** and His merciful **indwelling.** Acts 2:38 - **Repent and each one from among you let himself be baptized for the forgiveness of sins. Thus you will receive the gift of the Holy Spirit.**

In the fourth place, **the hearing of prayers.** 1 John 3:21 - **If our heart does not condemn us, we have a friendship with God, and what we ask for we shall obtain from Him.**

In the fifth place, **deliverance from temporal punishments and plagues,** or otherwise the **alleviation** of them. 2 Chr. 12:7 - **When the Lord saw that the Israelites had humbled themselves** (in true repentance), **the Word of the Lord came to Shemaiah the Prophet and said, They have humbled themselves, therefore I will not destroy them. Instead I shall give them a bit of relief.** V. 12 - **Because** the King had humbled himself, **the Lord's wrath turned itself away from him so that not everything was destroyed.** Jer. 18:7-8, **Suddenly I speak against a people that I want to uproot, crush and destroy them. Where, however, they turn back from their evil against which I am speaking, I shall regret the misfortune which I had considered doing.** Jon. 3:10 - **When God saw from the deeds of the Ninevites that they had turned back** from their evil ways, He regretted the evil which He had said He would do against them and did not do it. Luke 13:3 - **If you do not better yourselves, all of you will also perish** like the Galileans whose blood Pilate had interspersed along with the blood of their sacrifices. Also, the **eighteen** upon whom the tower in Shiloh fell and killed them. From this it contrariwise follows that through true repentance a person may escape the misfortune that confronts him.

In the sixth place, **eternal salvation and blessedness.** In Acts 11:18, **God also gave the Gentiles repentance for life.** See then, these are truly great, heartfelt benefits of true repentance that one does well to take note of:

a) That such is not to be understood *ratione meriti*, as if repentance on its won is some kind of **vital, meritorious work** by which we are able to earn the great heavenly treasures and blessings. Rather it is *ratione medii*, since it is the blessed **means** ordained by God Himself whereby God the Lord wants to distribute and bestow these blessings to us.

b) That these accomplishments and benefits of repentance are attributed not so much *ratione contritionis*, **as a result of contrition and sorrow** over sin—as if one could achieve these treasures and blessings oneself in a meritorious manner. Rather it is *respectu fidei*, **as a result of faith in Christ**. This faith is the other essential part, and, so to speak, the **'soul' of repentance**. This faith clings to Christ—and in Christ there is God's grace, forgiveness of sin, the gift of the Holy Spirit and eternal life. *Quod partis est & quidem primariae, illud tribuitur totiper usitatam Scripturae Synecdochen**.

---

* "That which is indeed the chief part is attributed to the whole

c) That there is a second opportunity with **spiritual and heavenly blessings,** namely that of forgiveness of sin, righteousness, the gift of the Holy Spirit and eternal life, like with **the averting** or **mitigation of temporal punishment.** For what pertains to spiritual and heavenly blessings may not be obtained in any other way than through true, salutary repentance through which true, proper faith in Christ is obtained. However, the averting or mitigation of temporal **punishment** may at times also be obtained with a **hypocritical repentance,** with which there is no true faith, is demonstrated by the example of King Ahab in 1 Kin. 21:29.

d) That, indeed, through true, proper repentance the **averting of eternal punishment is obtained at all times.** However, with the temporal punishment it has this possibility, that God the Lord according to His all wise counsel and gracious will at times allows the repentant to remain stuck for a time under shame, even though they already have obtained forgiveness of sin through true repentance. That is why truly repentant people must humbly and completely leave it to God if, when, and in what manner He might avert and mitigate temporal misfortunes.

7. *Vitae impoenitentis noxa ac deformitas,* **the disgrace and shame of the unrepentant life.** An unrepentant life is nothing other than a **separation from God** and the holy angels. It is a disgraceful and shameful **enslavement to sin** and the evil devil. It is **a straight and ever straighter path to hell.** Through non-repentance a person heaps upon himself God's wrath, temporal, and eternal punishment. Rom. 2:4-5, **Are you despising the riches of blessing, patience**

---

thing through the usual synecdoche of Scriptures."

and longsuffering of God? Don't you know that God's goodness directs you to repentance? You, however, according to your proud and unrepentant heart are heaping up for yourself wrath for the day of wrath and the revelation of the righteous judgment of God. (Just as a stingy, greedy person daily accumulates something so that it finally amounts to a huge treasure, so also an unrepentant person daily piles upon himself the wrath of God so that later on it all at once shall be poured out upon him **like a hidden "treasure."** That's what the holy Apostle actually implies in what he is saying. God the Lord also speaks of this unblessed "treasure" in Deu. 32:34, **Is not this hidden by Me and sealed up in My treasure chest?**, i.e., they don't believe it until they experience it, because it is hidden from their eyes. V. 35 – **The fury is Mine, I shall repay. At the proper time their foot shall slip, for the time of their misfortune is near and their due is rapidly approaching.** And from the Prophet Jeremiah (50:25), **The Lord has opened His treasure chest, and has brought out of it the weapons of His wrath.**) An unrepentant person is an enemy of God. For **the holy angels**, an unrepentant person is a **monstrous beast**, a bodily-owned **slave**. And he is a latrine for the **devil**. He is an **abomination to all creation**. An unrepentant person **takes from God** the **glory** that is rightly God's. Rev. 16:9 – **They blasphemed the name of God and did not repent to give God the glory.** Just as God is **glorified** by true repentance—that total glory for all the righteousness and mercy is thereby given to Him (Psa. 51:6). So also, contrariwise, God the Lord is **dishonored** and shamed by non-repentance because an unrepentant person does not want to acknowledge or feel that

God the Lord is righteous and is enraged over sin. An unrepentant person brings about his own loss of the gracious **indwelling of God the Lord.** For in the same way God the Lord desires to **dwell** in those who are of a **crushed and humble spirit** (Isa. 57:15), so also He wishes to turn away from those who live in impenitence and arrogant self-assurance (Isa. 59:2): **Your misdeeds separate you and your God from each other.** Ch. 1:4 – **Wisdom does not reside within a body that is subject to sin.** An unrepentant person robs himself of the **protection of the holy angels.** For just as **there is joy among the angels in heaven over one sinner who repents** (Luke 15:10), so also the holy angels are saddened over a sinner that does not repent. They turn away from him with their protection and their heroism. An unrepentant person belongs to, and **more readily follows after**, the evil **devil than God** the Lord. For God the Lord cries out to us: **Today, as you hear My voice, do not let your hearts fill with pride and stop up your ears** (Psa. 95:8; Heb. 4:7). Contrariwise, the **devil** calls out to us men to serve him for today with sin and to postpone our repentance until tomorrow morning. And when the following day arrives he once more says, give me yet this one more day, for you can spare yourself for the Lord God tomorrow. So what is an unrepentant person doing other than that he is following the devil more than God the Lord? An unrepentant person robs himself of the **merit** and the power of **Christ's suffering and death.** For where there is no true repentance, there Christ's blood and death can not be efficacious for eternal life. If a precious **balsam** is poured upon a hard stone, it is of absolutely no benefit to that rock. In the same manner, the blood of Christ is unable to achieve its efficacious power for salvation in a stone hard, stuck-up and unrepentant heart. Isn't it a shame that the hard **Demanstein** can be softened by **ram's blood** while our hard, unrepentant hearts do not want to allow themselves to be turned to repentance by the **blood of Christ,** the only, true **Ram of Atonement** (Lev. 16:21)? An unrepentant person deprives himself of the gracious **forgiveness of sins** since without true, genuine repentance the forgiveness of sins has no status (Luke 24:47). Likewise, a unrepentant person deprives himself of all very same **heavenly blessings** that we become partakers of through repentance.

    8. *Scandali aliis dati atrocitas,* the **great offense** that is given to the neighbor by impenitence. The Lord Christ cries out to us in Mat. 18:7 – **Woe to that person by whom offense comes.** St. Paul cries out to us in 2 Cor. 6:3, **Let none of us give offense to another.** But now then the huge offense of the unrepentant does not only harm **them,** but it also harms **others** by wicked example. That's why they load on themselves the **curse** that is pronounced on all those who give offense.

    9. *Vitae nostrae fragilitas & fugacitas,* **the insignificance and fleetingness of our life. Our life passes away quickly as if we fly away from it** (Psa. 90:10). **It is all a dew-drop that exists for a short time and then disappears** (Jam. 4:14). We can no more add a single **minute** to our lives than we **are able to add even a teeny smidgen to our body's height** (Mat. 6:27). Why then would we deliberately and consciously want to remain in such danger by which we might fall into **eternal damnation?** We do not know whether we will live through **tomorrow**—indeed, whether we will live for **another hour.** Why would we then postpone our repentance? From God's Word, we can be certain that we shall obtain God's grace and forgiveness through true repentance. But whether we will live through **tomorrow**—of that we have no assurance. That's why it is foolish and dangerous for a person to postpone repentance until the next day if one's life were to turn **into fog** and the body **into a corpse.** Then later would be useless for one to repent.

   10. *judii divini severitas,* **the serious and final Judgment of God.** St. Paul holds this reason before us in Acts 17:30-31, **God bids all people in every place to repent. That's why He has set a Day upon which He shall judge the end boundaries of the earth with righteousness through one Man by whom He has finalized it. God the Lord will present every deed, every word, ... and yes, every thought before His judgment** (Ecc. 12:14; Mat. 12:36; 1 Cor. 4:5). If at that time God the Lord wanted to deal with us according to His strict righteousness and according to our merits—we would not be able to stand. That's why we must repent yet during this present time of grace, and from a repentant heart longing sigh with David in Psa. 143:3 – **Do not enter into judgment with Your servant, for before You no living person is just. Pray,** Christ says in Luke 21:36 – **that you may be become worthy to escape all of this that will take place and to be able to stand before the Son of Man.** Such a prayer has to arise from a repentant heart if it is to be heard. That's obviously why genuine repentance is part of it if one someday wants to stand before the Son of God on Judgment Day. These are the main reasons that should cheer and motivate us to true repentance. Whoever takes these to heart will let himself to be awakened from the sleep of arrogant self-assurance and impenitence. However, whoever disregards this will in the end discover the reality that he himself has brought upon himself the greatest disaster.

Chapter Three

In what manner a true Christian should exercise himself with true repentance.

True, genuine repentance, which not only is beneficial for every person but also is in all aspects necessary, does in no way consist *in nuda oris professione,* of **a naked profession by mouth,** where a person wants to boast orally about his true repentance. For just as we are not only to love with **word** and with the **tongue** but in **deed and truth** (1 John 3:18), so also we should not only repent with the **words** and with the **tongue,** but it also has to be accompanied by **deed and truth** so that God the Lord need not lament over us (Isa. 29:13). Mat. 15:8 – **These people draws near to Me with their mouths and honors Me with their lips, but their heart is far from Me.** In the same way, God the Lord spoke to Samuel in 1 Sam. 16:7 – **a person sees what is before his eyes, but the Lord looks into the heart,** so also we here may say: a man hears what comes to his ears if a person exalts repentance only with words, but the Lord **looks into the heart.** That's what James says in his epistle, ch. 2:14, **What good does it do if someone says he has faith and yet does not have works?** V. 17 – **The faith** of a person who boast with his mouth alone **if he does not have works is dead**

inside himself. So we also may say here: What good is it if someone says he has true repentance and yet there is no **deed and work** along with it? The repentance of the person who only boasts about it with his mouth, if there is no work and deed accompanying it, is **dead** inside of himself.

Nor does true repentance consist *in simulatione externa*, that a person **presents himself with external appearances** as if he is truly repentant. For that is merely a **hypocritical repentance** that is in no way pleasing to God the Lord, since He does not **look** at the outward appearance, but **into the heart.** That was what Cain's repentance was (Gen. 4:8). When God the Lord punished him on account of his sins and admonished him to repent, **he spoke with his brother Abel.** Outwardly, he presented himself in a friendly manner to his brother, but it did not come from his heart. For the sake of a shameful sham, he had to present himself outwardly and speak with his brother because he had been chastised—even though, as it is recorded in the marginal note, he had thoughts of murder in his heart. That's what Ahab's repentance consisted of (1 Kin. 21:27) as he heard from the mouth of the Prophet Elijah what a huge misfortune had been established for his household. **He then tore his garments, he laid a sack on his body and fasted and slept in a sack and went forth in misery.** But it was not in his heart. He did not even feel any sorrow over the fact that he had enraged God by his great, grievous sins. Instead, he heard about the great misfortune that had been decided upon for him. True Christians should guard themselves against such hypocritical Cain-like and Ahab-like repentance, and take to heart the admonition of Sirach in ch. 1:34:

See to it that your fear of God (your repentance) **not be hypocritical, and serve Him** (turn yourself to Him) **not with a false heart.**

Instead, true God-pleasing repentance consists *in interiore cordis mutatione,* of an **inward change of the heart.** For true repentance must be a **heart-repentance, an inward movement and change of heart.** Joel 2:12-13 - **Thus says the Lord: Turn yourselves to Me with your whole heart. Tear apart your hearts and not your clothes, and turn yourselves to the Lord your God.** Mal. 4:6 - **Elijah shall turn the hearts of the father to the children and the hearts of the children to their fathers.** 2 Chr. 6:37-38, **If they** [the Israelites] **turn back to You with their whole heart and soul, then You shall also desire to hear their prayer.** Likewise, the Fall of Eve did not just merely consist of an **outward bite from the apple, but rather the inward turning away** of the heart from God and His command. So also, repentance is not simply a barren, **outward deed, but a turning back of the heart to God the Lord.**

Likewise, the heart of man is the true, **main source** from which sin springs up. Jer. 6:7 - **Just as a well gushes forth its water, so also their wickedness flows forth.** Mat. 15:19-20, **Out of the heart come vile thoughts, murder, adultery, fornication, thievery, false witness, slander. These are the things that make a person unclean.** Thus, true repentance must once more well up out of the **well of the heart,** and the foundation for true **repentance** must be sought within the heart. If a person wishes to draw a circle he then must properly set the *centrum* or the middle point and begin from that point. The same holds true if a man wishes to turn himself back to GOD—from whom a person has turned himself away through sin—so that he can return once more to his Origin. Thus one has to set the *centrum* **in the heart** and begin the turning back in the heart and not with words or outward appearances. 1 Sam. 7:3 – **If you turn yourselves back to the Lord with your whole heart, then the Lord will direct your heart.**

This **change of heart,** of which true repentance consists, has of **two** essential parts. **1.** *Seriam contritionem,* **true contrition and sorrow over sin,** so that a person, from the heart, acknowledges his sin against God's Law. That he is inwardly contrite and sorrowful. That he gleans a displeasure over the fact that he previously had borne desire and pleasure over sin. **2.** *Fiducialem Christi apprehensionem,* a **true faith in Christ,** so that a person amidst such contrition and anxiety of heart seizes the gracious promise of forgiveness of sin and by faith is seen before God as being sure of this forgiveness. In keeping with God's gracious promise, our sin is forgiven for Christ's sake. As fruit springs forth from a good tree, from these two points it follows: **3.** *Vitae emendatio,* **the betterment of ones life.** Mat. 3:8 – **See to it that you produce proper fruits of repentance.** For whoever has in his heart a sincere **contrition** and a sincere hatred and displeasure against sin, such a person will never again deliberately sin and will consciously go forth. Whoever in true faith seizes Christ's merits, and in whomever's heart **Christ resides by faith** (Eph. 3:17), in such a person **Christ shall live and he in Christ** (Gal. 2:20). However, wherever Christ lives and rules **there sin shall no long rule** (Rom. 6:22). Since true, proper repentance consists of both of these two essential parts, it is sufficient to conclude therefrom that anyone who wants to exercise himself in true repentance, must also exercise himself in both of these two essential parts of repentance. Now as to how this can and should take place shall be dealt with comprehensively and extensively in the chapters that follow.

At this time, we want to remember only this in concluding this chapter: true repentance is not a work of one's own natural human powers. Rather, it is **a gracious work of God** the Holy Spirit—as is proven by many passages of Holy Scripture. That's why it is quintessential for the exercise of true, proper repentance that a man from the heart longingly sigh to God for true conversion and daily pray like this:

O Holy and righteous God, merciful Father! I confess and lament the hardness of my heart and my impenitence, that I have not turned back to You with my whole heart. Alas Lord, **take away from me this stony heart and give me a heart of flesh. Give me a new heart and a new Spirit** (Eze. 36:26). **Turn me back, Lord, thus I shall be turned back, and if You turn me back I then shall repent** (Jer. 31:18-19). **Bring me back to You, Lord, so that I once more may come home** (Lam. 5:21). **I am like an erring and lost sheep. Search for Your servant, Lord** (Psa. 119:176). **O Lord Jesus Christ**, You who came to earth **to seek and save the lost** (Luke 19:10), seek out also me, a **poor lost little lamb** (Luke 15:5). **God has exalted You at His right hand in order to bestow on Israel repentance and forgiveness of sin** (Acts 5:31). By grace, You also desire to give me repentance. Let Your **holy**, worthy

suffering not be lost on me. Instead, grant grace that through true repentance it redounds for my good. **O Holy Spirit,** You heavenly Light, enlighten the eyes of my heart (Eph. 1:18), so that I do not remain in my inborn **darkness and blindness** (Luke 1:79). Give me a **heart** that has understanding, **eyes** that see, and **ears** that hear (Deu. 29:4). **Create in me a clean heart** (Psa. 51:12). Thus I may say in true, proper repentance: **I will get up and go to my heavenly Father and say to Him: Father, I have sinned against heaven and before You and am from now on no longer worthy to be called Your son** (Luke 15:18–19). You, eternal heavenly **Life,** awaken me from the **death of sin** (Eph. 2:1), and bring me **to the life that is from God** (Eph. 4:18). Thus, I will praise You for these and all Your benefits and blessings both here in time and there in eternity. Amen.

Chapter Four

That true, proper repentance encompasses within itself contrition and sorrow over sin and a true, living faith in Christ.

In the previous chapter, we established this rule: that anyone who wishes to exercise himself with true, proper repentance must also exercise himself in the fundamental parts of repentance. Also, that the essential **parts of repentance** are the following two: **contrition and sorrow over sin,** and then a **true,** living **faith in Christ.** Such has to then be carried out and demonstrated so that one not fail in one's true repentance. But this is generally demonstrated:

1. *Ex natura poenitentiae*, **from the nature and distinctive characteristic of true repentance.** Repentance is a **turning back,** as it is repeatedly called in the holy Scripture, especially in Jer. 31:19; Acts 26:20. Thus each individual repentance is found to be **twofold: first,** *terminus a quo,* **the particular thing from which a man turns away.** Secondly, *terminus ad quem,* **the thing to which a person turns.** Both of these parts are to be found in repentance. For here we turn from **darkness** to **light** and away from **the power of the devil to God** for the reception of the forgiveness of sins—as Christ says in Acts 26:18. Because we then turn away from godless living with repentance, there then ensues as a result heartfelt **contrition and sorrow** over sin. In certain passages of the Holy Scripture in particular this is referred to as **repentance.** The fact that we with repentance turn back to God ensues as a result of faith in Christ through whom alone we have an entry to God the Lord and to His grace (Rom. 5:2). That's why Scripture in every respect sets **repentance**—i. e., the acknowledgment of sin, including true contrition and sorrow on account of it—side by side with **faith in Christ.** Mark 1:15 - **Repent and believe the Gospel.** Acts 20:21 - **I have testified both to the Jews and the Greeks repentance towards God and faith in our Lord Jesus Christ.** In these passages, the **word 'repentance'** does not utilize everything that **pertains** to true conversion. Instead, it refers to the **first part of this turning back,** namely concerning true acknowledgement of sin and heartfelt contrition over it. As a result, this should be viewed as expressly and specially also having faith in mind.

2. *Ex natura Dei,* **from the nature and distinctive characteristics of God** the Lord, to whom we turn ourselves with true repentance. There are mainly **two** essential **attributes of God** the Lord with which He deals with us humans. First of all is **His righteousness**, and secondly His **mercy**. From an inward contemplation of divine **righteousness** there arises within us a heartfelt contriteness and sorrow over sin. For if we consider that God the Lord is a **righteous God** who has a heartfelt enmity towards sin and wants to temporally and eternally punish it, there consequently rises a contriteness of the heart over the fact that we have stirred up God's wrath against us with sin. Also, we have laid upon ourselves temporal and eternal punishment. When we contemplate that GOD the Lord is a **merciful Father** who, for the sake of Christ His beloved Son, has by grace promised and announced to us forgiveness of sins, there then as a result arises a **believing trust** in His goodness and mercy. He also wants to show us this and forgive us our sin. The repentant **sinner** in Luke 7:38 **moistened both feet of the Lord Christ** with **tears,** kissed them and anointed them with ointment. By these two **feet** of the Lord Christ are prototypically portrayed God's **righteousness** and **mercy.** Here we must with true repentance not only have wetted the feet of divine righteousness with repentant tears, but also with true faith grab and kiss the feet of divine mercy. The Prophet **Daniel**—as he conducted his and the entire Israelite nation's prayer of repentance before God the Lord—he said in Dan. 9:5 - **We have sinned, committed wrongs, are godless, and have become rebellious. We have turned away from commands and judgments.** V. 7 - **You Lord are righteous, we however have to be ashamed.** This is true contrition—the first essential **part** of repentance. V. 9 - **However,**

Lord our God, Yours is the mercy and forgiveness. V. 18 - **We prostrate ourselves before You with our prayer not on the basis of our righteousness, but on the basis of Your great mercy.** V. 19 - **Hear us Lord, for Your own sake.** That's true faith, **the second** essential part of repentance. **Manasseh** states in his prayer: **Your wrath is unbearable, for You Lord threaten sinners. However, the mercy that You promise is immeasurable and incomprehensible.**

   3. *Ex natura verbi divini,* **from the nature and characteristic of the divine Word.** There are basically **two chief parts** of divine doctrine from which everything that has been written for us in God's Word may be summed up, namely the **Law** and the **Gospel**. The Holy Spirit also uses these [two chief parts] for the purpose that He may work repentance in the hearts of people. Through the Law, the Holy Spirit bring us to the knowledge of sin and works true, proper contrition over sin in our hearts. Rom. 3:20 - **Through the Law comes knowledge of sin.** Ch. 4:14 - **The Law brings on only wrath.** Ch. 7:7 - **I did not know sin except by the Law.** Through the preaching of the **Gospel**, the Holy Spirit works **faith** in us by which we seize Christ along with His merits for the forgiveness of sins. Rom. 10:18 - **Faith comes out of preaching. Preaching however through God's Word**; namely, through the preaching of the holy Gospel. In v. 8, this Gospel is called **the Word about faith.** Also in Gal. 3:2, [it is called] the **preaching about faith.** Even though both of these chief points of divine doctrine—Law and Gospel—**are distinguished** from each other in many ways, nevertheless they are actually quite precisely **intertwined** with each other *in Praxi* [*in practice*], in the exercise of true repentance. Also, each point has its individual **special function** in the conversion of a person so that consequently both essential parts of repentance consist of this and from it the entire work of conversion. The following passages of God's holy Word speak of this. 1 Sam. 2:6 – **The Lord slays** through the preaching of the Law. He **makes alive** through the preaching of the Gospel. **He leads one into hell** by means of heart-anxiety and contrition over sin, **and leads one out from it again** through the comfort of faith (Psa. 118:8). **The Lord thoroughly chastises me** so that He might bring me to the acknowledgment of sin, **but He does not turn me over to death**—He does not let me remain stuck in such anxiety of the heart so that I'm not overcome by it (Psa. 119:28). **I am grieved** to the point where my heart despairs on account of my sins. **Strengthen me with Your Word** through the comfort of the Gospel. Isa. 57:15 – **I reside within those**, says the Lord, **who are of a shattered and humble spirit, so that I may renew the spirit of him who has been humbled and the heart of him who has been shattered.** Such renewal takes place through the Word of the holy Gospel. Hos. 6:1 – **Come, let us return to the Lord, for He has ripped us apart, and He will also heal us. He has smitten us and will also bind us together.** That is the voice of faith that amidst anxiety of heart once more raises us up again. In Mat. 11:28 echoes forth the voice of God's Son: **Come to me all of you who are weary and overburdened. I will refresh you.** In these and other passages, about killing off, crushing, and chastisements are to be understood as referring **true contrition** and sorrow over sin. With making alive, sanctification, and renewal are indicated the faith that lives in Christ, health for the soul, and the rest which the heart once more finds.

4. *Ex praxi vere poenitentium,* **from the example of those who have God-pleasingly repented.** As we look at the examples of those who through **true repentance** have turned back to God, we find in them the following two parts in their repentance: [1] From the Law, they acknowledged their sin, regretted and lamented it from the bottom of their hearts. [2] Also, in true faith, they were comforted, uplifted, and pleaded for forgiveness. **Our first parents** fell into grave sin. God the Lord dealt with them in such a way that He first cited them before His judgment through the voice of the Law. He gave them the opportunity to acknowledge their sin, in that He said to Adam: **Did you eat from the tree about which I commanded you, "You shall not eat of it"?** (Gen. 3:11). And He said to Eve, **Why have you done this?** (v. 13). However, He comforted them after that and directed them to the promise **of the Seed of the woman who would step on and crush the head of the** hellish **Serpent** (v. 15). In true faith, they seized this promise and were once again ripped away from the anxiety of conscience. **David**, after his fall into sin, had to first hear from the Prophet Nathan, **Why have you despised the Word of the Lord in that you have done such evil before His eyes? You have smitten with the sword Uriah the Hittite, taken his wife to be your wife. Him, however, you have killed with the sword of the children of Ammon** (2 Sam. 12:9). However, as he regretted his sin from the bottom of his heart after that, and said, **I have sinned against the Lord** (v. 13), there was presented to him the gracious promise of the forgiveness of sin. **The Lord has taken**

away your sin, you shall not die (v. 13). John the Baptist preached to his hearers **about the wrath of God** (Mat. 3:7), and admonished them to proper repentance (v. 2). Along with that, he direct them to **the Lamb of God who bears the sin of the world** (John 1:29). The repentant **sinner** in Luke 7:38 showed with tears and outward signs her **inward contrition** and sorrow over sin. Immediately she heard the evangelical **promise** about the forgiveness of sin (v. 48). She seized it with true faith (v. 50). **Your sins have been forgiven you, your faith has helped you, go forth in peace.**

    5. *Ex analogia*, from the **comparison of the sickness of our bodies and souls.** Sin is otherwise nothing more than a **deadly poison and sickness of the soul** that no one can heal—other than **the heavenly Physician, Christ.** He Himself speaks of this in Mat. 9:12 – **The strong do not require a physician, but rather the sick.** V. 14 – **I have come to call sinners to repentance and not the pious.** In the healing of a physical illness, two things are called for; namely, the acknowledgment of its existence, and then next its **removal**. In the same way also these two parts are to be found in true repentance (as the soul's sickness is thereby healed). Namely, that a person by means of the Law properly recognize this fatal illness of the soul and then also that a person through faith in Christ take care of it and be rescued from it. On this basis, it can be shown that true, proper repentance consists of remorse and sorrow over sin, and of a true, living faith in Christ. From this it follows that **anyone** who wishes to exercise himself with true repentance must also exercise himself in both of these essential parts of repentance.

Chapter Five

That true remorse and sorrow over sin is an essential part of repentance, and thus also of godliness.

The fact of remorse and sorrow over sin being an essential part of repentance and thus also of true godliness is especially established on the following bases.

1. *Ex divina jussione,* **from God's command,** since God the Lord Himself requires acknowledgment of sin and heartfelt remorse for it from a repentant person. Psa. 51:17 – **The sacrifice that pleases God is a concerned, crushed spirit.** Isa. 46:8 – **You transgressors, take it to heart.** Isa. 66:2 – **I look upon the person who is of a miserable, broken spirit, and who is in fearful awe of My Word.** Jer. 3:12–13, **I am merciful,** says the Lord, **and will not be eternally enraged. Just confess your iniquity that you have sinned against the Lord your God.** Jer. 4:3–4, **Plow a new furrow and do not sow among the thorns. Be circumcised for the Lord and do away with the foreskin of your hearts.** V. 8 – **Put on sacks and lament and howl.** Joel 2:12–13, **Turn yourselves back to Me, says the Lord, with your whole heart, with fasting, weeping, with lamentations. Tear apart your hearts and not your clothing, and turn yourselves back to the Lord your God.**

2. *A poenitentiae conditione,* **from the characteristic of true repentance.** True repentance and forgiveness of sins have no status without the acknowledgment of the sin and a heartfelt remorse over it. For just as a sick person who does not feel sick disregards the physician about his being sick, so also one does not seek out the Physician of the soul if one does not recognize his severe, deadly illness. Mat. 9:12 - **The strong do not need the physician**—they regard themselves as being healthy and strong disregard the Physician—**rather the sick do.** Whoever is not grieved disregards the comfort. Thus, **godly sorrow produces a remorse towards salvation which none regrets** (2 Cor. 7:10). Anyone who does not recognize his **poverty** and need does not long for the gifts that are offered. Rev 3:17-18, **You say, 'I am rich and am satiated and am quite satisfied. And I actually need nothing.' But you don't realize that you are pitifully poor and miserable, in poverty, blind and naked. I counsel you that you buy gold from Me that has been refined by fire, so that you may become rich. Also, that you put on white garments so that the shame of your nakedness may not be revealed, and anoint your eyes with eye-ointment so that you may see.**

  3. *Ex praxeos confirmatione*, **from the example of repentant people.** The example of every repentant person testifies to the fact that there is found in them a true acknowledgment of sin and heartfelt remorse and sorrow over it. **Our original parents were fearful**, and they hid themselves from the face of God on account of their fall into sin (Gen. 3:8). **David** speaks from a repentant heart *peccavi*, **I have sinned** (2 Sam. 12:13). As he let the people be counted, **his heart was crushed** and he said: **I have severely sinned in that I did this. So now, Lord, take away the transgression of Your servant, for I have behaved foolishly. Manasseh**—as he was in anxiety and imprisoned—**stood before the Lord his God and deeply humbled himself before the God of his fathers, and he prayed to and pleaded with Him** (2 Chr. 33:12). **I have sinned,** he said in his prayer, **and my sins are more than the sand upon the seashore. Also, I am bound in heavy iron bonds, and I have no rest because I have awakened under His wrath. I have done great evil before You by the fact that I have done such gruesome and offensive things.** In his penitential prayer, King Hezekiah states (Isa. 38:13), **Like a lion, He crushes all my bones.** As John the Baptist admonished his hearers to repent, they came and **confessed their sin** (Mat. 3:2 and 6). When Peter preached repentance, **it pierced the hearts of his hearers** (Acts 2:37). Take a note of every example of those who truly repented and you will discover that they began by acknowledging their sins with a heart-felt lament over them. What else are the **penitential Psalms** of David other than longing sighs and laments over the sins that weighed so heavily upon him?

Chapter Six

In what manner should a repentant heart exercise itself in the acknowledgment of, and remorse over, sin.

The first part of repentance—namely remorse and sorrow over sin—includes the following points:

1. True acknowledgement of sin. For how can a person bear remorse and sorrow over sin if he does not yet admit to it? Can also a sick person be concerned about his illness if he does not yet acknowledge or feel that he is sick? God the Lord requires such acknowledgment of sin from the repentant person. Jer. 3:13 – **Acknowledge your transgression, that you have sinned against the Lord your God.** Such acknowledgement is to be also found by every repentant human being. Psa. 51:5 – **I acknowledge my transgression, and my sin is constantly before me.** Jer. 14:20 – **Lord, we acknowledge our godless ways, and the transgressions of our fathers. For we have sinned against you. I have sinned,** says Mannaseh, **and acknowledge my transgression.**

2. **The discovery of divine wrath against sin.** For where sin is properly acknowledged, a person will also feel that one has **through sin evoked God's wrath**, because that is the fruit and product of sin. It incites and loads wrath upon a person. However, such a discovery of divine wrath finds itself in a repentant person. Psa. 6:2 and Psa. 38:2 – **Oh Lord, do not punish me in Your wrath, and do not chastise me in Your fury.** Psa. 32:4 – **Your hand was heavy upon me day and night so that my sap was dried up within me like it does during the drought of summer.** Psa. 38:3-4, **Your arrows are stuck within me, and Your hand presses down upon me. There is nothing healthy in my body on account of Your threat, and there is no peace in my bones on account of my sin.** Psa. 88:17 – **Your fury passes over me, and Your terror crushes me.** Psa. 102:10-11, **I eat ashes like bread and mix my drink with wine. On account of Your threats and wrath You have picked me up and shoved me down to the bottom.** Jer. 4:8 – **Lament and wail, for the gruesome wrath of the Lord does not depart**

from us. Lam. 3:42-43, **We have sinned and have not been obedient. That's why You have rightly so not spared us. Instead You have poured out wrath upon us.** Mic. 7:9 – **I shall bear the Lord's wrath, for I have sinned against Him.** Manasseh says in his prayer: **Your wrath is unbearable, for You threaten the sinners. I have no rest because I have awakened Your wrath.**

3. **Anguish and terror of conscience.** For where a person truly feels God's wrath, there also immediately ensues anguish of heart and conscience in that God the Lord exercises His judgment against sin. Once again, such anguish and terror is also found in the repentant person. Psa. 25:17 – **The anguish of my heart is huge. Guide me out of my need.** Psa. 31:13 – **I became like a broken bowl.** Psa. 34:19 – **The Lord is near to those of a broken heart, and helps those with a mind that has been shattered.** Psa. 38:5 – **My sins are piled up on top of my head, like a heavy load they became too heavy for me.** V.9 – **I'm wailing on account of the unrest of my heart.** V.11 – **My heart trembles, my strength has forsaken me, and the light of my eyes is no longer with me.** Psa. 51:10 – **You have shattered my bones.** Psa. 102:5 – **My heart is crushed and dried up like grass to the point where I forget to eat my bread.** Psa. 109:21 – **I am poor and miserable, my heart is crushed within me.** Isa. 57:15 – **I renew the spirit of the humble and the heart of the crushed.** This refers to the **poverty of the spirit** that is spoken of in Mat. 5:3 and Luke 4:18, **the spiritual captivity and bonds in which the anxious heart is stuck** (Isa. 61:1). It is the **sorrowful heart** (Jer. 23:9; Lam. 1:20; 2 Cor. 7:10) from which sometimes also **bodily burdens** and weaknesses arise when it gets the upper hand. This

can be seen from the penitential Psalm of David (6:3), **My bones are terrified and my soul is very much terrified.** V. 8 – **My face has fallen with sadness and has become old.** Psa. 38:4 – **Because of Your threats there is nothing healthy within my body.**

4. Humiliation before God's judgment and His high majesty. For whoever confesses from his heart that he has enraged **God, the highest Good,** and has enraged the highest divine Majesty, such a person humbles himself from the heart before God. He especially does so when he discovers that God the Lord—if He wanted to deal with him in accordance with His righteousness and the fury of His might—could **smash him to smithereens in the twinkling of an eye.** Lev. 26:41 – **At that time, their uncircumcised hearts will humble themselves in true repentance.** Psa. 44:26 – **Our soul is bowed down to earth, our belly is glued to the ground.** Isa. 57:15 – **I dwell in those who are of a humble spirit.** Jer. 36:7 – **Read this book to the children of Israel, so that perchance they may wish to humble themselves before the Lord and turn themselves back from their evil ways.**

5. Confession of sins. For where sin is truly acknowledged and regretted, such heartfelt anxiety erupts forth with **the confession of the mouth**, as once again is show by the examples of the repentant. Lev. 26:40 – **They will confess their misdeeds with which they have sinned against Me and lived in opposition to Me.** 2 Chr. 30:15 – **The priests** and the Levites **confessed their shame.** Neh. 9:2 – **The children of Israel confessed their sin and the misdeeds of their fathers.** Psa. 32:2 – **When I tried to keep silent, my bones ached.** V. 5 – **Therefore I confessed my sin and**

did not try to hid my misdeed. I said, I will confess my transgression to the Lord. The You forgave me the iniquity of my sin. Mat. 3:6; Mark 1:5 – **John's hearers came and confessed their sins. God the Lord calls** for such confession of sins from every repentant person (Num. 5:7), and **promises** that He wants to forgive all those who in true repentance confess their sin. Pro. 28:13 – **Whoever denies his misdeeds shall not prosper, however, whoever confesses and leaves it will obtain mercy.** 1 John 1:9 – **If we confess our sin, He then is faithful and righteous in that He forgives us our sin and cleanses us from all vice.**

  6. **An earnest disapproval and hatred against sin.** For anyone who bears a heartfelt remorse and sorrow over his sin and truly feels that he has thereby ladened himself with God's wrath, such will from henceforth bear an earnest disapproval of sin. And, he will also from the bottom of his heart **shun** it so that he does not once more, or from anew, heap such a burden upon himself. Lev. 26:41 – **Then their uncircumcised hearts shall humble themselves, and then they shall be pleased with the punishment of their transgressions.** That is to say, just as they had a desire for their sins and found My judgment to be putrid, so now they will once more have a delight and pleasure in the punishment and say: "O how justly we have been dealt with! Thanks be to You, O dear righteous God—O righteous One—that our sin has been condemned!" ... as it is reads in the marginal notes. Isa. 38:15 – **I shall shun such sorrows for my soul for the rest of my life.** And, from now on I will all the more earnestly and diligently guard myself against sin. Eze. 20:43 – **You will think back about your ways and about your**

doings by which you were made unclean. And you will disapprove of all your evil that you have done. So take note, these are the six parts of which remorse and sorrow over sin mainly consists. It occurs in various ways with outward signs, behavior and deeds—like with **fasting**. It manifests itself by **tearing one's clothing** (1 Sam. 7:6; 2 Chr. 20:3; Neh. 9:1, etc.). Also with the **shedding of tears** (1 Mac. 3:47, etc.). By **prostrating oneself on the ground** (Joel 2:12; Mat. 26*). By **heaping dirt upon their heads** (Neh. 9:1; Jon. 3:6). By **putting on a sack**, i.e., gross, plain clothing (Est. 4:3; Jon. 3:5; Mat. 11:21; Luke 10:13). By **striking one's breast** (Luke 18:13). By **clasping one's hands over one's head** (2 Sam. 13:19; Jer. 2:37). By **striking one's hip** (Jer. 31:19). These outward behaviors are at times found by the repentant, however if there is no **true, inward remorse** alongside, then they rightly are regarded as hypocrites before God the Lord. That's why the Prophet Joel says in ch. 2:13 – **Shred your hearts, not your clothes.**

If true remorse over sin consists of the parts presented above, one can readily conclude that these six parts have to be found in each true, repentant person who properly regrets his sin. Namely, he must **acknowledge** his sin, feel **the wrath of God,** and have **pangs of conscience, humble** himself before God the Lord, **confess** his sin, and have an **earnest disapproval** over and against his sin. However, the ability to carry this out is not to be found within the **natural powers** of mankind. Instead, **God the Holy Spirit,** who alone works conversion in a person, has to do this. For mankind's **reason** has been so **darkened** by inherited

---

* Tr. note: then Gerhard writes "*v. ult.,*" possibly referring to v. 39 as the '*ultimatum*' verse.

sin that he is unable to recognize the severity of God's wrath against sin. Instead, the **Holy Spirit** has to place them **before his eyes.** Psa. 50:21; Psa. 90:8, the **will** of human being has been so corrupted through inherited sin that he only desires sin and focuses his pleasure in it. Consequently, if an earnest disapproval and hatred against sin is to arise in the heart of a person, God the Holy Spirit has to work that in him. Of course, a person is able to recognize the **outward**, gross sins from the light of nature. However, the **inward** sins are **hidden** from him. Psa. 90:7; Rom. 7:8, Thus, a person may also to a certain degree be able by his own natural power, to scoop some remorse and sorrow over gross, outward sin. However, that is still not **the true, blessed remorse,** but, rather, a **hypocritical remorse** that can be distinguished from the contrition unto salvation in many ways.

For **first of all** in their contrition, the truly repentant first and foremost look **to God the Lord**, and that's why they are distressed that they have **enraged** their dearly beloved **Father** who is the highest Good. The **hypocrites** are far more afraid of the **punishment.** If they do not experience this they shall not discover any remorse and sorrow.

Secondly, truly repentant people do not only **acknowledge** the **outward,** gross sins, but they also acknowledge the **inward,** hidden **sins of the heart.** And by the light of the Holy Spirit they acknowledge that they **were conceived and born in sin** (Psa. 51:7). However the hypocrites look only at the **outward** sins, and when they don't see any, they regard themselves as being innocent.

Thirdly, true repentant persons do not just look

at the **temporal punishment, but also at the eternal punishment.** And they acknowledge from the heart that they not only have deserved **temporal** but also **eternal** punishment. The hypocrites cast their eyes solely upon the **present, temporal punishment** that hangs on their necks and suppresses them.

Fourthly, the truly penitent regard their sin as being huge. And with true humility they say: **Lord, You are righteous and all Your judgments are righteous** (Psa. 119:137). The hypocrites regard their sin as **insignificant** and constantly think that God is doing them such a great injustice.

Fifthly, the truly penitent indeed have a **heartfelt,** inward **contriteness** over their sin. However, through the comfort of the Gospel they **once more get up** with **true faith** in Christ. The hypocrites have no upright faith. So when sin and the heat of divine wrath really shines before their eyes **they fall into doubt** on account of it.

Inasmuch then as **true contrition for salvation** has been distinguished from **hypocritical contrition** by the five points enumerated above, so once more the following can sufficiently be concluded. An upright, repentant person must first of all look **to God** and, as a result, have remorse and sorrow that with his sin he has offended **this most high Good.** Also, he must not just look at his outward sins, but also at the **inward** turning away and corruption of his heart and regret it. He must acknowledge from the heart that he has not just earned temporal, but also **eternal,** punishment with his sins. He must not regard his sin as being **insignificant** but as being serious. Also, he must with such remorse and anxiety of his heart once more comfort and raise himself up again with true **faith** in Christ. Where these parts are found, there also is a **true remorse unto salvation that nobody regrets.**

But someone might say, if it is the case that true, blessed contrition is a work of the Holy Spirit, well then, I will count on it that the Holy Spirit will in **His own good time**, work such remorseful repentance in my heart. With that in mind, I will continue to **live in sin** as I have before. The response to this is that the Holy Spirit indeed works this blessed **repentance**, but **not without means.** Instead, He works **through means,** in particular through the means of **the preaching of the Law** by which He **exposes** our sin (Rom 3:20; ch. 7:7). He smashes our **stony hearts** as with a hammer (Jer. 2:3, 29). And it places before us the **wrath of God** against sin (Rom. 4:15). To this point also then chimes in the **inward testimony of one's conscience.** It accuses us on account of our sin. At the same time, the Holy Spirit additionally utilizes towards this end the **contemplation** of divine judgment and **punishment**—with which God the Lord **visits** the sins of others as well as our own, Jer. 30:11 – **I will chastise you sufficiently so that you do not regard yourself as being innocent.** Hos. 5:15 – **If it goes evil with them, then they shall have to seek me early.** Hos. 4:9–11, **I have plagued you with a drought. Yet you do not turn yourselves back to Me, says the Lord. I sent pestilence among you, yet you did not turn yourselves back to Me, says the Lord. I turned some of you under as God did Sodom and Gomorrah, yet you did not turn back to Me, says the Lord.** 1 Cor. 11:22 – **If we are judged, we shall be chastised by the Lord so that we are not all condemned with the world.** Furthermore, the Holy Spirit also uses to this end the **contemplation of Christ's suffering.** In it we have placed before us a clear **reflection** of divine **wrath** against sin. Accordingly, anyone who desires to obtain and come to a true remorse and sorrow over sin, must not neglect this **means** through which the Holy Spirit wants to be mighty. Instead one should take it in hand. One dare **not deliberately** go forward with sinning against conscience. For the Holy Spirit will not be mighty for repentance and conversion in the heart of a person who evilly proceeds with contemptibly wicked sins against conscience. And, while the Holy Spirit will, of course, not complete the **entire perfect work** of conversion in the **twinkling of an eye,** one must not **resist** the workings of the Holy Spirit. 1 Cor. 6:19, a person must not destroy or ruin the **spiritual building** within oneself. Rather, one should let the Holy Spirit do and complete His work within one.

To this pertains **first of all [1.]** *verbi praedicati auditus lectio** that a person love the **Word of God** as the office and workshop of the Holy Spirit, that he gladly **hear, read,** and **contemplate** it. When the **angel of the Lord** held up their sins to the Israelites, the **people lifted up their voices and wept** (Jud. 2:4). When the **Book of the Law** was read before King **Josiah, he tore up his clothing** (2 Kin. 22:11). When Esdra read from the Book of the Law to the Israelites, they assembled with **fasting** and **sacks** and with **dirt upon them** (Neh. 9:1). When **John** the Baptist preached repentance from the **Word of God, the city of Jerusalem and the entire Judean country and all lands on the Jordan went out to him and let themselves be baptized and confessed their sin** (Mat. 3:6). When **Peter** presented to the Jews

---

* Tr. note: "the proclamation of the Word by hearing and reading"

the seriousness of their sin that they initiated by crucifying Christ, **it pierced their hearts** (Acts 2:37). When **Paul** spoke before Governor Felix about **righteousness** and about **chastity** and about **the future judgment, it frightened Felix** (Acts 24:25). Such is the character of what the Holy Spirit still today wants to efficaciously work in the heart for repentance and remorse over sin through the **preached, heard and contemplated Word.**

2. *Meditatio*, that a person **with utmost devotion ponder** that which can awaken and increase proper remorse over sin in our hearts. For here we need to consider, **1.** *Peccati atrocitatem*, **how gruesome and horrible sin is.** What is sin other than the **venom of that hellish Serpent** that poisons a person with the poison of eternal death? Sin **offends GOD the Lord.** But now God happens to be the unending **highest Good.** Therefore, sin must be an **immeasurable evil**—since the unending Good is offended by it. Through sin against conscience is lost **God's gracious blessings,** the gracious **indwelling** of the Holy Spirit, a **clear** conscience, and eternal **salvation.** Now all these are overwhelmingly **heavenly blessings.** Therefore, sin must be a **huge, overwhelming evil,** in that we through sin are robbed of these great, heavenly blessings. Every time a person sins, he simultaneously has a scale in his hand. On the **one side** and in its scale pan lies **common entertainment,** ordinary perishable **desires,** the little, inferior **benefits** that a person hopes to get from sin. On the **other side** and scale pan lies **God's wrath,** which becomes enraged by sin. A person who sins is doing nothing more than that he **tips the balance,** and would rather lose God's **blessed favor and grace**

than the **inferior desires** and the little **benefit** that he hopes to gain by sinning. What could you think of that would be more **frightful and harmful** than that a person, for the sake of temporal inferior things, things of worthless **benefits** and worthless **desires**, would **set aside** the **grace** of the eternal **God** and the **kindness** of the unending, eternal **Good?** Every time a person is tempted by sin, he likewise sits with **Pilate upon the throne of judgment.** There stands before him on the one side, Christ, upon the other side, Barabbas. If he willingly and deliberately sins, **he condemns Christ** and **releases Barabbas.** For sin is a true **murderer** of souls. Here it chooses Barabbas instead of hanging on to Christ with His merits and blessings. **The hatred** with which God the Lord is hostile towards sin is an **immeasurable, eternal hatred.** The eternal hellish agony of the damned sufficiently proves that. Consequently, sin must obviously be an **immeasurable evil.**

3. *Peccatorum varietatem*, **the huge host** and various **forms of sin. Who can realize how often he fails? Pardon me also for my hidden failures,** David says in Psa. 19:18. **My sin has gripped me with fear to the point at which I am unable to see. My sins are more than the hairs on my head,** he says in Psa. 40:13. **You place our unknown sin before Your divine countenance,** Moses says in Psa. 90:9. From this it can be concluded that our sins have to be **very** many. No human being can **enumerate** or **remember** all the sins that he has merely committed against a single commandment of God over his lifetime. How then could one be able to enumerate or remember the **huge host** and various **forms of all his sins?** Take a look at each and every commandment of the Lord in the **Ten Commandments.**

Remember just a little bit of how often you with **deeds, words, and thoughts,** have sinned against each one of them. How you sometimes **inwardly** and **outwardly, unknowingly** or **out of weakness,** and also, at times, **out of wickedness** have sinned. Remember how often you have done a bad thing and neglected the good thing. Remember how often you have not just sinned **on your own**, but also have caused a **stranger** to be a participant. Thus, you will realize how multitudinous and varied your sins are. Also, you will then realize that you cannot remember or count them all.

  4. *Dei majestatem*, **the high majesty of God** the Lord. God the Lord, who is offended by sin, is such a Lord of heaven and earth that leaves and grass and all creatures **tremble before His majesty.** The holy **angels cover their faces** before His high, incomprehensible majesty (Isa. 6:2). How then do you, sinful man, **dare presume** that you need have no shyness about enraging this great, mighty Lord? **In the twinkling of an eye**, He could **destroy your body and soul in hell** (Mat. 10:28). How is it then that you have no shyness about **opposing** Him by sinning? **His eyes are bright like the sun and see into the hidden corners** (Sir. 23:28). How do you arrive at the **blind and foolish** conclusion that you think **darkness surrounds me; and the walls hide me so that nobody sees me? Why should I be shy? The Most High doesn't notice my sin**, v. 26.

  4. *Beneficiorum divinorum ubertatem*, **the huge host of divine blessings.** Remember the various and many blessings God the Lord has shown to your **body** and **soul** for your **glory** and **good,** that He has created you, nourished you, redeemed you, sanctified you, protected you from various misfortunes. For as

many creatures there are in this world and as many **members as** there are in your body, that's how many **witnesses** there are to God's blessings. Is it not then wrong and a damnable thing that you repay God the Lord **for so many blessings with so much wickedness,** that you think such evil of all of His **benefits,** that you with your sin so grossly enrage your most gentle **Father** and beneficent Lord?

  5. *Irae divinae gravitatem,* **the heavy burden of divine wrath.** Think about **God's wrath,** that with your sins you have enraged Him to be **a destroying fire** against you (Deu. 4:2; Heb. 12:29), that it is a **heavy, unbearable burden**—as Manassah says in his prayer. Take a look, the Lord's wrath **burns** and is severe. His lips are full of fury and His tongue is like a destructive fire. Also His **breath** is like flooding water that comes up to one's neck (Isa. 30:27). Who can withstand His wrath? And who can remain before His fury? His **wrath burns like fire and the boulders explode before Him** (Nah. 1:6). When this **fire** of divine wrath truly ignites, **it burns down to the depths of hell** (Deu. 32:22). Should you not rightly then have shied away from having ignited this burning, destructive fire of divine wrath by sinning? For **as many sins** that you have undertaken against conscience, that's how many times—so to speak—you have piled on **wood** and **straw** so that this fire might continue and burn you up.

  6. *Passionis Dominae acerbitatem,* **the bitter suffering of our Lord Jesus Christ.** Just look at your Lord and Savior **Jesus Christ,** at how He, with such miserable shame, is dealt with in His suffering! **Inwardly,** within His holy soul, He suffers such **heartfelt agony** that He perspires with **bloody sweat** like a delicate little bunch of grapes that lies at the bottom of the wine-press gives off red juice. He suffers such need that He groans and cries out: **My God, My God, why have You forsaken Me? Outwardly,** He suffered such pain in His holy **body** that also a **heathen heart** complained in that he said *Ecco homo,* **Look, what a Man this is!** He was captured, bound, struck in the face, scourged, crowned with thorns, spit on, given vinegar and gall to drink, nailed to the cross and killed. All this He suffered **on account of your sin.** All this **He suffered for the sake of your sin.** Your sin thus dealt miserably with Him. It was your sin that was the very same heavy burden that then pressed Him. Your sin brought upon Him such heartfelt agony. From this, then, you indeed can see what an **abominable thing** sin has to be for God, because it then dealt such evil to His only-begotten, most-beloved Son.

7. *Judicii extremi severitatem,* **the final Day of Judgment.** Think about what will happen on Judgment Day. **At that time all your works, words and thoughts will be revealed** (1 Cor. 4:5). At that time everything shall stand **naked and exposed** before the eyes of the holy angels and all mankind. **The righteous will barely be able to be upheld, what will it be like for the godless and sinners?** (1 Pet. 4:18). Such is the burdensome, unbearable judgment that you have brought upon yourself with your sins, and if God the Lord wanted to proceed with you on that basis, **you would not be able to stand before Him** (Psa. 143:2).

8. *Gaudiorum coelestium suavitatem,* **the loveliness and sweetness of the heavenly joy.** Think about what a great, exuberant blessing **eternal life** with its **eternal heavenly joy** will be. It is an **eternal and im-**

portant glory beyond all measure (2 Cor. 4:17). **No eye has seen, no ear has heard, nor has it entered into the heart of man** (1 Cor. 2:9). However, with your sin you forfeit this eternal, exuberant benefit, and by your **disobedience** you cast aside this **Fatherly inheritance.** As huge as such a forfeiture is, that's how huge and serious you should rightly regard your sin—as something through which you lose your **eternal blessing.**

9. *Infernalium poinatum aeternitatem*, **the eternal, unending pain of the damned.** Consider the **manifold torture** and pain the damned shall suffer in **body** and **soul.** They will be **separated** from **God**, from the holy angels, and the elect; from all joy, comfort, and salvation while they shall receive **wailing and tooth gnashing.** Just remember that this torture and pain of the damned will **endure for all eternity without ceasing.** By your sinning, you have made yourself guilty of this unceasing agony and pain. With your sins you have earned this **punishment of the damned. As huge** then as the pangs of hell are to be regarded, so huge and serious should you rightly regard **your sin**, as if through it you have earned this serious punishment and loaded it upon yourself. Take note that whoever with devout inward contemplation diligently exercises these nine points, in such a person through the gracious workings of the Holy Spirit, shall be wakened and increased true remorse over sin.

Though it would indeed be salutary and beneficial that such contemplation would be taken in hand **daily,** it especially and mainly should, above all else, occur if we perchance have **fallen into a grievous sin**, or, also, if we desire to find ourselves in the **confessional booth.** Or, if God the Lord through an **unusual tribula-**

tion or a general time of **national testing** reminds us of our sin, that we then remind ourselves of our sin and its serious burden and indeed place it before our eyes, and with heartfelt contrition confess it before God the Lord.

However especially and thirdly there pertains to this *Oratio [prayer]*, **a humble, inward longing and sighing before God** so that He through His Holy Spirit would work in us true acknowledgement of the sins and a heartfelt contrition for salvation. That's why a repentant heart should longingly sigh before God: O holy and righteous God, merciful Father, I confess and lament to You my inborn blindness, that I do not so forthrightly acknowledge my sin and so heartily regret it as I should. Alas Lord, You place our unknown sins into light before Your countenance (Psa. 90:9). Grant me the grace to acknowledge my sin and place it before my eyes in this life (Psa.50:21), so that it may not be placed before my eyes on Judgment Day and I thereby be put to shame before angels and men. Alas, LORD, You can see and know the hardness of my heart with which I was born (Mark 16:14). Take it from me and soften my heart through Your holy Word so that I may inwardly regret my sin. O LORD Jesus Christ, You shed Your blood on the tree of the cross so that You might soften up my heart thereby. Don't let this Your holy blood and holy suffering be lost on me. You, precious Teacher, cried out during Your days in the flesh, **Repent** (Mat. 4:17). You also desire to powerfully cry out to my heart: Repent and regret the sin. You are standing before the door of my heart and are knocking (Rev. 3:20). Oh, grant me grace that I may hear Your voice, that I do not lock up my heart but open its door.

Oh, Holy Spirit! You, who descended upon Christ in the form of a little dove (Luke 3:22), also grant me the genuine skill of a little dove that I with true regret and sorrow over my sin may coo [mourn] like a dove (Isa. 38:14). Oh, You eternal heavenly Light, enlighten my dark heart so that I may confess the darkness of my sin in Your light and may heartily regret it, Amen. Also, the **Acknowledgment of sins,** which is found in the first part of the volume [written by Gerhard] under the title of *The Daily Exercise of Godliness* and is divided into **ten** distinct chapters, may be useful for the contemplation and prayer of a repentant person.*

Chapter Seven

That a true, living faith in Christ is an essential part of repentance and also for godliness.

True, proper repentance by which a person should obtain forgiveness of sins, God's grace, and eternal salvation not only consists of **remorse and sorrow** over sin, but also **a true, living faith** in Christ. This is to be seen from the following unchangeable reasons.

    1. *Ex poenitentiae descriptione,* **from the description of repentance.** When the Holy Scriptures describe true repentance, or **require** it from people, it also regards faith in Christ as the **second essential part** of true repentance. Mat. 21:32 – **Even though you indeed saw it, you still did not repent so that you might**

---

* Tr. note: This volume is available from Repristination Press under the title of *The Daily Exercise of Piety*, translated by the Rev. M. C. Harrison.

have consequently also have believed. In Mark 1:15, Jesus says, **Repent and believe the Gospel.** In Acts 19:4, **John** had baptized with the baptism of repentance and told the people **that they should believe in the One who would come after him,** that is, in Jesus who is the Christ. Ch. 20:21 - **I have given witness to both the Jews and the Greeks of the repentance before God and the faith in our Lord Jesus Christ.**

2. *ex poenitentiae operatione,* **from the working of repentance.** The Holy Scriptures ascribe to repentance that it is the blessed **means** by which we obtain the following: **The grace of God, forgiveness of sins, righteousness** that avails before God, **the gift of** and the indwelling of **the Holy Spirit, the hearing** of prayer, and **eternal salvation and blessedness**—just as has already been shown in the foregoing Chapter Two. Now, however, these heavenly blessings and merits are altogether provided in such a way that they may not be obtained without faith—especially since **it is impossible to please God the Lord without faith** (Heb. 11:6). Indeed, faith in Christ is the sole and only **means** through which we **seize** these benefits and become partakers of them. Obviously **remorse** and sorrow over sin is also a necessary part of repentance. However, it is not a **meritorious work** by which we can earn forgiveness of sins—especially since **it is imperfect** and cannot *adaequaren* [*equalize*] nor requite the hugeness of sin and the divine wrath against sin. Thus, it also is in no way the **means** by which we can **seize** the gracious promise of the forgiveness of sins and possess it. For it [remorse and sorrow] come from the **Law** which **instigates only wrath** (Rom. 4:15). Nor does it have the **attribute to be able to seize** Christ, the only sin-bearer and sin-reconciler, along with His merits. Instead, that applies solely to **faith:** it solely and alone has this attribute that it can seize Christ—and in Christ, seizes these heavenly treasures and blessings. That is why there is no way that faith in Christ may be excluded from the parts of **true repentance.** All along in **taking a look at faith,** it is ascribed to repentance—that faith is of service for the **forgiveness of sins and eternal life** (Acts 11:17–18).

3. *Ex verae & falsae poenitentiae distinctione,* **from the difference between true and false repentance.** True repentance and contrition for salvation is distinguished from false and non-beneficial repentance in this way: that with **true repentance** and contrition for salvation is to be found **faith in Christ**—which the non-beneficial repentance decimates. **Cain** and **Judas** heartily regretted their sin, but there was no accompanying **faith** by which they could once more have let themselves be comforted and restored. That's why their repentance was a false and non-beneficial repentance. Contrariwise, **Peter** regretted his sin, but he once again allowed himself to be restored by **faith** and seize the gracious promise of forgiveness of sin. That's why his repentance was a **proper, blessed repentance.** Since genuine, blessed repentance is distinguished by **faith** from non-beneficial repentance, how could faith in Christ be separated from the essential parts of repentance?

4. *Ex poenitentiali concione,* **from the preaching of repentance.** Those who ever preached true **repentance** not only held before their hearers the **Law** in order to thereby bring them to **acknowledge their sins,** but they also preached to them the promise of the **Gospel** about the grace of God in Christ in order to thereby bring them to faith and to the **forgiveness** of sins. Those who ever truly **repented** did not only through the **Law** acknowledge their sins and inwardly regret them, but they also through true faith once more grasp the comfort of the **Gospel** and thereby obtained the forgiveness of their sins before God the Lord.

5. *Ex absurdorum consecutione* [*from the ensuing absurdity*], if a person tried to exclude faith in Christ from the essential parts of repentance, there would ensue many **ridiculous things** therefrom. The repentance would not be a **conversion to** God the Lord, for without faith in Christ we cannot come to GOD (Rom. 5:2; Heb. 11:6). Repentance would not be **a sorrow for salvation** (2 Cor. 7:10), and **for life** (Acts 11:18). For without faith neither life nor salvation has any status for humanity. There would no longer be **any difference between the true**, blessed, and beneficial repentance and the false, hypocritical, non-beneficial repentance. The consciences of mankind would have **no solid, steadfast comfort.** For no person can rely upon the worthiness of his **remorse.** Instead, the believing **trust for forgiveness** of sin must totally and solely be founded **upon Christ.** From this is it sufficiently proven that faith in Christ may in no way be excluded from the essential parts of repentance.

Chapter Eight

In what manner should a repentant heart exercise its faith in Christ.

Search yourselves, says Paul in 2 Cor. 13:5, **whether you are in the faith. Examine yourselves. Or do not you yourselves acknowledge that you are in Christ? Or perhaps it's a case that you are unworthy.** With these words, all true Christians are required to search and examine themselves to see if they are in the faith. Also, that they are to exercise themselves in the faith so that they may become ever more perfect. Such faith in Christ consists of the following parts: **1.** *Notitiam*, of **a knowledge** and **conception** that a person from the Word of God truly acknowledge Christ according to His **Person** and holy **Office.** Job 19:25 - **I know that my Redeemer lives.** Isa. 53:11 - **By His knowledge My Servant, the Righteous One, shall make many righteous.** Luke 1:77 - **That You give to His people the knowledge of salvation which consist of the forgiveness of their sins.** John 17:3 - **This is eternal life, that they know You—the only true God, and the One whom You have sent—Jesus Christ.** 2 Tim. 1:12 - **I know in whom I have believed.**

2. *Assensium*, an **agreeing**, that a person not only knows from God's Word what is to be held concerning Christ's Person and Office, but that one also approves of it. Rom. 4:21 - **Abraham**—the father of all believers—**gave God the glory** and **most certainly** knew that what God promised **that He also can do.** In Rom.

1:5; ch. 16:26, the approval is called **the obedience of faith.** Heb. 4:2, a κρασις, **or unification of the Word and faith.** Ch. 11:1, ελεγχος, **an undoubting approval.**

3. *Christi apprehensionem,* **the seizing of Christ and His merits.** For since **on God's part** Christ and His merits are **presented** to us in the Word of the Gospel, we then **on our part must** with true faith **seize** Christ and His merits. John 1:12 – **All those who received Him (Christ), to those He gave power to become children of God who believed on His Name.** Ch. 3:14-15, **In the same way as Moses lifted up a serpent in the wilderness, so also must the Son of Man also be lifted up, so that all who believe on Him**—all who fasten the eyes of their hearts on Him and through faith partake of His merits—**shall not be lost but have eternal life.** Ch. 4:14 – **Whoever drinks of this Water that I will give him to drink, such a person shall forever never thirst.** Ch. 6:50 – **I am the Living Bread that comes from heaven. Whoever eats of this bread shall live forever.** V. 54 – **Whoever eats My flesh and drinks My blood has eternal life.** Rev. 21:6 – **He who thirsts, him I shall give the living Water from the well of life for free.** A person must not only just **look at** food and drink but must also **receive it** and **partake of it** if it is to be of benefit to him, so also we must not only know the Word of the Gospel about Christ and give approval to it. Instead, we must by true faith seize and take unto ourselves Christ as our soul's spiritual food and drink. Gal. 3:27, Through faith we can **put on** Christ, so that His righteousness becomes **our cloak and decoration** by which we are able to stand before God and please Him (Rev. 19:8).

4. *Fiduciam,* **a child-like trust.** Psa. 2:12 – **Blessed are all those who trust in Him.** This is also offered in Mark 16:16 - **Whoever believes shall be saved.** Psa. 31:2 - **Lord, I trust in You. Let me never again be put to shame.** Rom. 4:19-20, **Abraham**—the father of all believers—**was not weak in faith. He did not by unbelief doubt the promises of God. Instead He was strong in the faith.** 2 Cor. 3:4 - **Through Christ we possess such a trust towards God.** Eph. 3:12 - **Through Christ we have fellowship with and access to Him, with all confidence, through faith in Him.** Heb. 11:1 - **Faith is a sure confidence that one has hope.** 1 John 5:13-14 - **I have written this to you who believe in the Name of the Son of God so that you may know that you have eternal life and that you believe in the Name of the Son of God. And this is the joy that we have before Him, that if we pray according to His will, He will hear us.** Jam. 1 - **Let him who prays pray in faith and not doubt.** These are the four parts of which true faith in Christ consists. From this it can be sufficiently concluded that whoever wants to exercise himself in faith must, first, **know** the teaching of Christ. Next, he must **assent** to it. Thirdly, he must **seize** Christ's **merits** for himself. Also he must say: "**Christ has loved me and given Himself up for me**, Gal. 2:20. **I know that my Redeemer lives,** Job 19:25." Finally, he must rely upon God's goodness and grace **with certain trust.**

Now again, such true, saving faith is not a **work** of natural **human power.** Instead, it is **the work of the Holy Spirit.** Mat. 16:17, **Flesh and blood did not reveal this to you, rather My Father in heaven.** John 6:29, **This is the work of God**—which is not only acceptable and pleasing to Him, but which He also works and creates—**that you believe in Him who sent Me.**

Phi. 1:29, **To you has been given** (by grace) **that you believe in Christ. Col. 2:12 – In Christ you have arisen through the faith which God works.** 2 The. 3:2, 3 – **not all have faith.** However, **God is faithful. He will strengthen you.** Heb. 12:2 – **Jesus is the Initiator and the Perfector of our faith.** At the same time, however, the Holy Spirit will not work faith **without means.** Rather, He does so through certain means He Himself ordained for that purpose. That's why it is necessary that if we want to come to faith and grow in that faith that we must take in hand these very same means. Consequently, for this it is required:

1. *Verbi autitus ac lectio,* **that a person hear and read the Word of the Gospel about Christ.** For through the Light of the divine Word, God the Holy Spirit wants to **ignite, sustain,** and **increase** the light of faith in one's heart. In John 17:20, Christ says: **I pray for those who through their** (the Apostles') **Word shall believe in Me.** Rom. 10:17 – **Faith comes from the proclamation, the proclaiming however comes through the Word of God.** 1 Cor. 1:21 – **It pleased God very much to save through the foolish proclamation those who believed it.** Ch. 2:5 – **Who is Paul? Who is Apollos? They are servants through whom you became believers.** 2 Cor. 4:6 – **God, who called the light to shine forth out of the darkness, has given a bright reflection into our hearts, so that through us arose the enlightenment about the knowledge of the brightness of God in the face of Jesus Christ.** That is to say, just as God the Lord by His mighty Word created the **natural light** at the first creation, so likewise He still today desires to ignite the **spiritual light** of faith in us through the Word. Consequently, whoever wants the coming of faith and the increase of same, such a person must cling to the **Word**. For just as God the Holy Spirit wants to work remorse and sorrow over sin in a person's heart **through the Word of the Law,** so also He wants to work, sustain, and increase **faith through the Word of the Gospel.**

  2. *Sacramentorum usurpatio,* **that a person utilize the holy Sacraments.** For the holy Sacraments are the *verbum visibile,* **the visible Word.** That's why they are just as powerful and blessed a **means** whereby God the Lord wants to **work, increase,** and **sustain faith in us** as the preached Word. That is why **circumcision** is called the first Sacrament of the Old Testament, **a seal of the righteousness of faith** (Rom. 4:11). In place of this Sacrament, **Baptism** came into being in the New Testament (Col. 2:12), since it is a **bath of re-birth and renewing by the Holy Spirit** (Tit. 3:5). Thus it is also a blessed means through which the Holy Spirit wants to **awaken** faith in us, increase it, and seal it. In the **holy Lord's Supper**, our faith is mightily **strengthened and sealed** inasmuch as we in the Holy Supper receive the very same body that was given into death for our sin, and drink the very same blood that was shed for our sin. Accordingly, whoever wants to obtain faith and the increase of it must not set aside the salutary **use** of the holy Sacrament.

  3. *Pia meditatio* [*pious meditation*], so that **foundation** and **pillar** by which our faith can be established and made solid may be **indeed be taken to heart.** For here a repentant person does well to contemplate in opposition to the anxiety over his huge and grievous sin and against all sorts of evil attacks of the devil which can cause one to doubt:

1. *Misercordiae divinae ubertatem*, the **overwhelming and immeasurable mercy of God the Lord.** Just as God's **Essence** is immeasurable and unending, so also is His **mercy** immeasurable and unending. The reason for the mercy of God is that it is the **essence of His character.** Sir. 2:21 – **His mercy is indeed as large as He Himself is.** 1 John 4:16 – **God is love.** Why, just think of how blessedly lovely and comfortingly God the Lord speaks of His mercy. Jer. 31:20 – **Is not Ephraim My precious son? For I indeed remember what I said to him. Therefore My heart breaks over him so that I must have mercy on him, says the Lord.** Hos. 11:8–9, **What shall I do with you, Ephraim? Shall I protect you, Israel? Should I not right turn you into an Admah and deal with you like Zeboim? However, My heart is of a different mind, My mercy is too intense, so that I do not want to deal with you according to My gruesome wrath. I actually want to turn away from destroying you, for I am GOD and not a man, and I am the Holy One among you.** Remember that God's wrath lasts for a brief moment, but His mercy is an **everlasting mercy.** Psa. 30:6 – **His wrath lasts for an eye blink, and He has a desire for life.** It is written in Psa. 117:2 – **His grace prevails over us into eternity.** Psa. 118:1 – **His goodness endures forever.** Isa. 10:25 – **It actually won't take too long and My disfavor and My wrath over your vice shall cease.** Here again, it is written in Isa. 54:9–10, **I have sworn that I do not wish to show wrath or scold you, for mountains shall depart and hills fall down, but My grace shall not depart from you, and the covenant of My peace shall not collapse, says the Lord who has compassion on you.** V. 7 – **I have forsaken you for**

a brief moment, but with great mercy I will gather you up. V. 8 – **For a twinkling of an eye moment of wrath I have hidden My face from you, but with eternal grace I will have mercy on you, says the Lord your Redeemer.** Mic. 7:18 – **He does not remain wrathful forever, for He is merciful.** Remember that God's mercy is immeasurably **greater** than **sin.** For the mercy of God is a huge, unfathomable ocean, compared to which our sin is to be regarded as a **little speck of dust** or a **little droplet.** Mic. 7:19 – **He shall hurl all our sin into the depths of the ocean.** Sin is the work of the **devil** and of sinful, errant humanity. **Grace** is a **work of God,** of the immeasurable and unending majesty of God. How could it be possible for that which **emanates from** the devil and from **mankind** overturn that which **comes from God?** Much rather it is called what Paul says in Rom. 5:21 – **Where sin was mighty, there grace became much mightier.** Whoever truly contemplates this mercy of God shall thereby be mightily strengthened with believing trust and the forgiveness of sin.

2. *Meriti Christi infinitatem,* **the unending power of the sufferings and merits of Christ.** Christ our Redeemer is in the unity of Person not only true **Man,** but also **true God.** That's why He was able to achieve and accomplish an all-important and totally adequate payment for our sin that also avails in deed and truth. The **blood** that Christ shed from His body is **God's own blood** (Acts 20:28), **the blood of God's Son** (1 John 1:7). Therefore, it is a complete, perfect payment for the sin of the entire world. This His holy, precious **blood** Christ shed meekly. **In the garden** on Mt. Olive, His sweat over His entire body became like drops of blood.

In the **judgment hall**, He was scourged and whipped so that the blood meekly flowed forth from His entire body. That crown of thrones was so deeply pressed into His head so that the blood flowed down from His holy head. On the **tree of the cross**, His hands and feet had nails driven through them, and He was pierced in His side with a spear so that His blood no longer was flowing in droplets but rather like a **gushing stream.** That's why with Him there is **abundant redemption** (Psa. 130:7), because He did not just shed His blood in droplet fashion in His circumcision but in the **fashion of a gushing stream** with His sufferings. Ponder how the Holy Scriptures speak so comfortingly about this precious, costly suffering and perfect payment. Isa. 43:24–25, **With your sins you have caused Me labor and have crafted a burden for Me with your transgressions. I, I expunge your transgressions for My sake, and do not remember your sin.** Isa. 53:4–6, **He really did carry our sickness and loaded upon Himself our suffering pain. We, however, viewed Him as the One who was plagued and beaten and tortured by God. But He was wounded on account of our transgressions, and was beaten on account of our sin. The punishment was laid on Him so that we could have peace, and through His wounds we have been made holy. We had all gone astray like sheep, but the Lord hurled all our sin upon Him.** John 1:20 – **See, This is the Lamb of God who bears the sin of the world.** Rom. 5:8–10, **Therefore, God be praised for His love toward us in that Christ died for us despite the fact that we were sinners. Thus, even more so we shall be kept from God's wrath after we having been made righteous through His blood. For since** we have been reconciled to God through the death of His Son while we still were enemies, even more so we shall then be saved through His life since we now have been reconciled. 2 Cor. 5:21 – **God made Him who knew of no sin into sin for us so that we in Him became the righteousness that avails before God.** Gal. 3:13 – **Christ has redeemed us from the curse of the Law in that He became a curse for us. For it is definitively written, "Cursed is everyone who hangs on the tree."** Col. 2:14 – **In Christ and through Christ, God has presented us with the free gift of forgiveness. And He has erased the handwritings that were against us and stood opposed to us. God expediently disposed of them by stitching them to the cross.** 1 Pet. 2:24 – **With His own body Christ sacrificed Himself on the tree for our sin.** 1 John 1:8 – **the blood of Jesus Christ, the Son of God, cleanses us of all our sin.** Rev. 1:5 – **Christ loved us and washed us of our sin with His blood.** Whoever inwardly contemplates and ponders these and similar passages that speak about the power of Christ's sufferings and about His perfect payment, such a person will thereby be strengthened in his faith. Also, He will be shielded from the doubts and anxieties over his sin.

    3. *Christi benignitatem,* **the love and kindness of Christ.** Yet today Christ also is of the same mind towards all repentant sinners like He was minded towards us humans with His suffering and death. Still today He is **the faithful Shepherd** who **seeks for the lost and erring sheep** (Luke 15:4). **He spreads out His hands** and calls and beckons us to Himself in such a very kindly way (Isa. 65:2). Why should He not then receive the repentant sinner who comes to Him and seeks grace? His promise is sure and immovable. John 6:37 – **Whoever comes to Me I will not shove aside.** Why would a repentant sinner have any doubts about His kindness, willing compliance, and obsequiousness? 1 Tim. 1:15–16, **This is most certainly true and a precious, worthwhile statement, that Jesus Christ came into the world to save sinners—among whom I am the foremost one. But that's why I experienced the mercy of God, so that with all patience Jesus Christ might be shown especially to me, as an example to those who were to believe in Him for eternal life.** If this is a **precious,** worthwhile and sure **statement**, then a repentant person has no reason to have the least bit of doubt about it. If Christ came into the world to **save sinners**, then He will not shove aside the repentant sinner, nor deal with him contrary to His most holy office. If Christ still is minded towards all repentant sinners like He dealt with Paul, then He also will exercise total **patience and longsuffering**, total kindness and human affability towards them, too.

    4. *Promissionum Evangelicarum universalitatem,* **the universal promises of the Gospel.** In no way has God out of **pure hatred** excluded certain people from His grace. Instead, He much rather explains in His Word the point that He **from the heart** desires the salvation of every human being. Psa. 145:8-9 – **Gracious and merciful is the Lord. He is patient of great goodness. The Lord is good to all and has mercy upon all of His creations.** Eze. 18:23 – **Do you think that I delight in the death of the godless, says the Lord, and not much more want that he turn from his ways and live?** 1 Tim 2:4-6, **God want for all mankind to be helped and come to the knowledge of the truth.**

For there is one God and one Mediator between God and mankind, namely the Man Christ Jesus. He offered Himself up for the redemption of all. 2 Pet. 3:9 – God does not want for anyone to be lost, but that everyone, with repentance, be turned back. Since these divine promises are universal, a repentant sinner should never exclude himself from them. Instead, he should much rather receive them with true faith and appropriate them especially for himself.

5. *Juramenti divini stabilitatem*, **the certainty of a divine oath.** God the Lord **truly** is indeed Himself the **Truth.** Rom. 3:4 – **He remains faithful, He cannot deny Himself.** 2 Tim. 2:13, Consequently, also His **Word** and His **promises** are also **true.** 2 Sam. 7:28 – **Your Words shall be truthful.** The word of men and the promises of men are unreliable and uncertain. A person should not steadfastly rely on them. For **all men are liars** (Psa. 116:11). However, God's Word and God's promises are truthful, sure, and unfailing. A person can boldly and steadfastly rely upon it. Num. 23:19 – **God is not a person who would lie, nor a child of man who would regret something if He were to say something and not do it. Would He say something and not keep His Word?** There is no way that we can in the slightest manner have a reason to doubt His promises. So also He has **with simple words** not only promised all repentant and believing persons forgiveness of sins and eternal life, but He has also **empowered** His promise to them with a **precious oath.** Eze. 33:11 – **As surely as I live, says the Lord, I have no pleasure in the death of the ungodly, rather that the ungodly person turn back from His ways and live.** John 5:24 – **Truly, truly I say to you, if anyone keeps My word and believes**

in Him who sent Me, he has eternal life and does not come into judgment. Instead, He has squeezed through from death to life. Ch. 8:51 – Truly, truly I say to you, if anyone keeps My word, he shall not see death eternally. From this, the Epistle to the Hebrews concludes in ch. 6:16-18, **People actually swear by someone who is greater then they are, and the oath puts an end to all quarreling—so that it steadfastly abides among them. However, since God wanted to convincingly prove the inheritance of the promise so that His counsel not waver, attached an oath to it, so that we might have a strong comfort through two parts that do not waver. For it is impossible for God to lie. We have a refuge in it and cling to the proffered hope.** Why would a repentant person have doubts about God's grace and about the forgiveness of sin since it is empowered with such a precious oath? **Whoever does not believe God makes Him into a liar** (1 John 5:10)—and yes, even **into a perjurer.** That would first of all be the **greatest of all sin** that a person could ever have instigated in his entire life.

6. *Sacramentorum utilitatem,* **the great benefit of the holy Sacraments.** God did not just promise His grace to repentant sinners with **plain words.** Instead, He also attached to His promises the **holy Sacraments as a seal of the grace** which is offered to every repentant person by the **Word** of the Gospel. So once again, a repentant person will not have the slightest thing to doubt about the grace of God and the forgiveness of sin. Through **repentance, the door** to the **covenant of grace** that God the Lord established with us in **Holy Baptism** once more stands wide open, for it is an **everlasting covenant.** In Absolution, the forgiveness of sin

is announced to each person individually. A repentant person has nothing to doubt about this either, for Christ expressly states in Mat. 18:18: **What you loose upon earth shall also be loosed in heaven.** John 20:23 – **Whoever's sin you forgive, they shall be forgiven.** In the **holy Lord's Supper,** we are fed and given to drink of the true body and blood of Christ so that through it we become strengthened and reassured in our faith. Also, that we also especially become beneficiaries of that which Christ earned for us by offering up His body and shedding His blood. How, then, could a repentant sinner have any doubts about the grace of God and the forgiveness of sin when he takes into account that Christ is placing into one's mouth to **eat** and to **drink** that **precious ransom payment** through which He has won for us the forgiveness of sin?

7. *Testimonii Spiritus sancti interni veritatem,* **the inward witness of the Holy Spirit within our hearts.** God the Lord does not only witness about His grace **outwardly** through His Word about what He has promised to repentant, believing persons. Rather, He also gives into their hearts the **Holy Spirit** by which He **inwardly** testifies of His grace. For the **very same Spirit gives witness to our spirit that we are God's dear children** (Rom. 8:16). **Since we are children, God has sent the Spirit of His Son into our hearts through which we cry out, "Abba dear Father!"** (Gal. 4:6). **We have received the Spirit of God so that we may know what has been given to us by God** (1 Cor. 2:12). **God has solidly stuck us onto Christ and has anointed and sealed and given into our hearts the security deposit of the Spirit** (2 Cor. 1:21–22). **When you were brought to faith you were sealed by the**

Holy Spirit whom He promised. He is the security deposit for the inheritance of our redemption (Eph. 1:13, 4:30). As you, by the Holy Spirit, are **strengthened in your heart by the grace of God, how can you have any doubts about the forgiveness of sins and the grace of God? If we accept the testimony of men, God's testimony is greater** (1 John 5:9). Why would we want to doubt this? Since we are **sealed** by the Holy Spirit, why would anyone want to doubt this divine Seal which God the Lord has imprinted into our heart?

8. *Ex auditionis promissae infallibilitatem*, **the unfailing promises of God about the gracious hearing of prayer.** Our faithful Savior Christ Jesus promised that our prayers shall be heard. Mat. 18:19 – **Truly I say to you, where two among you become unified upon earth as to what it is that they want to ask for they shall experience from My Father in heaven.** Ch. 21:22 – **Truly I say to you, everything you ask for in prayer, as you believe so you shall receive.** John 16:23 – **Truly, truly I say to you, If you ask the Father for something in My Name, He will give it to you.** Now, Christ has likewise prescribed for us in the Our Father [the Lord's Prayer] that we should ask for the forgiveness of sins (Mat. 6:12). That's why we can be sure that God the Lord, by grace, wills and desires to forgive us our sin. That is the most certain and comforting concluding speech.

9. *Exemplorum claritatem*, **the examples of the repentant persons** whom God the Lord by grace forgave their sins. God the LORD has not only promised in His Word to forgive the sin of all true repentant believers. Instead, He has also shown with clear, comforting examples that He faithfully and unchangingly wants to

keep His promises. Did not our **first parents** sin very grossly in that they turned away from God's command not to eat of the tree of forbidden fruit, and did they not thereby plunge themselves into eternal destruction? Nevertheless, God the Lord once more received them back into grace when they repented. Had not **Aaron** grossly sinned in that he consented to the idolatry of the people of Israel and erected a golden calf? All the same, God once more received him back into grace when he repented. Had not **David** grossly sinned in that he simultaneously instigated adultery and murder? Even so, God the Lord once again received him back into grace when he repented and prayed his *Miserere*, **have mercy upon me, O Lord God** (Psa. 51:1). Had not king **Manasseh** grossly sinned in that he over and over again erected idolatrous images, and allowed his son to pass through fire? Nevertheless GOD the LORD received him back into grace when he repented. Had not the **tax collector** in Luke 18:10 grossly sinned? All the same, God the Lord received him back into grace when he in true repentance smote his breast and longingly sighed: **God be merciful to me a poor sinner.** Had not **Peter** grossly sinned by denying Christ? Nevertheless, God the Lord received him back into grace when he bitterly wept in true repentance. In the same way God the Lord dealt with these, so also He wants to deal with all truly repentant sinners. For with these people God the Lord has **placed before us an example of His patience**, long-suffering, kindness, and grace (1 Tim. 1:16). If they are to be an example, then they must also be of comfort to other repentant sinners. **Behold,** these are the *fulcra* and support with which we may undergird and secure our weak faith. We should contemplate these examples with all diligence and devotion if at any time our faith wants to become weak.

To the fourth and last part of increasing and empowering faith belongs also *ardens oratio*, **an eager, zealous prayer.** For just as all other gifts of God flow forth to us from the **little fountain of divine goodness** through the little **pipeline** of prayer, so also must the increase and empowerment of faith be obtained with prayer. Accordingly, a truly repentant person should longingly sigh to God the Lord in this manner:

Almighty, eternal GOD, merciful Father, from the bottom of my heart I confess and lament before You that I by nature continually have desired unbelief, mistrust, and doubt. Also, I have not so steadfastly trusted Your Word and promises as I should have. Alas, dear Father, forgive me this sin and ignite in my heart the light of faith. Increase and strengthen it within me daily so that I constantly grow and increase in faith, and become a fruitful tree of righteousness (Psa. 1:4). O Lord JESUS Christ, You who initiate and finish our faith (Heb. 12:2), Your heavenly Father has promised regarding You that You will not extinguish the glimmering wick of faith nor break apart the crushed reed (Isa. 42:3). You also desire to fulfill this promise for me and my weak faith. In the same way that Your beloved disciples prayed, Lord strengthen our faith (Luke 17:5), so also I longingly sigh before you: "O Lord! Strengthen my faith." You, my heavenly Bridegroom have promised that You want to become betrothed with me by faith (Hos. 2:19). You also desire to fulfil this promise in me, and through faith reside within my heart (Eph. 3:17). You are the Way. You do not want to allow me to err in faith. You are the Truth. You do not want me to doubt Your promises. You are the Life. Through faith, You want to bring me out from the death of sin into life (John 14:6). O Holy Spirit, You heavenly eternal Light, enlighten my heart and drive from it all darkness of unbelief and doubt. You heavenly little Dove, also grant to me the form of a 'dove' so that I in true faith may hide myself in the wounds of Christ as a little dove hides itself in a rock crevice (Song of Sol. 1:14). Grant that I through faith become a new creature (Gal. 6:15), and be grafted into the spiritual Vine, Christ Jesus (John 15:3). May I obtain from that Vine the sap and life of eternal salvation. Amen.

Chapter Nine

That the new obedience is a necessary part of godliness.

Of course **the new obedience** and the **good works** actually are not an essential part of repentance but rather a salutary **fruit of repentance**, as John the Baptist clearly testifies in Mat. 3:8 – **See to it that you bring forth true fruits of repentance.** v. 10 – **Any tree that does not produce good fruits is chopped down and hurled into the fire.** Nevertheless, the new obedience and the good works can in no way **be separated** from repentance and true godliness. Instead, they **follow after** true, genuine repentance like a wholesome, necessary **fruit** of it. Also, they belong to it as an essential part of it. It is found to be:

    1. *Ex poenitentiae descriptione* from **the description of true repentance.** Because **new obedience and**

betterment of life is described as a constantly resulting fruit of true repentance. Pro. 28:13 – **Whoever denies his transgressions shall not prosper. However, whoever confesses and allows** (desists from it) **shall obtain mercy.** Isa. 1:16–18, **Wash, cleanse yourselves, take your evil ways from My eyes. Desist from evil, learn to do the good, strive after what is right, help the oppressed, deal justly with the orphans, and help the widows with their matters. Even though your sin is blood-red, it shall yet become snow-white, and if it is the color of a plum, it shall nevertheless become like wool.** Jer. 18:8 – **If a people turns from its wickedness against which I have spoken, then it will also cause Me to regret the misfortune that I had thought of doing to them.** Eze. 18:21–22, **If the godless person turns back from all his sins that he has done and keeps all My commands and does right and well, then he shall live and not die. All the transgressions that he had instigated shall not be remembered.** Jonah 3:10 – **God saw the works of the Ninevites that they had turned back from their wicked ways.**

  2. *Ex fidei proprietate & contritione,* from **the attribute of true faith. True faith** in Christ an essential **part** and also—so to speak—**"the soul"** of true, honest repentance. True faith in Christ has the attribute that it **is active through love** (Gal. 5:6) and **shows itself through works** (Jam. 2:18). **For just as the body is dead without the spirit, so also faith is dead without works** (v. 26). That is to say, a body that no longer stirs nor moves nor breathes is rightly regarded as dead, so also if a person merely boasts about his faith with his mouth and does not show its works, such a faith is to be regarded as dead, false, hypocritical. Faith is a salutary, saving **acknowledgment** of God and His Son **Jesus Christ** (John 17:3). Such an acknowledgment—if it is honestly genuine—also brings with it the observance and **keeping** of God's commands. 1 John 2:3-4, **Here is how we take note of the fact that we know Him in that we keep His commands. Whoever says, I know Him, and does not keep His commandments, such a person is a liar and in him there is no truth.** Through faith we are born of God, 1 John 5:1, **Whoever believes that Jesus is the Christ is born of God.** Also, through such faith and through such **rebirth we become God's dear children,** John 1:12-13, **As many however who received him, to them He gave power to become children of God, those who believed in His Name, who have been born of God.** But now, with those who actually have been born of God it also so happens that they live towards God in childlike obedience and diligently watch out for sin. 1 John 3:9 - **Whoever is born of God does not sin,** i.e., he does not cling to sin, he does not allow the sin in his flesh to **rule, for His Seed abides with him,** i.e., the Seed of the Word of God. A person who has been born of God lets the Seed of the divine Word take root in his heart so that it produces fruit in him. V. 10., **Hereby is revealed those who are children of God and those who are children of the devil. Whoever does not do the right thing is not from God, also whoever does not love his brother.** If anyone who does not do what is right and does not love his brother is not of God, then such a person is also not by faith born of God. 1 John 4:7-8, **Whoever loves is born of God and knows God. Whoever does not love does not know God for God is love.** If a person who does not exercise love does not know God, then he most certainly will not believe in God. **Through faith Christ dwells in our hearts** (Eph.3:17). Where Christ dwells with His gracious presence, there also dwells the Holy Spirit. Where the Holy Spirit dwells, there are also to be found the **fruits of the Spirit: love, patience, long-suffering, meekness, kindness, chastity, and the like** (Gal. 5:23). Consequently, where Christ dwells with His gracious presence, there you will also find the fruits of the Spirit. Through faith Christ not only resides in us, but He **also lives within us.** Gal. 2:20 – **I live, yet not I, rather Christ lives in me. For what I now live in the flesh that I live by the faith of the Son of God who loves me, etc.** What is Christ's life other than love? Other than meekness, patience, humility, obedience, etc.? Consequently, wherever Christ lives there also is found the **works of the spiritual life.** Through faith we become—in a spiritual manner—**united with God.** Where, however, such a union has been established, there a person does not cling to sin. 1 John 3:6 – **Whoever remains in Him does not sin. Whoever sins has not seen Him nor does he know Him.** (Or, according to the manner of the Hebrew language—he sees Him but does not recognize Him). How could he actually believe in Him? Through faith our **heart is enlightened,** for faith is a spiritual **light for the soul.** Where, however, there is a light, it gives off its radiance. Mat. 5:16 – **Let your lights shine before men so that they see your good works.** Through faith, our **hearts become cleansed** (Acts 15:9). However, where one deliberately and wickedly wallows around in the mud of sin, how could there possibly exist any cleansing of the heart? It indeed is the case, as Christ says in Mat. 12:34 –

A good man bring forth good from the good treasure of his heart. By faith, we overcome the world. 1 John 5:4 - **Everything that is born of God overcomes the world, and our faith is the victory that overcomes the world.** But what is this world that faith overcomes? In 1 John 2:16 it is described like this: **Everything that is in the world, namely the lusts of the flesh, the lusts of the eyes, and an arrogant life is not from the Father but from the world.** Consequently, where one still trustingly clings to these things, there the world has not yet been overcome. As a result, there also exists no true faith there. By faith, we receive **the Holy Spirit.** Eph. 1:13 - **Through Christ you have been sealed with the Holy Spirit of promise, in that you believed.** Gal. 3:26 - **All of you are children of God through faith.** Ch. 4:4 - **Since you then are children, God has sent the Spirit of His Son into your hearts.** However, where the Holy Spirit is present, there He motivates a person to all sorts of good works. Rom. 8:14 - **Those who are motivated by the Spirit of God are the children of God.**

From all of these it is as clear as the sun that true faith cannot exist without new obedience. Consequently, since true faith is an essential part of repentance, repentance cannot exists without such new obedience.

3. *Ex comparatione,* **from certain comparisons.** Through repentance we become entirely **new people.** For through faith, which is an essential part of repentance, in Christ we become **transferred** and **transplanted** into Christ, the **Tree of Life**, so that we too become good, fruitful trees (Psa. 1:4). This is what John the Baptist is referring to in Mat. 3:10 when he states, **Each tree that does not produce good fruit shall be chopped down and hurled into the fire.** And Christ in Mat. 7:17 – **A good tree produces good fruit, but a lazy tree produces evil fruit.** Through faith, we become spiritual **tendril vines** on the heavenly Vine, Christ Jesus (John 15:1). **Whoever then abides in Christ** as a spiritual **tendril vine, and Christ in him, such a person produces much fruit** (v. 5). Consequently, there can be no doubt that the new obedience is a fruit of wholesome repentance, and that saving faith also, are an essential part of godliness.

Chapter Ten

In what way should a person exercise himself in the new obedience and good works.

The kind of motivational **reasons** which should stimulate, beckon, and drive each individual to busy himself with good works and godliness were extensively dealt with in the first volume of this Tractate. Therefore, we immediately engage in that which actually is pertinent at this point, namely, **the manner in which a person should exercise the new obedience and good works.** Thereupon this is the correct, sure answer for someone who wants to exercise himself in new obedience and good works. He must also exercise himself in that about which the **Holy Spirit** testifies that it **belongs to new obedience** as a necessary, essential part: We previously have shown that the person who wants to exercise himself in repentance has to also exercise himself in the essential parts of repentance. In the same way, it can be shown on the basis of the same grounds that he who wants to exercise himself in new obedience must also exercise himself in the essential parts of new obedience. These **essential parts of new obedience** are described in the Holy Scriptures in a two-fold manner. **1.** *In genere,* **in general, 2.** *In specie,* **in particular.**

Pertaining to the description of the new obedience **in general,** the Holy Scriptures testify that the new obedience consists of **refraining from wickedness** and furthermore **doing good.** Psa. 37:27 - **Forsake wickedness and do good.** Isa. 1:17 - **Refrain from evil, learn to do the good. Strive for justice.** Eze. 18:21 - **If the ungodly person turns from all the sins that he has committed and keeps all My statutes and does right well, he shall live.** The same thing is found in the **essential parts** of true repentance. They are **true contrition and sorrow** over the sin, and then **true faith in Christ.** Where there is true remorse and sorrow over sin that a person will also have **an inclination about sin** to henceforth hate it and forsake it. He who still has a lust and desire to sin, who still continues to strive after it so that he valiantly sins, how could such a person bear in his heart a proper contrition and sorrow over his sin? *Confessio peccati est professio desinendi* [*to confess sin is to promise to desist from it*], Hilarius says concerning Psalm 136. **Confessing one's sin and having remorse over it means to simultaneously promise that one wants to refrain from sinning.** It is a proper contrition if that which a person previously found pleasing and was sweet and acceptable to him is now greatly and bitterly opposed by him. Consequently, whoever still has a lust and desire for sin, such a person does not have a proper remorse over sin. Instead it is merely a hypocritical contrition. *Irrisor est, non poenitens, qui adhuc agit, quod poenitet,* [*He is a mocker, not a penitent, who is still doing what he repents*], Bernhard says in *Medit. devotiss.* Cap. 4. Col. 1194. A person who still deliberately sins and gives the impression that he is contrite and sorrowful over his sin is merely **a hypocrite and mocker.** However, where there is **true** faith in Christ, there a person busies himself with doing good, and performs this obligatory obedience to God the Lord. For true faith seeks and strives after **God's grace** so that a person once more may become reconciled to God and may please Him. Therefore faith motivates a person without relenting so that he serves the Lord with child-like obedience and does such works as are pleasing to Him. Through faith, a person **tastes** and extensively discovers the **sweetness of divine goodness** (Psa. 34:8; 1 Pet. 2:3; Heb. 6:4). Out of such inward discovery and tasting of the divine goodness springs up the **love** for the highest good. From love flows forth **obedience.** For I will obediently and appropriately busy myself to perform acceptable works for the person whom I love. From this it clearly becomes apparent that from remorse and sorrow over sin arises *odium & fuga pecatti,* that a person from henceforth **abstains from evil.** Also, he, out of true faith in Christ, will arise to *studium &amor operis boni* [*a zealous inclination and love for good works*], that a person from henceforth **busies himself to do good.** Both of these parts of the new obedience are called *carnis mortificatio & Spiritus renovatio,* **the crucifying, killing off, and subduing** of the sinful **flesh,** and the **renewal of the Spirit.** At the same time [it is referred to as] *sub abnegatio & Christi imitatio,* that a person **should**

deny himself and **follow after Christ.** Consequently, anyone who wants to properly exercise himself in the essential parts of the new obedience must **crucify** his sinful flesh with its lusts, and by the Spirit daily **renew** his mind. He must **deny** himself and **follow Christ**, his Lord and Master.

Pertaining to the **description of the new obedience in particular,** God the Lord here in His Word not only requires that we **in general serve Him with holiness and righteousness, abstain from evil and do good.** Instead, in His holy commandments He has also has prescribed for us a **complete doctrine of good works**—and thus also a complete **rule of new obedience.** He did this so that we dare not flounder back and forth with our own thoughts and dictate for ourselves a particular form and manner for serving God, for that would result in our being constantly in doubt about whether our actions and life actually please God the Lord. This has been extensively shown in the introduction of this second volume. Anyone who wants to exercise himself in new obedience and good has to set before his eyes the **Ten Commandments of God.** He should then contemplate what God the Lord requires of us in each individual commandment, and along with this to busy one's heart to **align his life in accordance with each of them.**

Indeed, in this life we cannot bring to these commandments the **perfection** that is prescribed for us in the Law of God. For we still constantly fail in perfectly **loving with our whole heart, soul, might, and mind.** Nor can we in this life be totally freed from the evil, sinful **lusts** that arise in the heart. Therefore, we daily must longingly sigh for and beg for forgiveness of sins from God the Lord—that He would pardon our **imperfection** and weakness for **the sake of the perfect obedience and merit of Christ.** Nevertheless, we must **initiate** a good **beginning** to provide from the heart obedience and compliance to the Law of God, to **long for** perfection, and constantly **grow and increase in it.** Also we must permit **God's Law to be** a **lantern** for our path for how we carry out all our actions and affairs. Therefore we also want to deal with, and consider in this second volume, the initiation of this part about new obedience. Later on, after the introduction of each individual divine commandment in particular, we want to deal with and consider in the third volume what God the Lord specifically requires from those who want to exercise themselves in good works and new obedience.

Chapter Eleven

What it is that should motivate a true Christian to crucify and kill off his sinful flesh and be renewed by the Spirit.

The crucifixion and killing off of the sinful flesh when a person has already been reborn through the Spirit of God does not come about as easily and gently as a raw, cockily self-assured worldly heart thinks. Instead, it requires the **power of the Spirit and diligent effort.** That's why the highly important, motivational **reasons** that drive us to such a crucifixion of the flesh and renewal of the Spirit should be given special consideration. We, however, place the **crucifixion of the flesh** and **the renewing of the Spirit** side by side since there is only one reason that motivates us to both. Also, because neither the crucifixion of the flesh can exist without the renewing of the Spirit nor can the renewing of the Spirit exist without the crucifixion of the flesh, if the **old man** [old Adam] **is killed off** then the **new man is raised up and made alive.** If the **flesh** is overcome, subdued, and killed off, then **the Spirit** rules and reigns in a person. The death of one is life for the other. The weakening of the one is the strengthening of the other. The subjugation of the one is the raising up of the other. Thus, the following should motivate us to crucify the flesh and towards the renewing of the Spirit:

    1. *Divinum praeceptum*, **the Law of God the Lord.** When God the Lord says in His commandments in Exo. 10:17; Deu. 5:21, **Do not let yourself lust,** He thus requires among other things all this from us—that we should not follow the sinful lusts of our flesh. Instead, we should subdue them and kill them off—as this passage from Sir. 18:30 explains, **Do not follow the evil lusts; instead, break your will.** In Gen. 4:7, God says to Cain, **Sin lurks at the door, but don't you let it have its way. Instead, rule over it.** In other words, do not follow your evil lusts that drive you to wrath and murder. Instead, subdue and kill the evil lusts.

    However, **Christ** and His **holy Apostles in the New Testament** have faithfully and frequently admonished us towards such crucifixion of the flesh and renewal of the Spirit. Mat. 18:8–9, **If your hand or your foot offend you, then chop it off and throw it away from you. If your eye offends you, rip it out and throw it away.** Christ does not say this about the hands, feet and eyes of a **natural** body. For it of itself is a creation of God which a person must not mutilate or dismember. Otherwise one would sin against the Commandment of God: **You shall not kill** yourself any more than another person. Instead, He understands it concerning the evil, **sinful lust** in these members—concerning the members of the **old Man** [Adam]. And He desires that a person chop them off and tear them out, i.e., the evil lusts in the members of the natural body should be killed. Rom. 6:12-13, **Do not let sin rule in your mortal bodies, to obediently serve it with its lusts. Also do not bequeath the sins of your member as weapons of unrighteousness**, etc. Gal. 5:16-17, **I say however, walk in the Spirit. Thus you will not fulfill the lusts of the flesh. For the flesh lusts against the Spirit and the Spirit against the flesh. They are opposed to each other, so that you do not do what you want to.** Eph. 4:22-23, **So then take off from yourselves the former life-style of the old person who through lusts destroys himself. But renew yourselves with the spirit of your mind. V. 14 - And put on the new man who is created after God with proper, genuine righteousness and holiness.** Col. 3:5 - **So then kill off your members that are upon earth: fornication, uncleanness, shameful desires, evil lusts and greed. V. 8 - Lay it all aside; wrath, rage, wickedness, slander,** etc. v. 9 - **take off the old person with his works. V. 10 - and put on the new one who shall be renewed in the knowledge according to the image of Him who created him.** 1 Pet. 2:11 - **Restrain yourselves from the fleshly lusts.**

    2. *Nostrum debitum*, **our indebtedness.** Rom. 8:12 - **Thus dear brothers we are debtors, not to the flesh that we should live according to the flesh, but**

rather to the Spirit that we should live according to the Spirit. From where does such indebtedness emanate? That can be concluded from the foregoing words of this chapter. V. 9-10, **You are not fleshly but rather spiritual, if it be the case that the Spirit of Christ resides within you. If however Christ is in you, then the body is actually dead on account of sin. The spirit however is alive on account of righteousness.** It is as if he wants to say, God gave the Holy Spirit into your hears through Christ and for Christ's sake. He redeemed you from your former fleshly life. Through the Spirit, He has re-birthed and renewed you for the purpose that you from now should not live according to the flesh but according to the Spirit. **If you then live in the Spirit, you should also walk in the Spirit**, he says in Gal. 5:25 (also chap. 6:1). That is to say, since God the Lord through His Holy Spirit has worked the spiritual life in you, you then no longer are indebted, so that you from now on also walk in the Spirit and through the **Spirit subdue the works of the flesh and kill them.** Through the covenant of holy Baptism we have denounced the lusts of the flesh. If we give in to them we enter the path of falling away and become **oath breakers.** 2 Cor. 5:15 – **One,** namely Christ, **died for all,** and through His death He won for us the spiritual life and the bestowal of the Holy Spirit, **so that those who then live henceforth do not live for themselves but for Him who died for them and arose again. Also, through His death and resurrection He brought them to the life that is from God, and has given His Holy Spirit into their hearts.** Col. 3:5 – **Kill off your members that are upon earth: fornication, uncleanness, shameful desire, etc.** v. 7 – **In which you also at** have walked as you lived therein. V. 8 – **Now however lay it all aside.** It is as if he wants to say, "Before your conversion and rebirth you lived according to the lusts of the sinful flesh. No longer, however, because through God's Spirit you have been re-born and have become true members of the Christian Church. Thus you have the duty to lay aside the former life-style and no longer live according to the flesh but according to the Spirit." 1 Pet. 1:14-15, **Do not place yourselves into your previous position, when you** (prior to your rebirth and conversion) **lived in uncertainty according to the lusts** (of your flesh). **Rather, live according to Him who has called you and is holy. So also you be holy in all your conduct.** Ch. 4:3 – **It is enough that we in the former life-style carried on according to the will of the heathenish, as we lived unchastely, lustfully, drinking and eating excessively, getting drunk, and lived in gruesome idolatry.** From now on we are obligated to live **differently** and to present our actions differently. The crucifixion of the flesh is the **daily repentance** in which we should at all times find ourselves (Mat. 4:17). The crucifixion of the flesh is the **daily sacrifice** which we are obligated to offer up to God the Lord (Psa. 51:19), just as in the Old Testament God the Lord had to be brought His daily sacrifice.

    3. *Passionis Dominieae meritum,* **the bitter suffering of our Lord Christ.** 1 Pet. 4:1-2, **Since Christ then suffered for us in the flesh, arm yourselves with the very same mind-set. For he who suffers in the flesh desists from sins, so that he from now on no longer lives in the past times of the flesh in the lusts of mankind, but rather lives according to God's will.** Why did Christ suffer for us and for the sake of our sins? Definitely not so that from now on we should follow after the lusts of our sinful flesh. Instead, that we from henceforth live for Him and strive against the lusts of the flesh. 1 Pet. 2:21 - **Christ suffered for us and left us an exemplary portrayal that we should follow in His footsteps.** V. 24 - **He Himself bare our sin in His body upon the tree so that we may die to sin and live righteously.** St. Paul explains the same thing in this way: as Christ was nailed onto the cross for the sake of our sin, our old man [Old Adam] was **crucified and killed** with Him, so that he no longer may live and rule in us. Rather, we should live in a new life with Christ who was raised from the dead and live according to the new man. Rom. 6:6 - **we know that our old man has been crucified with Christ so that the sinful man quits so that we no longer serve sin.** Gal. 6:14 - **Through Christ the world** (which includes the lusts of the eyes, the flesh and arrogant living [1 John 2:16]) **has been crucified to me and I to the world.** Consequently, anyone who wants to follow the lusts of his flesh thereby gives witness that his old self has not yet been crucified along with Christ. Anyone who will not renew his mind with the Spirit and live in keeping with the new man gives witness thereby that he has not yet arisen with Christ in a spiritual manner.

4. *Sepultura Dominicae speculum*, **the burial of Christ.** Rom. 6:3 - **We have been buried with Christ through Baptism into death so that just as Christ arose from the dead through the glory of the Father, so also should we walk in a new life.** As Christ was buried our **old Adam**, the old man, was laid to rest with Him and buried. Here we should kill, abandon, and bury the old man by the power of Christ's death and resurrection so that in **us a new man arises who lives in righteousness and holiness before God.** Whoever follows the lusts of the old man and does not want to crucify, kill, and bury him simultaneously violates Christ's grave and wants to bring to the fore that which GOD wants to have abandoned and buried. Whoever does not by the Spirit want to have his mind renewed, at the same time **denies** the resurrection of Christ and want to leave Christ abandoned in the grace because he does not want to arise with Him in a spiritual manner. Also, he does not want to live in righteousness and holiness before God according to the new man. Rom. 6:8–11, **If we have died with Christ we then believe that we shall also live with Him. And we know that Christ arose from the dead. Henceforth He no longer dies. Death shall from no own never reign over Him. In that He died, He died for sin one time. In that He lives, He lives for God. So also you look upon yourselves as having died to sin and living for God in Christ Jesus our Lord.**

    5. *Nostrum cum Christo consortiu*, **our fellowship with Christ.** Mat. 16:24 – **If anyone wants to follow after Me, let him take his cross upon himself**, i.e., he is not only with a cross so that others find him patient; rather, let him also take in hand the crucifixion of his flesh which I have bidden him to do. Gal. 5:24 – **Those who belong to Christ crucify their flesh along with the lusts and desires.** The reason, **For they have been baptized into Christ's death** and are thus in Him, and through **Him have died to sin** (Rom. 6:3). **Christ henceforth lives in them and they in Christ** (Gal. 2:20). **They have the Spirit of Christ. They are in Christ.** Now, those who are in Christ and have the

Spirit of Christ are described in Rom. 8:1 thusly: **That they do not live according to the flesh but rather according to the Spirit. V. 9 – That they are not fleshly but are instead spiritual.** V. 14 – **That through the Spirit they kill off the flesh's activities.** From this it follows that those who belong to Christ, who are the true, proper disciples of Christ and true Christians, they crucify their flesh along with its lusts and desires. Contrariwise, those who do not crucify their flesh along with its lusts and desires, **do not belong to Christ.** They are not true **disciples of Christ.** They are not true **Christians.** So take note here about how many true, proper Christians will remain among the great host of those who confess Christ. Christ and the new man are inextricably intertwined with each other. If Christ lives and resides in you, then also the **new man** must also **live** and rule in you. If the new man is to live and rule in you, then also the old man, along with his lusts, has to be subdued and **be killed** in you. There is no other way out of this. If we are to be completely spiritual in eternal life, then we must begin to overcome the flesh in this life.

6. *Breve hujus vitae curriculum*, **the short time of our life.** 1 Pet.2:11 – **Beloved brothers, I admonish you as strangers and pilgrims keep yourselves from the fleshly lusts that strive against the soul.** It's as if he wants to say, "Your life in this world is a short, insignificant, fleeting life. That's why you indeed should not imitate this world by fulfilling the lust of the flesh." **The world shall pass away with its lusts** (with its lusts of the flesh and lusts of the eyes), **but he who does the will of God** (he who subdues the lusts of the flesh and fulfills God's will concerning this) **shall**

abide in eternity (1 John 2:17). How is it though that it is actually such a wink-of-an-eye moment of joy if a person fulfills the lusts of his flesh? Even if a person were to soar with sheer lust every day, hour, and moment during the entire time of his life (which, of course, is impossible, since in this life misfortune and sadness don't constantly remain outside the sphere of one's life), this still would have to be regarded as a fleeting lust and joy because our life here upon earth, when compared to all eternity, only endures but for a blink of an eye. That's why, of course, the contemplation of the insignificance and fleetingness of our life should cause us to abstain from fulfilling the lusts of the flesh.

7. *Sactorum exemplu*, **the example of all the saints. Abraham**, the father of all saints, was prepared to sacrifice his beloved son to God the Lord when he received a special command (Gen. 22:4). There can be no doubt that fleshly affections were also found in him and wanted to hold him back from obeying. However, through the power of the Spirit he killed off and subdued them. If he had not first killed off his flesh along with its sinful lusts, he never would have been ready and willing to kill and offer up at God's command **his son.** Well then, **you also offer up to God the Lord the beloved son of your soul.** This does not mean that you perhaps should be willing to sacrifice one or more of your natural, physical children. For that would be an abomination to God the Lord (Eze. 16:21; ch. 23:39). Instead, you should be willing to kill off and sacrifice to the glory of GOD your flesh—which is a beloved son of your soul. Mic. 6:6 – **With what shall I make atonement to the Lord? V. 7 – Should I sacrifice my first born son from my transgressions, or the fruit of my**

body for the sins of my soul? V. 8 – **You have been told, O man, what is good and what the Lord requires of you. Namely, keep God's word and practice love and be humble before your God.** None of these things can happen without the killing off of the sinful flesh. However, **Paul** in particular prescribes for us a heartfelt example of how we should kill off the flesh with its lusts. In says in 1 Cor. 9:27: **I stifle my body and tame it so that I do not preach something else, and myself become dispensable.** Gal. 2:20 – **I have been crucified with Christ. I live. Yet it is not I but Christ who lives in me. For what I now am living in the flesh I live by faith in the Son of God.** Ch. 6:14 – **Through Christ the world is crucified to me and I to the world.** V. 17 – **I bear the marks of the Lord Jesus on my body.** What kind of 'marks' are these? They are not just external repulsiveness and various tribulations, but also the **inward**, daily crucifying of the flesh. We must follow this example by faith, as Paul admonishes us to that end in 1 Cor. 4:16; Ch. 11:1; Phi. 3:17. **Be followers of Me.**

8. *Promissum praemium*, **the great overwhelming reward.** Rom. 8:10–11, **If Christ is in you then the body is actually dead on account of sin. The Spirit however is life on account of righteousness. So then if the Spirit which raised Jesus from the dead lives in you, then He who raised Christ from the dead shall also make alive your mortal bodies by virtue of the fact that His Spirit resides within you.** That is to say, even though you actually are subject to temporal death on account of the sin that still remains in your flesh, nevertheless because the **Spirit of Christ** lives in you, it is He who makes you partakers of the spiritual life

that comes from God and through whom you subdue the sinful flesh. That is why the heavenly Father shall later wake you from temporal death to eternal life **because of the fact that His Spirit lives within you.** V. 14 - **If you by the Spirit kill off the works of the flesh, you shall live.** That is to say, you shall be preserved unto eternal life. For here especially it is not talking about natural life that all mankind in general have—also those who live according to the flesh. Instead, it is talking about spiritual and eternal life, as it is explained in v. 1: **There is nothing condemnable in those who are in Christ Jesus, who have not lived according to the flesh but according to the Spirit.** 1 Cor. 9:25 - **Anyone who fights a battle refrains from anything that** might be a hindrance to him obtaining the victory. That's why also we Christians as spiritual **warriors** should ourselves abstain **from spiritual desires** that are a hindrance to our salvation. In the former case [i.e., soldiers], they do it to obtain **a perishable crown. We, however, do it to obtain an imperishable one.** 2 Tim. 4:7 - **I have fought a good campaign. I have completed the course. I have held on to the faith** (to this battle also pertains that we fight against the sinful lusts of the flesh). V. 8 - **From now on there has been laid aside for me the crown of righteousness that the LORD, the righteous Judge, shall give me. However, not only to me but also to all those who have a fondness for His reappearance.** The more lusts that you subdue and overcome, that many more **crowns** your victorious Lord, Christ, has prepared for you. Rev. 2:7 - **He who overcomes I shall give to eat from the Tree of Life that is in God's Paradise.** V. 11, **He who overcomes shall not be harmed by the** second death. V. 17 – **He who overcomes I will give to eat from the hidden manna, and I will give him a good testimony and with the testimony I will write a new name that no one knows except for him who receives it.** V. 26 – **He who overcomes and possess My works to the end, him I will give power over the Gentiles, etc., and I will give him the Morning Star.** Ch. 3:5 – **He who overcomes shall be dressed up with white garments, and I will not blot out his name from the Book of Life. Also I will confess his name before My Father and before His angels.** V. 12, **He who overcomes I will make into a pillar in the Temple of God, and he will never again leave it. Also I will write the Name of My God on him, and the name of the new Jerusalem—the city of My God that will come down from heaven and from My Name, the new one.** V. 21 – **He who overcomes I will grant to sit with Me upon My throne.** To this overcoming pertains also the following: that we also **overcome** our sinful **flesh** and subdue its lusts, especially since the **flesh lusts against the Spirit and the Spirit against the flesh. They are opposed to each other** (Gal. 5:17). Here there is a constant battle of enmity and strife. Whoever is victorious in this battle and overcomes through the power of the Spirit, such a person shall possess and receive **divine comfort, peace of mind, the indwelling of the Holy Spirit,** the inward **testimony** from the grace of God. Ultimately, he will also possess and receive **happiness** on Judgment Day and the **estate of eternal life.** This is truly to be labeled as Christ speaks of it in John 12:25, **Whoever hates his life** (and himself) **here upon this world shall keep it unto eternal life.** Also, Mat. 11:12 – **The kingdom of** heaven suffers violent force, and those who commit the violent force are ripping it away for themselves.

9. *Consequens damnum,* **the great harm** that results if a person does not subdue the flesh with its lusts. In Mat. 18:8–9, Christ says, **It is better for you to enter into life lame or as a cripple than if you have two hands and two feet and end up being thrown into the eternal fire. It is better for you to enter into life with one eye than for you to have two eyes and be hurled into the hellish fire.** In other words, if you will not subdue the evil, sinful lusts in your hands, feet, eyes and other members but instead would rather follow them with cocky self-assurance, then you can not enter into eternal life. Instead you will be thrown into the eternal hellish fire. For anyone who deliberately follows evil lust sins **against conscience.** But then through sin against conscience are lost the grace of God and eternal life. John 12:25 – **Whoever loves his life shall lose it.** *Cyrill. Lib. 8. In Joh. cap. 14. Amat animam suam in hoc mundo, qui desideria ejus divinae legi repugnantia facit: at vero odit animam suam, qui non cedit neque bsequitur ei noxia concupiscenti & divinis praeceptis contraria.** Whoever loves this kind of life shall lose eternal life. The crucifixion of the flesh is the **spiritual circumcision** (Jer. 4:4). Here is how God the Lord wants Himself to be heard with extreme seriousness: Whoever is not circumcised† **his soul shall be uprooted** (Gen. 17:14). So then, if the crucifixion of the flesh is

---

* "He who causes the desire of his soul to be in conflict with the divine Law loves his life in this world. But he who neither yields to, nor obeys, that lust for harmful things that are contrary to divine commands hates his life."

† Tr. note: that is, with the aforementioned "spiritual circumcision" of crucifying the flesh.

neglected, the result will be the death of the soul. Rom. 8:13 – **If you live according to the flesh you will definitely die,** namely that second and eternal death. Gal. 5:16–17, **Walk by the Spirit. Thus you will not fulfill the lusts of the flesh. For the flesh lusts against the Spirit, and the Spirit against the flesh so that you do not do what you desire.** V. 19 – **The works of the flesh however are publicly known,** etc. V. 21 – **About them I have told you before and tell you once more: Those who do them shall not inherit the kingdom of God.** Ch. 6:8 – **Whoever sows upon his flesh, he shall from the flesh harvest destruction.** Col. 3:5 – **So then kill off your members that are upon earth: whoring, impurity, shameful desires, evil lusts, and greed.** V. 6 – **On account of these, the wrath of God comes over the children of unbelief.** Consequently, anyone who does not wish to load upon himself God's wrath must kill off the members of the old man [old Adam]. 1 Pet. 2:11 – **Refrain yourselves from the fleshly lusts, which strive against the soul.** Such a striving has everything to do with the **soul's salvation.** If the fleshly lusts retain the upper hand, then the soul must die the eternal death. Jam. 1:15 – **Each individual person is tempted when he is strained and lured by his own lusts. Thereupon, when lust has conceived, it produces sin. However, when sin is completed, it produces death.** This is a disgraceful birth, it transpires like the **birth of an adder.** In order for it to be born, it chews its way through the body of its **mother.** So likewise sin, if it is to be born, brings eternal death to the person who completes it. The **wages** that this **sin pays is death** (Rom. 6:23). Mic. 7:6 and Mat. 10:36 say it correctly: **A man's enemies are those in his own**

home. For our flesh is the **true Delilah,** that harlot who wants to seduce the **Samson,** i.e., our flesh. As Samson chased after that harlot, Delilah, he lost his strength. Consequently, the Philistines overpowered him. These are indeed powerful, urgent reason why we should be motivated to crucify the flesh and be renewed by the Spirit.

Chapter Twelve

How a true Christian is to exercise himself in the crucifixion of the flesh and the renewing of the Spirit.

The situation with **the lusts of the flesh** is such that they are not with stem and root completely uprooted and swept out of the heart of a Christian. Instead, they stick and cling to the re-born person for the rest of his life until they finally are shredded after that person dies. That's why a person is not only irritated and lured by sin for just one day but frequently—every day. That's why St. Paul so obviously laments in Rom. 7:22-23, **I have a desire for God's Law according to the inward man. However I see another law in my members. It strives against the Law in my mind, and it takes me captive to the law of sin that is in my members.** That's why it is of the utmost necessity that we diligently take note of how we are to daily exercise ourselves in the crucifixion of the flesh and the renewing of the Spirit. It can and must take place:

1. *Verbi divinie meditatione,* **through diligent, devout hearing, reading, and contemplation of the**

divine Word. However, it can especially take place even more so by means of the previously enumerated **nine reasons** that should motivate us to crucify the flesh. For through these the Holy Spirit will be efficacious in us so that we do not consent to the lusts of the flesh. *Ama scientiam Scripturarum & carnis vitia non amabis.* [*Love knowledge of the Scriptures and you will not love vices of the flesh.*] Anyone who diligently engages himself with God's Word, daily hears, reads and contemplates it will not so readily consent in the fulfillment of the lusts of the flesh. In the same way that **our body** is strengthened **through food,** so also the Word of God—as **food of the soul**—gives our inward man strength and power so that he can subdue and overcome the outward, old man [Adam]. 1 Pet. 2:2 - **Like a newly born baby, with sensibility greedily long for the pure milk, so that through it you may grow.** By this he means the spiritual **milk of God's Word** through which we are nurtured and strengthened in our soul and inward man. The Word of God is the **Sword of the Spirit**, Eph. 6:17—**the sharpest two-edged Sword** that flows forth from the mouth of Christ (Rev. 1:6). With it, we are able to **chop off** the evil lusts of the flesh when they try to sprout up within us (Mat. 18:8). The word of God is **a spiritual Fire** (Jer. 23:29). It is able to destroy and burn up the evil, sinful lusts. *Verbum DEI est gravium affectuum fugatorium instrumentum, & ignis animae insitum extinctorium magisterium,*[*] says Justin, *serm. 2. Ad Graec. Pag. 31.* The Word of God is our Teacher and Trainer, directing us how we should fight against the sinful fleshly lusts. Accordingly, it behooves us that in this School of the

---

[*] "The Word of God is the tool of serious feelings, and it is the tutelage of the spiritual fire located in things that will pass."

Holy Spirit we diligently learn how we should crucify our flesh. For example, when your sinful flesh tries to **provoke** and motivate you to be **greedy**, then immediately wrap yourself in a **saying** that forewarns you against greed. It is Mat. 16:26, **What does it help a man if he were to gain the entire world and yet receives harm to his soul?** Does your sinful flesh provoke you towards **whoring?** Then immediately seize for yourself a little verse from God's Word that will guard you against it. It is 1 Cor. 6:16, **Shall I take Christ's members and make them into members of harlotry?** May it never be so! Does your sinful flesh **provoke you to wrath and rage?** Immediately seize the Sword of the Spirit and protect yourself with it. Eph. 4:26 – **Don't let the sun go down over your wrath.** Also the same applies to all other lusts. There is none that can be named but what there is to be found a special verse in Divine Scripture to counter it.

2. *Primorum motuum repressione,* **through the prompt suppression of the very first sinful movement.** When an evil lust rises up in the heart, a person should not hang on to it in order to inflame oneself with lust, carry a desire for it, continually stir it up and think about it. Instead, one should immediately throw it out and direct the thoughts of one's heart to something else. Of course, we cannot prevent a sinful desire to **arise** in our heart like a flame that flares up. However, at the same time, we can guard ourselves that we do not bear a love and affection for it and cling to it. Just as we cannot prevent the birds from **flying over our heads,** we can take precautions that they do not sit on our head and build their nest in our hair—as our ancestors used to say. **The children of Babylon were**

smashed against a rock while they were still young (Psa. 137:9). Some exegetes indicate that this means a person has to smash the **evil lusts** against the Rock and Cornerstone of salvation while they are still new and fresh, and subdue and kill them off by contemplating the sufferings of Christ. Jam. 1:15 – **Lust, when it has conceived, produces death.** Anyone who does not desire that sin produce death in him, let him be on guard that the evil lust does not **conceive** in him. He should not obligate himself to it. He should not delight in it nor kiss it. Instead, he should kick it out of the house of his heart. Consequently, take the **circumcision of the flesh** with its lusts to means the Old Adam with his fruits as it is presented to us in Gal. 5:19. **The works of the flesh are revealed as being adultery, whoring, uncleanness, fornication, idolatry, witchcraft, enmity, hatred, greed, wrath, disputations, deceit, corruption, hatred, murder, drunkenness, overeating, and the like.** If any of these actions try to arouse and lure your sinful flesh, then immediately subdue such a sinful impulse and affection before they ever come to fruition. If ever there are found **the weeds of evil lusts** in the acreage of your heart, you must not wait until they grow tall. You must not **sprinkle and moisten them** with tender affection. Instead, you must immediately pull them out and uproot them the moment they sprout from their roots. Evil lust is a true **Seed of the Serpent** that one must not allow to grow but instead sternly step on and crush. If the **hellish Serpent** of the forbidden tree of the knowledge of good and evil is placed before you and portrays its fruits as being so beautiful that it is lovely to behold (Gen. 2:5), you must not with **Eve** believe him nor follow him.

Instead, you must immediately turn the eyes of your away from this tree. If **Ishmael,** i.e. your sinful flesh, wants to start **mocking** and mess around—if he wants to subdue **Isaac,** i.e., your inward man—then he must immediately be driven out of the **house of Abraham,** i.e., out of the house of your heart (Gen. 21:12).

    3. *Occasionum declinatione,* **through the shunning and turning away from the opportunity to sin.** The beloved ancient fathers used to say: *Vitare peccata, est vitare occasiones peccandi.*[*] Whoever wants to protect himself from sinning must on all counts shun the opening and opportunity to do so. Whoever does not want to be burned must not get too close to the fire. Whoever does not want to be **poisoned** must protect himself from the poisonous places. Whoever does not to be **wounded** must not get too close to a sword of war. That's also how things proceed here. Whoever does not wish to be ignited, poisoned, wounded, such a person should shun the opportunity for such evil lusts. In Pro. 23:29–30 Solomon says: **Do not look at wine when it looks so very red and shines so brightly in the glass that it flows down so smoothly, but then it bites like a snake and stings like an adder.** In other words, anyone who does not wish to let himself be motivated towards drunkenness must not allow himself to become carried away with the beautiful, shady character of the wine and become infatuated with it. Instead he should turn his eyes away from it. Whoever does not wish to become inflamed with **forbidden love** should not become infatuated with the forms of beautiful females and have a burning desire to look at them. **Had Eve** not so meticulously and with such desire looked at the

---

[*] "A sin regarded as precious, is a precious occasion for sinning."

fruit of the forbidden tree but had instead turned her eyes from it, then she would not so readily have been persuaded by the hellish Serpent to eat of the forbidden tree (Gen. 3:6). **Had Dinah** not gone out for a walk to visit the daughters of the country, she would not have lost her virginity (Gen. 34:1). **Had David** not so intensely looked at Bathsheba from the roof of the royal palace as she took off her clothes to bathe, he would not have become inflamed with forbidden love for here (2 Sam. 11:2). Had not the Apostle **Peter** entered into the Palace of the High Priest to warm himself at the fire of the ecclesiastical prelate, he would not have been approached to deny Christ his Lord (Mat. 26:72).

Recta corporis gubernatione, **through proper, sensible controlling of the body** in eating, drinking, sleeping and the like. Of course, it is true that a person's body has to have nourishment and have its thirst quenched, because through natural warmth, natural moisture, and labor the *spiritus* or living mind becomes drained every day. Yet, at the same time, **food and drink** must be kept at an appropriate level so that **the heart does not become burdened with gluttony and drunkenness,** and the body becomes excessively filled. For if one does not confine oneself to appropriate amounts, it results in the evil, sinful lusts show up in great number. Deu. 32:16 – **When he became satiated and full, he became fat and thick and strong. He forsook the God who had created him.** When the children of Israel **sat down to eat and drink, they then got up to play** and fulfilled the lusts of their flesh (Exo. 32:6; 1 Cor. 10:7). When they **ate with the Moabites and committed harlotry with them, the son began to fornicate with the daughters of**

the Moabites (Num. 25:1). That's why Solomon says in Pro. 23:29, **Do not look at the wine when it is so red, looks so beautiful in the glass that it goes down so smoothly,** v. 31 – **then your eyes will look at other women and your heart will say wrong things.**

Consequently, every person must examine himself, live moderately. Also, as opportunity arises, he should occasionally stop his body and his situation to humble his body through work and fasting so that he does not become foolhardy, lest the person that more readily give in to the evil lusts of the flesh. If the mule becomes too frolicsome, you take away his oats and give him hay. If the servant of the house wants to get too fresh, you simply hang his breadbasket up higher. In similar fashion, one has to deal with the control of the body in accordance to the example of St. Paul in 1 Cor. 9:27: **I stifle and tame my body so that I do not preach to others and myself become a castaway.** Obviously, as recorded, in this matter one must deal cautiously and one has to strike the middle of the street. For **anyone** who hurts the body destroys God's creation and hinders himself from performing the deeds of his calling and of godliness. However, anyone who leans too much to the other side and **caters to his body so that he becomes vile** and nurtures his own enemy.

4. *Seria oratione,* **through believing, earnest prayer.** Since the crucifixion and subjugation of the flesh with its lust requires the special power of the Spirit, it is essential that we obtain the same through a believing, earnest prayer, a longing sigh and pray to God the Lord like this:

O holy and righteous God, I confess and lament to You from the bottom of my heart that I have not been very diligent in the crucifixion of my sinful flesh and the renewing of the Spirit like it rightly should be. **Instead, my body and soul has become besmirched so many times with the evil lust of the flesh that strives against the soul** (1 Pet. 2:11). I have not always fought against them with the power of the Spirit. O faithful God, forgive me this severe sin for the sake of the pure and perfect obedience of Your beloved Son, my dear Savior, Christ. **Henceforth turn away from me all evil lusts** (Sir. 23:6), and grant grace that I subdue and kill off these lusts in my members. O Lord Jesus Christ, You for the sake of my sin let Yourself be crucified so that my old Adam might be crucified with You in order that the sinful body cease (Rom. 6:6). Give me, through the precious merits of Your crucifixion, the power and grace to crucify my sinful flesh along with its lusts and desires (Gal. 5:24). Grant to me that I arise with You and, by the power of Your resurrection, kill off my sinful members that are upon earth (Col. 3:5). Help me so that I as a true disciple daily take up my cross—not just with patience in external tribulations and persecutions, but also with the crucifixion of my flesh (Mat. 16:24). O Holy Spirit, You admonish me to strive against the flesh—externally through the Word and inwardly through Your witness. Give me power to become strong in the inward man and for Christ to live in my heart through faith (Eph. 3:16–17). Grant that the Spirit rule in me and that He overcome the flesh in me. You are, of course, a Spirit of holiness and cleansing (Rom 12:4). You also want to cleanse my heart (Act. 15:9), and thus also guide, rule and guide me so that my heart be Your holy temple and remain such forever more. Amen.

Chapter Thirteen

What should motivate a Christian to deny himself.

In the same way that the crucifixion of the flesh and the renewal of the Spirit are required of all true Christians, so also the **denial of self** is carried out in similar fashion. Accordingly, the following should admonish towards the same:

 1. *Discipulorum Christi proprietas,* **the true attributes of Christ's disciples.** Mat. 16:24, Mark 8:34, Luke 9:23 – **If any one wants to follow after Me**—i.e., whoever wants to be a genuine Christian and a true disciple of Mine—**let him deny himself.** It's just like the Apostle Paul says, **Those who belong to Christ crucify their flesh along with its lusts and desires** (Gal. 5:24). Thus, we can also say that **those who belong to Christ deny themselves. If anyone is in Christ, he is a new creature**, Paul says in 2 Cor. 5:17. This **new creature**, i.e., the rebirth and renewal, has no status unless a person denies himself. That's why we became Christians, that's why we are called Christians, since we are to be **Christ's heirs**, and **live in Him** (2 Cor. 5:15). If we are to be Christ's heirs and live in Him, then we must **deny ourselves and die to ourselves.** The person who has stated Gal. 2:20 – **I am crucified with Christ. I live, yet not I but Christ lives in me. For what I now live in the flesh I live by faith in the Son of God,** such a person has denied himself and is a true disciple of Christ. As a result, he no longer lives to himself because he has denied himself.

2. *Necessitas,* **the basic need. If anyone wants to follow after Me, let him deny himself,** Christ says at the indicated place. From this ensues the counterpart, **whoever does not wish to deny himself** also cannot follow Christ, i.e., he cannot be His true disciple. Christ Himself demonstrates to us this *antithesis* or counterpart in Luke 14:26: **If anyone wants to come to Me and does not hate his father, mother, wife, children, brother, sister, and, in addition, his own life, he cannot be My disciple.** V. 33 – **Whoever among you who does not renounce everything that he has cannot be My disciple.** This **hatred and renunciation** is nothing other than that one **denies himself.** Namely, it consists of a person denying and setting aside everything of this world that is dear to him for the sake of Christ. Since a person may not come to Christ nor follow Him, i.e. be His true disciple, unless he denies himself, it is obviously to be concluded that without the denial of self a person can have no status in Christ's kingdom, nor obtain His merits. Nor can he rejoice over His future. Why is that? Without the denial of self a person cannot be a **true disciple of Christ.** But anyone who is not a disciple of Christ is also not a **true member** of His kingdom. He cannot obtain His merits. He does not rejoice over his future.

3. *Utilitas,* **the benefit** that we receive from it if we deny ourselves. **If anyone wishes to follow after Me**—or as it actually reads in the original Greek, "come to Me"—**let him deny himself,** Christ says. From this, it is easy to conclude that he who denies himself **also comes to Christ.** As a person has his essence and life more **in God,** his Creator and Preserver, than in his own self, he is far better off with God than with his own self. Indeed, the more a person denies himself, and with this denial and renunciation distances himself from himself and every creature, he actually draws all the more near to God the Lord. When **Abraham** left his fatherland and its fellowship and went out from his father's house, he was **blessed** by GOD (Gen. 12:1). So also when you through your self-denial depart from yourself and all creatures, God the Lord will enter your soul with his **heavenly blessings.** When the daughter of the heavenly Father, the **bride of the heavenly King and Bridegroom** [i.e., members of Christ's body—the holy Christian Church] **forsakes her people and her father's house, the King** immediately then **delights in her beauty** (Psa. 45:11-12). Within us by nature there is nothing else but sin, death, and damnation. In God there is nothing else but righteousness, life, and salvation. As a result, when we deny ourselves, we draw away from sin, death, and damnation to righteousness, life, and salvation. Since denying one's self is so essential and beneficial, that's why the gracious God utilizes **crosses** to this end in order that thereby He may motivate us towards denial of self. For if amidst tribulations a person recognizes and acknowledges his insignificance, his weaknesses, his vanity, thereby he will be prepared for the denial of self. This is what true Christianity consists of.

Chapter Fourteen

How a true Christian should exercise himself in the denial of self.

In Luke 14:26, Christ describes the denial of one's self as hating oneself. By comparing the Evangelists one arrives at such a conclusion. For in what is written in Matthew and Mark, Christ says: **If anyone wishes to follow after Me, 1. Let him deny himself, 2. And take up his cross, and 3. Follow Me.** Luke records it this way: Christ says, **If anyone wishes to come to Me and 1. Does not hate his father, mother, wife, child, brother, sister, as well as his own life he cannot be My disciple. 2. Whoever does not bear his cross, 3. And does not follow Me cannot be My disciple.** From this, it is quite sufficient to see that to want to **follow** Christ or want to **come to Him** is called being His true disciple and denying one's self. It means to **hate oneself** as well as hating that which a person loves in this world, and to set it aside for the sake of Christ. In Mat. 5, this denial is called **spiritual poverty** [being poor in spirit], if a person divests himself of his personal and inordinate love for material things and acknowledges his spiritual poverty and his nothingness. This denial of self is also the **inner Sabbath** of the soul, when a person relinquishes his own work so that God may have from him the inward constant Sabbath that the Commandment about celebrating the Sabbath directs us to. Isa. 58:13–14, **If you turn your foot from the Sabbath so that you do not do what pleases you on My holy day, then it shall be called a desirable Sabbath in which to sanctify and praise the Lord. Then you will have your delight in the Lord.** Consequently, self-denial is called nothing other than renunciation and denunciation.

1. *Proprio amori*, **love of self.** By nature a person loves himself more than God the Lord. A person must denounce such inordinate love of self. If the **fruit of divine love** is to grow and flourish in the heat, then

the **poisonous root of self love** must first wither away. Love of self hinders the love of **God.** Isa. 28:20 – **The bed is so cramped that there is no room left and the blanket is so short that a person has to snuggle up in it.** Consequently, if God's love is to enter in, love of self has to leave, in the same way that a **pot** cannot gather up costly balsam water unless the foot-washing water inside it is first poured out. However, this will be dealt with more extensively at the proper time and place.

    2. *Proprio honori,* **one's own honor.** By nature a person glorifies himself. He thinks highly of himself. He seeks his own glory for every deed. A person has to renounce and kill off this search for self-glorification with his own self denial. Whoever seeks his own glory cannot seek God's glory. John 5:44 – **How can you believe,** and through faith seek God's glory, **you who seek to take glory from one another?** In other words, because you seek your own glory, **your do not seek the glory that comes from God alone.** It is a **huge sin** to seek God's own glory, for St. Paul in Rom. 1:30 ranks among the greatest sinners those who **speak boastfully.** That is to say, those who, out of their own desires, boast about their own glory and want to be exalted as if they were something special—and yet are nothing, 2 Tim. 3:2 sets those who think so highly of themselves to be among the stingy, the disobedient, unspiritual, unchaste, and the greatest of transgressors. All glory belongs to **God the Lord alone,** since everything we have belongs to Him. As far as we are concerned however, it is inappropriate for us to seek our own glory, since we have nothing from ourselves. Psa. 115:1 – **Not us LORD, not us, but to Your name be given all glory.** If you truly, from the bottom of your heart regard yourself as nothing, and do not seek your own glory, then God the Lord shall glorify you with a greater glory than what the entire world is able to give you. In John 12:26, Christ says: **whoever shall serve Me, him My Father shall glorify.** However, there is none who can properly serve Christ unless he renounce his own glory and deny himself. It follows from this that whoever denounces his own glory, God the Lord Himself shall glorify that person. In John 8:50, Christ says, **I do not seek My own glory. There is however One who searches and judges you.** It can be concluded from this that he who does not seek his own glory, God Himself wants to seek him.

3. *Propriae voluntati*, **one's own will.** Mankind's **will** was **ruined** and destroyed after the Fall into sin. At the same time, his understanding was darkened. That's why a person must denounce his own wrong will and deny it. Gal. 5:17 – **The flesh lusts against the Spirit and the Spirit against the flesh. They are opposed to each other so that you do not do what you want to.** One's own will leads to **depravity and damnation.** Mankind fell into death on account of the fact that he set God's will aside and followed his own will. **Your will be done, and not My will,** Christ prayed in Mat. 26:39, even though His will at all times was holy and good. He wants to teach us with this that we should denounce our wrong and depraved will and submit and subjugate our will to God's will. That's why He also taught us to pray: **Lord, Your will be done, like in heaven so also on earth** (Mat. 6:10; Luke 11:2). Our will is a **human** and thus also an **unreliable, wavering-minded will.** That's why it must likewise be embedded into the reliable will of God, i.e., be submitted to it. **If Christ's kingdom** is to

have a place in our hearts, then we must denounce our own will. That's why Christ placed these petitions side by side: **Your kingdom come, Your will be done—as in heaven so also on earth.** To the extent that your will departs, that's the extent to which Christ's kingdom enters into your heart. To the extent that your will is clung to, that's the extent to which Christ's kingdom departs from your heart.

  4. *Propriae voluptati,* **one's own lust.** A person has his desires and affections within him by nature. But that's not how it should be. Instead, he should seek his desires and affections in God. He is the **one greatest God** and He alone is able to give us what we seek and desire. Psa. 37:5 – **Have your desire in the Lord. He shall give you what your heart wishes for.** This highest Good is **unchangeable and eternal.** That's why this God alone is able to give us lasting desires and joys. However, we along with all creatures will perish. That's why we cannot obtain any lasting desires and joy from ourselves or from creatures. In death we must **depart** and will be **forsaken by all of creation.** So if you have placed all your desires and joy in creature things, what will be your desire and joy, your comfort and your life amidst death? **Your body** may indeed for **a time** find desire and joy in creature comforts. However, the **soul** cannot be satisfied with this. It can have its desire and joy nowhere else than in God.

  5. *Propriae utilitati,* **one's own benefit.** After the Fall into sin, man by nature seeks his own benefit. This seeking after one's own benefit has to be denounced by a true Christian. Also he has to replace it with seeking the benefit of **the neighbor.** There can be not true love where one's own beneficial interests reign supreme.

But now love is a characteristic of a true Christian. Where there is no true love, there can exist no true Christianity. **Love does not seek its own**, says Paul in 1 Cor. 13:5. The reason for this is that love gives itself to be owned by the neighbor and to serve him—just as Christ did. Out of love, He totally and completely gave Himself to be possessed by us. Just as He did not seek His own glory, so He also did not seek **His own benefit.** Mat. 20:28 – **The Son of Man did not come in order to let Himself be served, but that He serve and give His life as a redemption for many.** Everything that He did and suffered, He did and suffered for our benefit. That is the true way of love.

  6. *Propriae sapientiae,* **one's own wisdom.** By nature a person **thinks** he is **wise** (1 Cor. 3:18). In matters of faith, he wants to follow his own understanding. And that which appears inconsistent or absurd to his reason, that he doesn't want to accept. However, this his natural wisdom a person must renounce in matters of faith. **He must take his reason captive under the obedience of Christ** (2 Cor. 10:5). Plotting **to be fleshly minded is animosity towards God** (Rom 8:7). The natural **man takes nothing from the Spirit of God. It is for him a foolishness and he cannot know it. For it has to be accomplished spiritually** (1 Cor. 2:14). Consequently, whoever thinks that he is wise, **he must become a fool in this world** so that he can become truly wise before God (1 Cor. 3:18). This means that he must denounce his own wisdom.

  7. *Proriae vitae,* **one's own life.** By nature, a person regards his life so dearly and worthy that he at various times behaves contrary to God's commandments, **does evil**, and **neglects the good**; for example, when many a person **in times of persecution** denies Christ and His Word so that his body and life may not fall into danger on account of this. Such a wrong love for the natural life a person must also denounce, and must learn with St. Paul **to not regard his life as being more important** (Acts 20:24). **He must be prepared to give up his life for the sake of the brother**—even more so **for the sake of confessing Christ** (1 John 3:16). Christ demands this of us when He says, **If anyone wants to follow after Me, let him deny himself. For whoever finds his life shall lose it, and whoever loses his life for My sake shall keep it** (Mat. 10:39; ch. 16:25; Mark 8:35; Luke 9:24). **If anyone comes after Me and does not hate his own life, he cannot be My disciple** (Luke 14:26). **Whoever loves his life shall lose it, and whoever hates his life in this world shall keep it for eternal life** (John 12:25). This also means to **renounce one's own life.** From all this it is easy to conclude that since to deny one's self means to renounce one's own **passion**, one's own **glory,** one's own **benefits**, one's own **wisdom**, and one's own **life.** Also, that the person who wants to deny himself must also diligently **exercise** himself **in the following.** He has to renounce his own passion, his own glory, his own will, his own lust, his own benefit, his own wisdom, and his own life. We cannot in this life bring this to **perfection** since the sinful flesh still resists. Nevertheless, by the Spirit of Christ, a **beginning** has to be initiated. Since, however, this does not exists within our natural **powers**, we have to ask for the help and support of the Holy Spirit by inwardly praying for this and say:

  O holy God, merciful Father, I confess and lament to You that I have not been very diligent and eager in denying myself as I should have. Alas, faithful God, pardon this my sin and negligence. Give me power through Your Spirit to become strong in the inward man, so that I through Him may deny myself. O Lord, take me and give me Yourself. O God, guide me out of myself and constantly draw me to take me and to give me to Yourself. O God, guide me out of myself and constantly draw me to You. Rescue me from evil. Within me and in my flesh exists the greatest evil. Rescue me from it and grant me grace that I turn myself over completely to You and Your will. O Lord Jesus Christ, You made Yourself known for my sake, and You took upon Yourself the form of a servant (Phi. 2:9). You did not seek Your own glory, Your own will, Your own benefit. Instead, You sought the will and glory of Your heavenly Father and the benefit of all of us. You thereby had placed before us a perfect example of self-denial. O precious Savior! Help me that I follow Your perfect example, and from the bottom of my heart may deny myself. O Holy Spirit, work in me by Your power that I may deny myself. You, Holy Sprit, graciously protect me that that I do not follow the hellish spirit that glorifies itself and fulfills its own will (John 8:44). You heavenly Fire, draw my heart to You that I do not rest on my laurels and cling to myself. Instead, draw me to You that I through self denial lift my heart up to God, die to myself, and in God, the living God, live forever, Amen!

Chapter Fifteen

What should motivate a true Christian to follow after Christ His Lord.

Just as the old **Adam** has a distaste for the crucifixion of the **flesh** and **self-denial,** so also is it the case with **following after Christ.** All of us gladly allow ourselves to be called Christians, but we do not gladly want to follow after Christ. *Volunt omnes Christo frui, at non eum imitari. Non curant quaerere, quem tamen desiderant invenire, cupientes consequi sed non sequi,** says Bernhard (*Serm. 21. Cant. Col. 550*). We all want to be **recipients** of Christ and His blessings, but **the following after Christ** disgusts us. We gladly want to **find** Christ and follow Him. However, it strikes us as an arduous inconvenience that we should **seek** Him and follow Him. When the **rich young man** heard from Christ in Mat. 19:21 – **sell what you have and give it to the poor and come and follow after Me, he sorrowfully turned away from Christ's countenance.** This young man still has many students today, and there are more who follow him that there are those who follow the Lord. When the people at **Capernaum** heard Christ say, **No one can come to Me unless it is given to him from My Father** (John 6:65), **many of His disciples turned away from Him and no longer followed Him,** (v. 66). That's what still

---

* "They all want to take pleasure in Christ, but they don't want to imitate Him. They don't care to look for the One they nevertheless want to find, as they wish to catch up with Him. But they don't care to follow Him."

happens today. Christ's Word and Christ's life becomes **an offense** to many so that they turn away from Him and do not want to follow Him. That is why we must somberly take to heart the **reasons** that should motivate us to follow after Christ. Of these there now are mainly nine, such as:

1. *Christi mandatum,* **the command of the Lord Christ.** In the Old Testament, **God the Lord set Himself** before His people, the Israelites, **as an example of** holiness to be followed, in that He spoke to them in Lev. 11:44; ch. 19:2, **You shall sanctify yourselves so that you become holy, for I am holy.** In the same way, **Christ** in the New Testament also wanted to place before His people and His true disciples Himself as an **example** to be followed. He says in Mat. 11:29, **Learn of Me**, and in John 13:15 – **I have given you an example that you do as I have done.** In the same way, He spoke to Peter and Andrew, James and John: **Follow Me** (Mat. 4:19), so to a certain degree He also still says to us all: **Follow Me.** During the days of His flesh, He began both **to do and to teach** (Acts 1:1), not only to teach with **words**, but also to do with **the works.** Likewise, He has also prescribed for us this rule and mandate in Mat. 5:19, **He who does it and teaches shall be great in the kingdom of heaven.** Christ has not only demanded of us that we should **believe** in Him, and through such faith become partakers of His blessings; He has also required of us that we are to **follow** Him. That's why we should not only hear the one thing, but also the other. **Teachers and Preachers** must not only preach **about faith** in Christ, but also about **following after Christ.** For otherwise they would only preach one half of Christ.

2. *Christi nomen & officium,* **Christ's Name and**

Office. Christ not only calls Himself the **Truth and the Life,** but also **the Way** (John 14:6). If He is **the Way,** then it indeed is right that we should **follow Him.** For why would He call Himself the Way if He did not wish for us to walk as He walked? Christ calls Himself the **Light of the world** in John 8:12 not just because He **enlightens** our hearts through His Word and Spirit, but because He also **shines the light** for our way so that we should follow after Him. That's why He immediately adds on: **Anyone who follows after Me shall not walk in darkness.** What good is the Light for those who will not follow the Light, but walk in darkness? Christ, of course, is our **Master and Teacher** (Mat. 23:10). That's why it is proper and right that we follow Him and step in His footprints. That's how He directs us in John 13:13-15, **You call Me Master and Lord, and you say it rightly. For I am that. Now since I, your Lord and Master, have washed your feet, you too should wash each other's feet. I have given you an example that you do like I have done.** Each individual **teacher and master** strives as much as possible that his **disciples and students** become **like him,** so also Christ, our **Teacher and Master** gladly wants us to become conformed to Him. Once again, just as the **students** and **disciples** not only take note of the **words** but also of the **deeds**—many times also of **the demeanor**, and they busy themselves to experience the same themselves. For just as this is what is especially testified about the students of Plato, so also we should as **students of Christ** not only take note of **His Word**, but also of His life and deeds, and imitate them. Christ is **our Shepherd** (John 10:12). We are His **lambs.** Now, just as a lamb follows after its **shepherd** as he goes ahead of it, so also it is appropriate that we also follow after **Christ**, our Shepherd. V. 27 – **My sheep hear My voice and I know them and they follow Me.** Christ is our **Bridegroom** (John 3:29). Now just as a **bride** busies herself to **follow** her bridegroom, so also we must faithfully follow our Bridegroom. Rev. 14:4 – **These are the ones who are not soiled with women, for they are virgins and follow the Lamb wherever He goes.** Christ actually came into the world foremost of all to **complete** the work of redemption, and through His obedience and suffering to once more **bring back** what had been **lost by Adam.** Along with this, He also came so that He could set before us an **example to follow after. We should follow Him and walk in His footsteps** (1 Pet. 1:21). That's why He not only grants us by grace the **righteousness** that avails before God and **eternal life** but He also gives us **His Holy Spirit** and through Him **new power** spiritually to live blessed lives and follow after Him.

    3. *Divinum Decretum*, **God's decree.** Rom. 8:29 – **Those whom God the Lord had previously foreseen He also preordained that they should likewise be the image of His Son, so that He would be the first born among many brethren.** Such **conformity** with the image of the Son of God consists not only of **cross and suffering**. Of course, the holy Apostle does deal with and teach at this same place that the true Christian's cross and suffering must serve for his highest good and for glorification—no less than Christ Himself. However, this conformity with the image of the Son of God also consists of **being a child** [of God], that just as Christ is God's **natural, beloved Son,** so also the elect are **God's beloved, chosen children.** Also, that with holiness and virtue, just as Christ **walked in love, patience, humil-**

ity, and all **holiness and virtue,** the **elect,** too, are to **walk** in these same virtues and are to become like the **image of Christ**—all this in order that someday the **conformity** shall result in **glorification.** Thus, just as **Christ through suffering entered into glory** (Luke 24:26), **so also the elect shall through much tribulation enter into the Kingdom of God** (Acts 14:22). There Christ shall **transfigure their vain bodies so that they become like His transfigured body** (Phi. 3:21). 1 Cor. 15:49 – **Just as we have borne the image of the earthly, so also we shall bear the image of the heavenly.** This all **begins in this life with the renewing of the image of God** in our hearts, and by **following after Christ.** However, on **Judgment Day it will be truly perfected.** Thus, we must not withdraw from God's council-decision nor strive against it. Instead, we should subject ourselves to this holy ordinance of God so that we may conclude from it that we also are among the number of those whom God the Lord has **previously foreseen** and **has ordained** for salvation. Just as a **very talented artist** thinks through in advance **all the strokes** when he wants to paint a beautiful picture, so also God the Lord from eternity has thought through and ordained everything concerning how He wants to make us in time into the image of His Son.

    4. *Veri Christiani proprium,* **the characteristic of a true Christian.** In Mat. 16:24; Mark 8:34; Luke 9:23, Jesus says, **If anyone wishes to follow along,** i.e., who wants to be My true disciple, **he should follow after Me.** John 12:26 – **Whoever wants to serve Me should follow after Me.** From this, it can be clearly concluded that this is a **true characteristic** of the true disciples of Christ: They **follow** their Lord and Master. **Whoever**

then says that he abides in Him should also live as He lived, John said in his first epistle (2:6). Accordingly, whoever does not live as Christ lived cannot truthfully say that he abides in Him—that he is a true disciple. *Frustra appellamur Christiani, si imitatores non sumus Christi, qui ideo se viam dixit, ut conversatio Magistri forma esset discipuli,*[*] says Leo (*Serm. 5. De Nativ. Dom.*). We allow ourselves to be called Christians in vain if we do not wish to be His followers. For that's why He called Himself the Way—to demonstrate that His life has been set before us to be followed by us. Whoever believes in Christ from the heart with an upright **faith** also believes that **Christ's life** has been set **before us to follow**, and it is the best life that a person can choose. Whoever believes in Christ with an upright faith also receives by faith **the Spirit of Christ.** Where, however, Christ's **Spirit is,** there the person also **is minded like Christ was minded** (Phi. 2:5). Where a person then is minded as Christ was, he **also loves Christ.** For how could a person believe in Christ from his heart if he did not simultaneously love Him as all the while **the faith is active through love** (Gal. 5:6)? Now, however, the characteristic of love is that it conforms itself to the One whom it loves. Consequently, whoever loves Christ from the heart will also endeavor to follow Him in life. **If you love Me then keep My commandments** He says in John 14:15. And again, **You are My friends if you do what I bid you to do** (ch. 15:14). To the degree that **conformity** and **likeness** to the **image** of Christ is found among us, to that degree **true Christianity** is

---

[*] "We are called Christians in vain, if we are not imitators of Christ, who said that He was the Way in such a manner that the behavior of the Schoolmaster was the form for his pupil."

to be found among us. **Learn from Me,** Christ says in Mat. 11:29. What are we to learn from Him? That He is **gentle and humble from the heart** so that we also may be gentle and humble from the heart. How may you demonstrate yourself to be a **pupil** and a **disciple of Christ** if you do not want to learn from Him? **Take upon yourself My yoke,** He says. This yoke is not only **cross** and **persecution,** but also **His holy life.** For to take Christ's yoke upon yourself means to carry His cross and to follow Him, the example of His life, to follow with humility and gentleness. This is difficult and hard for the **old Adam.** That's why Christ calls it **a yoke.** However, for the **new man** it is lovely and acceptable, gentle and light. That's why Christ says, **My yoke is gentle and My burden is light.** Gideon says to his people in Jud. 7:17, **As I do, so do you also.** The 'heavenly Gideon' still speaks these days. **I have left you an example** with My life **that you do as I have done** (John 13:15). If we want to be true proper disciples and true Christians, then we have to do as He did. If we want to be proper disciples of Christ, then **Christ** must **live in us** and work within us so that we follow Him. *Summa religionis est hunc imitare, quem colis,** says Augustine (*I. 8, ce Civitate Dei cap. 17.*). Therein consists the whole of Christianity: that one follow after Christ. And Lactantius writes *lib. 6. Institi. c. 10. Fol. 282. Religiosissimus cultus est imitari.*† It is true **worship** when a person follows God and places himself into conformity with Him.

    5.*Necessarium,* **the necessity. Whoever wishes to be My disciple, let him follow after Me,** says Christ. It contrariwise follows from this: Anyone who does

---
* "The sum total of religion is to imitate Him like a tendril vine."
† "Religion is a cultivation of imitation."

not want to follow after Christ can also not be a true disciple. **My sheep hear My voice and follow Me**, He says. From this it contrariwise follows: He who does not follow Christ the Shepherd is also not a true lamb. There is no need for us to prove this any further with *Consequentias* or successive deductions. It is written with clear, plain simple words in Luke 14:27 – **Whoever does not follow after Me can not be My disciple.** If a person is not a disciple of Christ, he boasts about his Christianity in vain. What does it help you that you falsely **present** yourself as a Christian and are not in **deed and truth** a Christian? How are you any better off in that you are in the **external fellowship** of Christendom and along with that are not a true disciple of Christ? But it here states very clearly: **Whoever does not follow after Christ cannot be Christ's disciple.** If a person is not a true disciple of Christ, then he also is most certainly not a proper Christian. For **Christ's disciple** and being a **proper Christian** is one and the same thing—as is to be concluded from Acts 11:26.

    6. *Dominicae passionis speculum*, **the mirror of the holy suffering of Christ.** St. Peter says in his first epistle (2:21), **Christ suffered for us and has left us an exemplary model that you should follow in His footsteps.** In the original Greek text, the Apostle uses the kind of word which actually means an instructive directive that a teacher and schoolmaster writes out for his disciples who are learning to write so that they copy it. Peter here places before us the **looking glass** of the virtues in Christ's suffering so that we should constantly view them and busy ourselves with the same virtues that shine forth in Christ's suffering. *Macarius* (*hom. 30.p.399*) explains this with a beautiful analogy:

An **artist,** when he wants to prepare the picture or portrait of a person, looks at him quite studiously and exactingly. Now, if that person looks directly and straight at the artist, then the artist paints a beautiful portrait. If, however, that person keeps staring off elsewhere, then the artist cannot correctly capture the portrait. So also **Christ** is the true heavenly '**Artist.**' If we steadily look straight at Him with the eyes of faith, then He prepares in us the **image of God.** He crafts in us that we become conformed to His image. 2 Cor. 3:18 – **The Lord's glory reflects itself within us all with the unveiled countenance. And we become transfigured into the very same image from one glory to the next, as from the Spirit of the Lord.** However, if we do not precisely look at Him, then He will not establish such an image of God in us. Christ in His life **gave Himself for us to own Him totally and completely.** Therefore, it is right and proper that we once again also **give ourselves to be His own** and to follow Him. **Out of love**, He conformed Himself to us. **He made Himself know, took upon Himself the form of a servant, and was found to be in conduct like a man. He became obedient to His Father unto death, indeed to death on the cross** (Phi. 2:9). Therefore, it is right that we, out of love for Him, also present ourselves conformed to Him and follow Him.

    7. *Sanctorum exemplum*, the **example of all the saints. Be my followers as I am of Christ**, says St. Paul in 1 Cor. 11:1. He does indeed point to his **own example**, but only insofar as it coincides with **Christ's example.** For all the examples of the saints have to be gauged and assessed on the basis of Christ's example. The spiritual **virgins,** who have kept themselves pure from the world, **follow the Lamb wherever He goes** (Rev. 14:4). The life of Christ is the **book** which all saints have studied for their entire lifetime. If we want to be among the blessed fellowship of the saints, then we also must daily study this Book and follow after Christ.

8. *Multiplex commodum*, **the many benefits** that we receive from following Christ. In John 8:12, Christ says, **I am the Light of the world. Whoever follows after Me shall not walk in darkness. Instead, He will have the Light of Life.** Christ is that **Light.** That's why anyone who follows Him comes out of **death to life.** Apart from Christ there is not else than darkness and death. If we do not want to remain in darkness and death we must follow Him. **Like the pillar of fire in the night and the pillar of cloud in the day led** the Israelites **through the wilderness** in Exo. 13:21, so also Christ leads us through the wilderness of this world as our **Precursor and Prince.** So long and far as the Israelites followed this pillar of fire and cloud they did not err. They did not walk in darkness. They had a **shade against the heat** and a **protection against the enemy** (Psa. 121:5-6). As long as we follow Christ we will not err. We will not walk in darkness. We have a shade against the heat of tribulation and a protection against the hellish enemies—for **He is our Sun and Shield** (Psa. 84:12).

9. *Consequens damnum*, **the great harm** that results if a person does not follow after Christ. **Whoever follows Christ does not walk in darkness, but instead shall have the Light of Life.** From this it can indisputably be concluded that whoever does not follow Christ still is walking **in the darkness of ignorance and sin.** Also, he cannot come to the Light of Life. Anyone who

does not follow Christ is a **member of the anti-Christ or against Christ**. For Christ clearly states, **Whoever is not with Me is against Me** (Luke 11:23). Just as it is an anti-Christian doctrine that strives against the Christian teaching, so also is it an anti-Christian life that strives against the Christian life. **Every spirit that does not confess that Jesus Christ came into the flesh is not from God, and it is the spirit of the anti-Christ,** John says in his first epistle (3:7). Such a person not only denies that Jesus Christ came in the flesh—which denies His **Person and Office**—but he also strives against Christ **with his life.** For since Christianity—as well as the Kingdom of God—**does not consist of words but of power** (1 Cor. 4:20), so also Christ is denied not just with **words**, but also and much more so with **deeds**. What does it help you if you have been redeemed from the anti-Christian **error of doctrine**, and you hear the **doctrine** pure and true, if you then alongside proceed to **live the anti-Christian life?** Anti-Christian **doctrine** and anti-Christian **life** are both death and darkness to anyone who does not want to follow Christ. Such a person will also not receive **Light and Life.** Whoever does not keep Christ as his Way and follow after Him, for such a person Christ will also not be his Life (John 14:6). Whoever does not want to be conformed by the **Spirit** to the **mind of Christ** will also not be able to beneficially understand and grasp His **Word which is Spirit and Life** (John 6:63). If it is to be beneficially and blessedly understood, then we must **walk in the Spirit** and have the Light of Life in following Him. **If anyone wants to do the will of the Father who sent Me,** He says in John 7:17 – **he will realize whether this teaching is from God or whether I am speaking**

it on My own. So then, whoever does not do the will of the heavenly Father, nor wants to follow Christ, he shall remain in darkness, and yes, he will dig himself in even more deeply.

Chapter Sixteen

How a true Christian should exercise himself in following Christ.

There are two kinds of **following after Christ.** First of all, one **special** kind that applies to certain **persons** and certain **times.** Then there is also a general kind that is called for from **all true Christians and for all times.**

Pertaining to the *sequelam specialem*, **the special following after** Christ applies, as noted, first to **certain persons.** One example of this is presented to us in Mat. 4:19 and 21 when Christ called **Peter** and his brother **Andrew,** and then also **James** and his brother **John**—the sons of Zebedee—and said to them, **Follow after Me.** With these words, they were called in a special manner to let themselves be prepared and allow themselves to be informed. Thus they **forsook everything,** committed themselves to be His pupils, and to be called to the **Apostolic Ministry** in order to proclaim the Gospel in the whole world. This kind of following after Christ is especially required of the **teachers and preachers** so that they in keeping with the example of Christ and the holy Apostles give up all the things that might be **a hindrance to their ministry.** Also, that they should teach and preach God's Word with faithful diligence.

Now, the **call** of the holy Apostles to follow Christ is to be somewhat **differentiated** from the call of other servants of the Church—especially since the beloved Apostles were called to preach the Gospel **in the whole world.** (That's why they forsook everything and had to follow Christ in His school.) This is not required from other teachers and servants of the Church in the same way—as when it is mandated to **graze** a **certain flock** and **congregation** at a **certain place** (1 Pet. 5:2). Nevertheless, there are some **certain parts** which the holy Apostles of Christ followed and in which also other teachers of the Church should follow Christ and the holy Apostles. In similar fashion, **Christ** and the holy **Apostles** did not preach **without a call.** Christ was sent into the world **by His heavenly Father**, and the holy Apostles were sent **by Christ.** John 20:21 – **Just as the Father has sent Me, so I send you.** So also, teachers and preachers should not preach without a call. Instead, they should first wait for an orderly call. Rom. 10:15 – **How shall they preach if they have not been sent?** Heb. 5:4 – **Nobody assumes this honor for himself unless he has been called by God in the same way as also Aaron.** Christ did not preach His teaching but rather the teaching brought forth from the **bosom of the Father.** John 7:16 – **My teaching is not Mine but the teaching of Him who sent Me.** Likewise, the teachers and preachers should follow Christ in this matter, so that they do not preach their own **dreams** but **only God's Word.** 1 Pet. 4:11 – **If anyone speaks, let him speak it as God's Word.** Likewise, Christ in His preaching did not seek His **own glory**, but the **glory** of His heavenly Father. John 8:50 – **I do not seek My glory.** So also the teachers and preachers should follow Christ in this matter, so that they do not seek their **own glory**, but instead God's **glory** and the salvation of **man.** John 7:18 – **Anyone who speaks on his own seeks his own glory. But he who seeks the glory of Him who sent Me is genuine, and there is not unrighteousness in him.** Likewise, Christ did not usurp worldly regimes and kingdoms, but instead much more **fled** from them **as they came and wanted to make Him into a king** (John 6:15). For **His kingdom was not of this world** (John 18:36). Teachers and preachers should also follow Him in this. They also should **not lord it over the people** (1 Pet 5:4), nor **want to be lords over their hearers' faith** (2 Cor. 1:24), in consideration of the mandates that Christ has given to His Apostles and all their faithful followers. Luke 22:25 – **The earthly kings rule, and the powerful are called gracious lords, but no so with you.** Christ earnestly chastised the **wicked** and the **hypocrites with the Law,** but He once more **comforted** and lifted up the **shattered hearts** with the soothing **voice of the Gospel.** In the same manner, teachers and preachers should also follow Him in this matter and promote both **Law and Gospel.** They are **to bring out old and new from their treasure chest** [i.e. the Scriptures] (Mat. 13:52). They are to sing **the song of Moses and the Lamb** (Rev. 15:3). Christ conducted His ministry in such a way that He could truthfully say: **Who among you is able to accuse Me of a sin,** i.e., show Me a single error [that I have committed] (John 8:46). In the same manner also teachers and preachers are to **be sure of their teachings,** so that they can say with Jeremiah (17:16), **What I have proclaimed is right for you.** That which Christ had taught to others, **He did Himself.** He began to both **do and to teach**

(Acts 1:1). In the same manner also, teachers should follow Christ and enlighten their hearers with a **good example.** To sum it all up, teachers and preachers are a perfect **mirror** for everything that they are obliged to do in the example of Christ.

Next, this following after Christ also happens at **certain times.** Namely, when a person in **times of persecution** has to forsake all his **possessions and goods**—also at times one's **body** and **life**—for the sake of confessing Christ. We have an example of such following in Mat. 19:21. Here Jesus began to reply to the **young man** who falsely boasted that he had perfectly kept all the commandments of God **from his youth on.** He said, **If you want to be perfect, go forth and see what you have and give it to the poor. Thus, you will have your treasure in heaven. And then come follow after Me.** That was an **outstanding**, special **command** by which Christ wanted to persuade this young man that it was a vain, false **exaltation** that he had kept all of God's commands. For he did not out of **love** and **obedience** want to give up his goods and submit himself as a pupil of Christ. Another such example of such following after is presented to us in John 21:20 where Christ says to **Peter, "follow after Me."** With these words, He was indicating the **kind of death** by which Peter was to **glorify God.** Namely, he was going to be crucified after the example of his Lord and follow Him therein. He had explained this to him previously: **When you are old, you will stick out your hand and another will gird you and lead you where you don't want to go. This He said however to indicate with what kind of death he would glorify God.** If such a special calling also goes out to us in a time of persecution so that we, for the sake of Christ, have to set aside our possessions and goods—and, yes, even our own lives—we are obligated to follow Christ. We are obligated to forsake everything, and to offer up our life to God the Lord. Mat. 10:37 - **Whoever loves father and mother more than Me is not worthy of Me.** V. 39 - **Whoever finds his life shall lose it. However, whoever loses his life for My sake shall find it.** Ch. 19:29 - **Whoever forsakes home, brother, or sister, or father, or mother, or wife, or children, or land for the sake of My Name shall receive a hundred-fold, and shall inherit eternal life.** Luke 14:26 - **If anyone comes to Me and does not hate father, mother, wife, children, brother, sister, also his own life, such a person cannot be My disciple.** Similar passages are to be found in Mark 8:35; Ch. 10:29; Luke 9:24; John 12:25. That's the way those to whom the letter to the Hebrews is addressed had followed Christ. It is stated about them in ch. 10:34 - **You endured the robbery of your goods with joy as those who know that you have with you a better and abiding possession in heaven.** It is **very difficult for flesh and blood** that a person should follow after Christ in this way. For it clings to **earthly** visible things and **loves itself.** That's why it is essential that a person **prepares** himself for this in time in such a way that a person **subdue in his heart the love for temporal things, turn away** from earthly and perishable things, and **cling** only to Christ. Whoever does not in this manner forsake in his heart everything **during times of peace** shall later, **during times of persecution**, actually have difficulties in forsaking everything for the sake of Christ. Also it is certain that **whoever** does not do this cannot be a true

Christian. For anyone who still loves **something more than Christ,** such a person does **not rightly love Him.** However, whoever is not prepared to set behind him and to forsake everything—including his own life—for the sake of Christ, such a person loves something more than **Christ.** Therefore, he does not truly love Christ. But if the **love for Christ is false** and deceitful in him, how can he be a true disciple of Christ? From this, consider how many true Christians are to be found nowadays.

Along with this special following after Christ, there still exists a **general following after** that is required of **all true Christians at all times.** Christ speaks of them in Mat. 16:24; Mark 8:34; Luke 9:23. **Whoever wants to be My disciple, let him follow Me.** John 12:26, **Whoever wants to serve Me , let him follow Me.** This simply consists of the fact that we did not want to, neither could we follow Christ. 1. *In operibus miraculosis,* by His **miraculous deeds.** For here it is called what the beloved ancient church fathers correctly said: *In quibusdam Christus est mirabilis, in quibusdam imitabilis.*[*] With certain deeds, Christ is presented to us as a **Wonder Worker** so that we should in faith marvel at His works and deeds. However, in others He is presented as our **Precursor** so that we should follow Him therein. For He has not said, Learn from Me how to raise the dead, fast for forty days, walk with dry feet upon the water. **Rather, learn from Me, for I am gentle and of a humble heart.**

We cannot nor should follow Him 2. *In factis heroicis,* **in his wondrous, heroic deeds,** as when He with his rod and whip **drove the buyers and sellers**

---

[*] "Christ is marvelous to some, imitatable in some."

out of the Temple in John 2:14. Instead, we are to follow Him:

1. *in doctrina*, **in teaching and with faith,** that we are to solely and alone let His holy **Word** be the **guiding principle for our faith,** because the heavenly Father has directed us that we should solely and alone hear **Him** (Deu. 18:18; Mat. 17:5; Mark 9:7; Luke 9:34). Christ speaks about this Himself in John 10:27. **My sheep hear My voice** (v. 5), **they do not follow a stranger.** The scholars of nature write that in Egypt there was an animal that supposedly had the name of **Hyena, Grave Animal,** or **"Eat Much."** (He is referred to in Sirach 13:22.) This animal came close to the sheep stall, learned **to imitate the voice of the shepherd,** called the sheep out of the stall, who then followed him. He then tore them apart and devoured them. That's the style of all **heretics and false teachers.** They imitate the voice of the Shepherd Christ and would gladly lure the sheep out of the Christians churches. Here, however, a sensible lamb must learn to properly **distinguish the voice** of his own **Shepherd, Christ,** from the howl of the wolves and the voices of the heretics, so that it is not misled and steered away from the way of salvation. One now could say a lot about **papal pronouncements,** about ancient **customs,** about the **decrees** and **councils,** about the teachings of the beloved **church fathers.** If a person wants to make commentary to you that is spun out of reason, then simply say: **I am a lamb of Christ,** it is incumbent upon me that I follow the voice of my Shepherd. For He has the **Word of eternal life** (John 6:69). Therefore, **whoever follows Him does not walk in darkness but shall have the Light of Life** (John 8:12). **His Word** is the **rod and staff**

of my Shepherd (Psa. 23:4), with which He will lead and guide me so that I do not err.

2. *In vita,* **in life and walk,** that we may follow Him with the **love, patience, humility, gentleness, kindness** and similar **virtues.** Christ speaks of this in Mat. 11:29, **Learn of Me.** What are we to learn from You, dear Lord? **For I am gentle and humble of heart** so that you follow Me with gentleness and humility. Ch. 16:24 – **Whoever wants to be My disciple let him renounce his own affections, his own glory, his own will, his own lusts, his own benefits** and follow after Me. For where there is no self-denial, that also can be no status for following after Christ. Eph. 5:1-2, **Be a follower after God** (and His Son Christ Jesus) **as dear children, and walk in love just as Christ has loved us.** 1 Pet. 2:21 – **Christ suffered for us and has left us a model that we should follow after in His footsteps,** v. 23 – **who did not scold as He was scolded, did not threaten as He suffered. But He placed it all into the hands of Him who judges justly.** 1 John 2:6 – **Whoever says that he abides in Him should also live as He lived.** From these and similar passages it is to be clearly seen that it is required of all true Christians that they should **follow Christ** with love, humility, gentleness, patience, obedience, and **similar good works.** They should be of **one mind and affection** with Christ (Phi. 2:5). They should constantly hold His **example** before their eyes, following after Him with their lives. His life is a **perfect mirror for all virtues.** Also there cannot be found in any science something that is perfect and more sure about true virtue than in the **book of the life of Christ.** For just as Christ is far above all the saints, so also His life is a perfect **Virtue Mirror** beyond all

the lives of the saints. Just as He has gone before us, so also we can confidently follow, for He calls Himself **the Way** (John 14:6). Whoever does not follow Him in his life walks in darkness, for He calls Himself **the Light** (John 8:12). Whoever does not follow Him remains in **lies**, for He calls Himself the **Truth**. Whoever does not follow Him remains in **death**, for He calls Himself the **Life** (John 14:6). Whoever does not follow Christ **in life** most certainly does not believe His Word. Let him boast about this with his mouth all he wants to, for this is indeed also Christ's Word: **Learn from Me that I am gentle and of a humble heart** (Mat. 11:29). **I mandate to you that you love one another** (John 15:17). Whoever does not love Christ's holy life also does not love Christ (John 15:14). **You are My friends if you do what I bid you to do.** Where true, proper, active **faith** exists, there also **Christ resides in the heart** of such a believing person. Eph. 3:17, where Christ is there also is the **Holy Spirit** who rests **over Him.** Gal. 5:21 – **If we live in the Spirit let us also then walk in the Spirit.** Where none of the fruits exist there also is not the Holy Spirit. There is no Christ there. There is not true faith, there is no **true Christianity.** Everything that **Christ did** became salutary and beneficial for man, as Peter speaks about this in Acts 10:38 – **He went about and did well**, i.e., wherever He went He did good. In this you must follow Christ and **direct all your activity towards that end,** so that it redounds to the **benefit of the neighbor** and is called a blessing. A wise heathen said, If we could be able to see the virtue we would immediately love to gain it. **Christ's life** in nothing other than a sheer virtue. Why is it that we don't love to gain Christ's life?

    3. *In cruce*, **in cross and tribulation.** That with

all patience we bear our cross **after the crucified Jesus.** Mat. 16:24 – **Whoever wants to be My disciple let him take up his cross upon himself and follow after Me.** Just as He through cross and suffering entered glory (Luke 24:26), so also must we through **much tribulation enter into the kingdom of God** (Acts 14:22). That's why all true Christians must also be true **Simons,** as he himself had to grab hold of **Christ's cross** and help carry it after Christ and followed Him. How may we **love** the crucified Christ if we do not also love **His cross**? He is a true **Guide and Leader.** He has shown us the **narrow gate** and the **small path** that through much cross and tribulation leads to life (Mat. 7:14). However, He Himself has **gone ahead** on this same path and has commanded us to **follow Him.** He is a faithful **Shepherd**; we are His obedient **lambs.** Consequently, as He leads us through **thorns** or through **roses,** we should follow Him. He is a **faithful Physician.** He gives us to drink from His **'tribulation beaker'** a bitter drink in order to withstand the illnesses of our souls. Psa. 75:9 – **The Lord has in hand a beaker and has graciously filled it full of strong wine and gives from it.** However, He Himself **drank** out of the same 'tribulation beaker' first and then **offers** from it to us all of our suffering so that we do not perchance think there is some sort of poison in it that would be harmful for our soul. This part of the following after leads us to the previous part. Especially so that **we** may be all the more willing to follow Christ in His holy life, He places us **under the cross** in order that **the flesh** with its evil lusts may be **subdued,** so that our **denial** of self may be mightily **effected** in us, and so that we may be prepared for the holy **following after** of Christ. **The rod makes for pious children.**

That is why God the LORD guides us towards patience and towards following Christ by means of the rod of the cross. If Christ burdens us with a cross in this manner, it usually actually transpires with us as it did with the Apostle **Peter.** When he heard Christ say, **follow after Me, he then turned around and saw the disciple whom Jesus loved and said: Lord, what about this one?** (John 21:20 and 21). That's also what we do. We look at the next person who has not been burdened with such a heavy cross, and whose following after Christ does not appear to become so sour. That's why we speak out: **What about this person or that one?** Of what am I actually so guilty that I am burdened with a greater cross than this or that person? But that's not how it should be. Instead, we should only look to Christ and follow Him. He will lead us properly and well.

    4. *In Morte,* **in death.** That we should willingly and gladly follow Him if He **calls us to Himself** through death. What is the believing, godly Christian's death other than **a call to Christ?** That is the reason why Paul says in Phi. 1:23 – **I have a desire to depart and be with Christ.** That is why we should eagerly follow Christ when He calls us to Himself. **Joseph** sent his father a chariot upon which he was to come to Egypt and **see his glory** (Gen. 45:27). Similarly, the death of a believer is nothing other than Christ's chariot that He sends to us so that we should come to Him and **see His glory that the Father has given Him** (John 17:24). He is doing nothing other with this than that He comes to us in death and says: **Follow after Me.** As the Apostles followed Christ, they later on heard Him teach and preach. So also, if we are going to follow Christ and will follow Him in and through death, then we shall later on personally **see and hear Him** in the heavenly kingdom. This final following after follows the first, for whoever follows Christ in **doctrine, in life, and in cross**, such a person will also later follow Him **in death and,** with Him, **enter into glory.**

Since, however, such a following after Christ **is not a work of natural human powers,** but instead has to be **worked in us through the Holy Spirit,** so also to that end we must cry out to God the Lord for help and support from the Holy Spirit every day. And we must thus longingly sigh:

O Almighty, merciful, and holy God, I confess and lament to You from my whole heart that I have not been so diligent in following after Christ my Lord and Master as I should have been. I have sometimes much more followed the world, my sinful flesh, and, indeed, also the evil foe and his cohorts instead of my faithful Savior Christ. By grace, You want to forgive me for this and bestow Your grace upon me so that I henceforth may follow Christ my Shepherd as an obedient lamb; so that I may follow Christ my teacher as a diligent pupil; so that I may follow Christ my guide and leader as an inexperienced Christian; so that as a faithful servant I may follow after Christ my Lord in faith, in life, in cross, and death. O Lord Jesus Christ, You unspotted Mirror of all virtues and the perfect Example of all holiness, You have said, "I am the Way." Grant me grace that I may follow You as the only true Pathway Guide, and walk in the footsteps of Your holy life with humility, gentleness, kindness, patience, love, and obedience. You have presented Yourself to us as a prototype so that we should follow in Your footsteps (1 Pet. 2:21). You have plainly and clearly said to us, "I have given you an example that you should do as I have done for you" (John 13:15). O please, grant grace that I may follow this most worthy Example and Prototype Image. You heavenly Bridegroom, draw me after You, thus we shall run after You (Song of Sol. 1:4). Let me be Your dwelling place, which You alone shall inhabit. Adorn and rule in it. You eternal Light, enlighten me. You eternal Way, lead me. You eternal Truth, teach me. You eternal Life, uphold me. O Holy Spirit, through Your sanctification and renewal, empower me that I by Your grace and power may follow after Christ my Lord. Make sure that You do not let me be a shameful, harmful tool of the evil spirit—that I not be a dwelling place of the evil foe in which he lives with pride, greed, wickedness, lies, and dirty filth. Instead, renew and rule me so that the image of Satan be subdued within me and that only Christ live in me with His humility, love, gentleness, chastity, and all other Christian virtues. Also, guide me upon the way of true faith and holy living to eternal life, Amen!

www.ingramcontent.com/pod-product-compliance
Lightning Source LLC
Chambersburg PA
CBHW062153080426
42734CB00010B/1673